PHILOSOPHICAL FOUNDATION OF EDUCATION

PHILOSOPHICAL FOUNDATION OF EDUCATION

P.K. Johri

ANMOL PUBLICATIONS PVT. LTD.
NEW DELHI - 110 002 (INDIA)

ANMOL PUBLICATIONS PVT. LTD.
H.O.: 4374/4B, Ansari Road, Darya Ganj,
New Delhi-110 002 (India)
Ph.: 23278000, 23261597
B.O.: No. 1015, Ist Main Road, BSK IIIrd Stage
IIIrd Phase, IIIrd Block,
Bangalore - 560 085 (India)
Visit us at: www.anmolpublications.com

Philosophical Foundation of Education

First Published, 2005
Reprint, 2008

PRINTED IN INDIA

Printed at Mehra Offset Press, Delhi.

Contents

Preface

The society has inherited in itself a transitional character and when the society is determined to change, everything gets changed automatically. The Education is also a significant facet of society. The history and the nature of education has also taken a new shape as the society has changed. We have come a long way, during last many centuries.

Now, we have stepped into 21st century. The Society has underlined marked changes. The era of computer is bound to conquer the society wholly. Science and Technology have advanced a lot and varied innovations and developments have become the order of the day.

People are beset with a lot of complex problems. Culture, morality and samskars, getting steadily eliminated from the society. Today, our society has become materialistic and we are walking in gloom.

The society today needs another Vivekanand, Tagore and Sir Syed to liberate the society with a new philosophical approach. Philosophical base of education has always mattered and will matter in a significant way, because this is the philosophical approach alone, which prevents us from deviating from the right path. We should bear in mind the fact that the existing materialistic society is transitory, which could not give us solace or peace.

Philosophy has always been a solid foundation for Education and we need this solid base today, more than ever. Hence, good books on the subject are most required. Here is one such effort to fulfil the vacuum.

The Editor expects a recognition by concerned circles and hopes that this modest work would satisfy the urge of the scholars, teachers and students.

Editor

1

Basic Principles

Philosophy is the theory of education in its most general phases as no educational structure can be built without the solid foundation of philosophy. According to Robert R. Rusk "a noteworthy feature of the doctrines of the great educators who are also great philosophers, is the emergence and reflection of their philosophical views in their educational schemes... we need only cite Plato's idealism and his cultural scheme of education ... Rousseau's anti-social philosophy and his negative or natural education, Spencer's hedonism and his discipline by natural consequences and, pragmatism and the project method in education.

This connection likewise subjects that the benefit may have been mutual, that in the development of the philosophical thought of such writers, their educational ideas may have played important". Nehru, Gandhi, Tagore, Vivekanand, Dayanand Sarswati, Shankracharya, Aurobindo and, a host of other Indian educationists were not philosophers by design, but reached philosophical heights while putting their educational concepts to practise. One may sum up that whereas education is the roof, philosophy is the root. Education should be the mirror of people's way of life i.e., philosophy, and philosophy should be the sum total of their aspirations, ideals, values finding worth and fulfilment in educational programmes and activities.

Philosophy, from the earliest times, has been not merely an affair of the schools, or of disputation between a handful of learned men. It has been an integral part of the life of the community and is, in fact, their way of life and not merely a way of thought. No wonder Jainism considers 'Do not live to know, but know to live' as its fundamental maxim, such is the closeness between the two. Similarly, Buddhism is the "most colossal example in history of applied metaphysics". (Whitehead) Kant also attempted to make his Pure Reason intelligible through Practical Reason. Mere thought might lead to abstraction, blinding one by its sheer brilliance, as in Samkra, ending up with *nirguna* and *neti neti*. Philosophy to be intelligible must be applied and not pure, in fact, be a way of life.

The Approach

Gone are the days when philosophy was considered to be a wild goose chase in looking for a black cat in a dark room where there is no cat. Philosophy is a reasoned recourse into the ultimate problem of substance, cosmos and truth. It is an overall, comprehensive and logical attempt at giving an overall world-view. Whatever the world-view thus projected, there must be relevance between it and society so much so, one's aims, aspirations, ideals and pursuits would be determined by such concepts prevalent from time to time, place to place, people to people. As such, philosophy may not be divorced from life, and would have no useful purpose in isolation. Abstraction leads to isolation, and isolation leads to decay.

According to R.W. Sellars, "Philosophy is a persistent attempt to gain insight into the nature of world and ourselves by means of systematic reflection".

Brightman defined philosophy as "the attempt to think truly about human experience or a whole, or to make out whole experience intelligible."

According to Bertrand Russell "philosophy is the attempt to answer ultimate questions critically after investigating all that makes such questions puzzling."

Going by its etymological meaning, Philos and Sophia, wherein philos stands for love, and sophia stands for wisdom, philosophy means "love for wisdom". Conversely, philosophy is the search for truth and wisdom.

Henderson defined philosophy as "a rigorous, disciplined and guarded analysis of some most difficult problems which man has ever faced."

The Analysis

1. Philosophy is an attempt, hence always dynamic and progressing.
2. It is a search, hence continuous and never ending.
3. It relates to human experience, hence experiential, and life-related.
4. It aims at gaining insight, hence goes beyond the appearances; does not restrict to observation alone.
5. It is "systematic reflection" but does not neglect experience. As a matter of fact, it is a reflection on what one receives through observation, or what is possible. In this sense, philosophy is defined as a science of the possible.
6. Philosophy is a rigorous, disciplined and guarded approach to such problems, hence, scientific in outlook and approach. It is, however, not merely reporting of observed facts, but is a "Reasoned recourse." Philosophy is to philosophise.

Chief Facets

Based on the above analysis, philosophy has the following essential features:-

Experiential and Situational : Philosophy comes out of experiences and situations. Even the climatic and topographical conditions help evolve a particular kind of philosophy. A warm and lazy climate, good and fertile land with plenty of river and ground water where one does not have to exert much to meet daily needs and requirements, might lead to the formulation of such concepts that take one beyond the experiential, and in to the realm of reflection and insight. On the contrary, a rugged, cold and barren topography may demand more physical labour leaving less time, or no time, for reflection and deliberation. Hence, the nature of experiences and demand of situations influence the emergence of a particular philosophical thought, and are its first essential feature.

Life-related **:** As philosophy is a way of life, it must be life-related and reflect the aspirations, values and needs of a people at a particular point of time. A changed social, economic and political scenario might blur this vision but the values so cherished would remain, howsoever dormant, in the former culture and ideology. Philosophy, therefore, should be a mirror of a society.

Scientific Attitude **:** Philosophy is not merely daydreaming; it is a reasoned recourse, a rigorous and disciplined way of thinking, a systematic reflection. It, therefore, does not restrict itself to observation of facts but goes beyond in providing them a rationale. So, whatever may be the experiences, circumstances, beliefs and situations, philosophy must rise above the empirical level, and provide a discerning explanation, in much the same manner as the scientific observation does, so as to provide experiences a necessary depth and direction. It should not end up in dogmas and doubts. Scientific attitude, therefore, is another essential feature of philosophy.

Deal with the Ultimate **:** Though experiential and situational, philosophy does not restrict itself to mundane existence alone and transcends experience in search of the ultimate. Even the Charvakas and the Hedonists, who consider pleasure as the sole ultimate value of life, go far beyond in search of the meaning, nature, extent and source of pleasure, and end up with "the greatest good of the greatest number" concept. So, whatever be its area and level of operation, philosophy aims at the ultimate. No wonder, in the transitional period when other values and practices are trying to fit in and foot the bill, philosophy keeps a dignified distance without compromising with the flux of life, as its position is at the top. Philosophy cannot be a handmaid of reason, it is its very condition. It is dynamic, invigorating, pulsating with life yet going beyond it.

Varied Role in Education

Education is described as the strongest instrument for the achievement of the ideals conceived by society, and is a civilised attempt to bring about the balanced, all round development of the individual. If education is the manifestation of the philosophical aspirations of a people, philosophy is its root, that is why it is said that education is the roof of philosophy and philosophy is the root of education. Adam goes as far as calling it the "dynamic side of philosophy." Fichte considered the relation between the two so integral when he said "the aim of education will never attain complete clearness without philosophy." Dewey described the relation as "philosophy may be defined as the general theory of education." Spencer went a step further when he said that "true education is practicable only by true philosophers." According to Ross, philosophy and education are the two sides of the same coin, presenting different view of the same thing, and that the one implies the other". According to Aristotle it is "some theory to guide practice" i.e. the theory given by philosophy to guide educational practices. It is, therefore, not a matter of accident that all great philosophers have been great educationist, for if you do not be the exponent of your own ideology, who else would be? The two must go together.

Growth and Development

The close relationship between philosophy and education led to the emergence of a new branch of knowledge: philosophy of education which "traditionally assumed the burden of formulating goals, norms, or standards by which to conduct the educative process" (Brubacher). It assures the "educator not only of the substance of the program of the schools but of its formal validity". In spite of variance amongst diverse philosophies of education—empirical, non-empirical, speculative-normative, commonsense-critical, and a host of other combinations—all seem to be recognising "the importance of interest and individual differences" (Brubacher).

Specific Rules and Regulations

Going with Brubacher, as mentioned above, let us examine the influence of philosophy in the areas of "traditionally assumed ... burden" of formulating goals, norms, standards, and of dealing with the whole lot of the educative process in its tripolar glory, content and process.

***Philosophy and Aims of Education* :** As seen in one of the earlier Chapters (Formulation of Educational Aims), "the nature of the values and aspirations that a society may have at a point of time or, may prescribe for its future growth and development, progress and prosperity would, to a very large extent, depend on the meaning that it ascribes to self, its nature and possibilities, and to the cosmological system that may help one achieve himself and attain his total possibilities" gives spurt to the formulation of educational aims. Hence, cosmological outlook and metaphysical viewpoint of a people determine their educational aims. Ross rightly remarked that "the educational aims and methods are corollaries of philosophical doctrines".

***Philosophy and Curriculum* :** According to Rusk "nowhere is this dependence of education on philosophy more marked than in the question of the curriculum, as specific curriculum problems demand a philosophy for their satisfactory solution". Curriculum is the content of education, and reveals the educational aims in expanded form. It has to be, therefore, in line-with the educational aims and should, sort of, help in their attainment. No wonder, all educational philosophies prescribe their own curriculum.

The curriculum prescribed by the idealists would differ from that of the naturalists, as the two differ as to their ideology and philosophy of life, the meaning and nature of self and cosmos. Hence philosophy determines curriculum, or the content of education. According to Briggs "it is just here that education seriously needs leaders—leaders who hold a sound comprehensive philosophy of which they can convince others and who can direct its consistent application to the formulation of appropriate curricula". Educational systems of various thinkers differ because of their philosophy which influences the entire domain of the educative process, curriculum being no exception.

Philosophy and Textbooks : As a matter of fact, it would be rather repetitious because just as the curriculum is the aim in expanded form, so are the textbooks indicative of the curriculum. Curriculum is the content of education and textbooks are the actual learning experiences/materials that would help transmit the desired curriculum. All under the same guiding philosophical doctrine which keeps them at a leash. Textbooks also reflect the aspirations of a people and help to create respect for higher values among the young mind. According to Wesely "textbook reflects and establishes standards" and indicates "too frequently, perhaps, what teacher is required to know and what the pupils are required to learn." Teacher must know what he is required to teach and a pupil must know what he is required to learn, yet maintaining the standards and values prescribed/approved by philosophy and allowing no tampering.

Philosophy and Methods of Teaching : "With the aims of education set and with the curriculum appropriate to the aim determined, we must next ponder how to teach that curriculum to ensure achieving our objectives as effectively as possible" (Brubacher). One generally thinks of the method of teaching as concerned with what a teacher does as he is considered to be an active agent in the teaching process. That would, perhaps, have been correct if the pupils were a mere passivity. But if one considers pupils to be as much active and participative as the teacher, one would have to focus as much on what the pupil does during the process of teaching-learning. Method should, therefore, concern both teacher and pupil, teaching and learning, as both are equally active and make teaching-learning a successful, meaningful and satisfying activity.

Much of the methodology would depend on the nature of learning: if learning is a "profound personal experience, a self-actualization, a coming to know oneself by his own efforts", (Brubacher) the method of teaching would be different as it would aim at simply help unfolding of what was already enfolded, and teaching would become an attempt to make explicit what was implicit. Method, therefore, would be so designed that it helps bringing out what is latent in one's faculties. This is how a rationalist would view his methodology

On the other hand, if learning is "acquisition of new behaviour patterns through conditioning and reinforcement" as with the behaviourist, it would have teaching method that helps instil desirable behavioural changes in the learner, and is "the actual building of new structures" (Robert M. Ogden)

Further, if mind is a tabula rasa, an empty chest of drawers, and learning is caused by the experiences acting on it and leaving their ideas and impressions, teaching would be merely pouring in information without any active participation by the pupil.

The activity based teaching-learning programmes, however consider learning to be rather an active affair, and therefore, have a corresponding methodology allowing pupils to exercise their judgement and imagination as in activity based project and experimental method.

So, in a nut shell, method of teaching would depend on the nature and meaning assigned to learning, which in turn, is affected by one's epistemological, cosmological and metaphysical viewpoint. Philosophy, therefore, exercises a deep control on the method of teaching.

Role of Teacher

Good teaching goes with good teacher, his knowledge, attitude, strategies and values. A teacher must be a lively wise, dynamic, energetic, scholarly, patient and sympathetic, with a clear philosophical views on teaching and education. A teacher, without any grounding in philosophy, may be as empty and barren as his teaching. Whatever may be his ideological and philosophical view point, he must be painstaking and considerate. Of course, much will depend on his philosophy of education as a teacher's approach will vary from idealism, where he is a guide, friend and philosopher, to behaviouristic tendencies where he is merely a prompter to cause desired response-behaviour as an indication of learning.

In between, Naturalism and Pragmatism have different expectations from a teacher, where he is more of a remote control having a behind the scene role. A teacher, however, is an active agent in the educative process irrespective of his philosophical training and learnings. He is a mediator between the learner and learning, his role is limited only by the meaning and significance ascribed to both in any philosophical doctrine. A teacher, therefore, must have a philosophy, a clearly defined and discernible outlook on all educational matters. "The belief that men may continue to educate without concerning themselves with philosophy means a failure to understand the precise nature of education, the process of education cannot go on right lines without the help of philosophy". (Gentile). A teacher's outlook toward teaching—autocratic-democratic, fixed-permissive, stern-friendly, distant-involved—would go a long way in developing similar attitudes and values among his students. A teacher should, therefore, not only be a man of learning, but also be imbued with lofty ideals, moral and spiritual values, be patriotic and democratic, so as to spread his message effectively and purposefully.

Thorough Discipline

The concept of discipline also goes in conformity with the philosophical views of a people, hence a philosophical problem needing a philosophical remedy. In a despotic and authoritarian society, discipline would be strict and rigid. Whereas in a democratic society it would be permissive and liberal, giving reasonable freedom of action to pupils in their day-to-day school programmes and activities. Further, discipline may be enforced from outside, or it may evolve from within the person, voluntarily. Does discipline mean repression or, subjugation into submission of the people or, is it to help a child grow freely in his situational environments? Can a teacher be a role model in this respect? All these questions seek philosophical intervention which will depend on the philosophical outlook of the people. Hence, the nature and extent of discipline in the school also depends on one's philosophical faith and belief.

We have discussed the role of educational philosophy with regard to the educative process under the following heads which would form the basis of studying any school of educational philosophy:—

(a) Aims

(b) Curriculum

(c) Textbooks
(d) Method
(e) Role of teacher
(f) Discipline.

One would not fail to observe a close affinity among the parameters wherein one implies the other and is the fulfilment and production of the total process: teacher-content-pupil in all its tripolar glory.

We have examined various aspects of education in relation to philosophy and realised that philosophy is essential for a productive and progressive outlook on education. We may conclude in the words of Rusk that "from every angle of educational problem comes thus the demand for a philosophical basis of the subject. There is no escape from a philosophy of life and of education. There is probably no worker whose practice is more affected by his philosophy than the teacher, it consequently, behaves him to secure as adequate a philosophy as he can command", and with Herbart that "education may have a holiday till philosophical questions are cleared up once for all."

Education as a Craft

Fichte in his "Address to the German People" observed that the art of education would never attain clearness in itself without philosophy: there is an interaction between the two, and either without the other is incomplete and unserviceable. Dewey defines philosophy in its most general phases as being the theory of education.

Rise of a Discipline

The word philosophy comes from the Greek word philosophia which is made up of the words phileo (love) and sophia (wisdom). Thus, the literal meaning of philosophy is "love of wisdom". One has often heard the phrase "What is your philosophy?" when questions are asked, relating to various problems. When an individual answers such questions, he is actually making statements which represent only partial segments of his philosophy. The word 'philosophy' refers to a certain way of thinking. It arises out of an attempt to arrive at the solution of a problem, it may be to resolve a confusing situation. But unlike most kinds of thought, philosophy has no immediate aim.

Philosophy relates not so much to solving an immediate problem, but attempts to find the deeper meanings of problems. Philosophy begins with the attempt to answer questions like "What is life?", "What is sorrow?", "Why do we suffer?", "What is goodness?", "Who is man?" These questions have been raised since the dawn of history, and the attempts to arrive at their answers, at various times, during different ages, in various countries, have given us philosophies.

Basic Issues

The areas of inquiry in all philosophies, generally, are: The Problems of Reality, of Knowledge, and of Value.

(i) *The Problem of Reality is:* What is reality? What is the nature of the Universe in which we live? The branch of philosophy which deals with this great problem is called Metaphysics. The Upanishads raise this question. Buddha looked at the universe in a new way after his enlightenment and called it "Maya". Confucius had a totally different view. Mahatma Gandhi and John Dewey's views of reality and the universe were different. The questions that are raised, regarding the nature of reality and the universe are profound and intricate, their wisdom and depth are astonishing, and the attempts to answer them, provide us with remarkable metaphysical themes.

(ii) *The Problem of Knowledge is:* How does a man know what is real? How do we get knowledge, and how can we be sure it is true and not error? This area of philosophy is called Epistemology. Here again, we find that the Vedas and the Upanishads raise these questions, and try to provide answers, which are different from those raised by the Buddha or Christ. The scientists and biologists, behaviourists and existentialists provide varied answers, after raising many issues.

(iii) *The Third Problem in Philosophy is:* The problem of Value. What are the important values that are to be desired in life? Are these values rooted in reality? How can we realize them in our experience? The branch of philosophy which deals with these questions is called Axiology. The religions of the world, and great religious books, expound ethical principles of life according to the view of reality that they support. The Bhagawad Gita and the Sermon on the Mount, raise and attempt to answer ethical questions in varying ways. Mahatma Gandhi's life style was evolved out of his own ethical principles based on his perception of values.

Wider and Narrower Meanings of Education

Mahatma Gandhi describes education as "an all-round drawing out of the best in child and man—body, mind and spirit." John Dewey regards education as "the development of all those capacities in the individual, which will enable him to control his environment and fulfil his possibilities". These interpretations converge into a two-fold meaning of the word 'education'. They point to education as the process of development of the individual from infancy to maturity, a life-long process.

John Stuart Mill explains the wider and the narrower meanings of the word education thus: "Not only does it include whatever we do for ourselves, and whatever is done for us by others for the express purpose of bringing us somewhat nearer to the perfection of our nature; it does more; in its last connotation it comprehends even the indirect effects of things of which the direct purposes are quite different, by laws, by forms of government, by the industrial arts, by modes of social life; nay, even by physical fact, not dependent on human will; by climate, soil and local position. Whatever helps to shape the human being, to make the individual what he is, or hinder him from what he is not, is part of his education". The narrower meaning the meaning as used in ordinary speech, John Stuart Mill has described as "the culture which each generation purposely gives to those who are to be its successors, in order to qualify them for at least keeping up, and if possible for raising the level of improvement which has been attained."

Indian Approach

The Rig Veda regards education as a force which makes an individual self-reliant as well as selfless. The Upanishads regard the result of education as being more important than its nature. The end-product of education, according to the Upanishads is salvation. Panini, the scholar and grammarian, identified education as the training one obtains from nature, while Kannad, the ancient philosopher considers to be a means of developing self-contentment. Yajanvalakya, the ancient legislator regarded education a means to the development of character and usefulness in an individual. Shankaracharya regarded education to be synonymous with self-realization.

Swami Vivekananda, modern exponent of Vedanta Philosophy, perceived education as the manifestation of divine perfection already existing in man. "Education" he said "should aim at man-making". By "man-making"—he implies the formation of character, increase in the powers of mind, and expansion of the intellectual capacities. Rabindranath Tagore's ideas of education is that, it should help the individual child realize in and through education, the essential unit of man and his relationship with universe—an education for fullness. The Indian Education Commission of 1966, condenses the various views on education thus:

"Education, according to Indian tradition is not merely a means to earn a living; nor is it only a nursery of thought or a school for citizenship. It is initiation into the life of spirit, a training of human souls in pursuit of truth and the practice of virtue. It is a second birth, 'dvitiyam janam'—Education for liberation."

European Approach

Plato held that education should enable one to attain the highest good or God, through pursuit of inherent spiritual values of truth, beauty and goodness. Aristotle, however, held that education exists exclusively to develop man's intellect in a world of reality which men can know and understand. St. Thomas Aquinas considered education to be the process of discerning the truth about things as they really are, and to extend and integrate such truth as is known. That education was to ensure proper morality and salvation was emphasized in the sixteenth and the seventeenth centuries by John Calvin and Martin Luther, who stressed that salvation was available through faith and this faith would be reached only through education in and study of the Bible. A more recent concept of education is that of twentieth century behaviour psychologists. According to them, education is a process of conditioning of providing stimuli, drill, repetition, rewards and reinforcement. The social scientists, however, define education as the transmission of the cultural heritage—which consists of learned behaviour, and includes tangible objects, such as tools, clothing, etc., as well as intangibles, such as language, beliefs, superstitions, etc.

Analysis : These varying definitions of education, through the ages, and there are a host of other definitions, past and present, point out the problems of the educator when he sets forth choosing from among them, for the purpose of educating children. Conflicting and inaccurate views may cause trouble in planning education and schooling for the young. Should the school aim at developing the powers of the child? Which powers, intellectual, moral, physical, spiritual, and to what extent should each be developed? Or, are we to condition the child's behaviour by providing various stimuli leading to responses, using drill, repetition, reinforcement, etc.? Or, do we gear the school to the transmission of the cultural heritage of humanity? A moment's reflection will make clear to us, that the differing views on education by various philosophers and educators are based on their varying concepts of reality, of knowledge, and of values. In other words, these definitions indicate that their philosophical positions as related to their views on education are of utmost relevance for the educator.

The Distinction

If philosophy is an enquiry into man's attempt to understand the universe in which he lives, and if education is, according to some definitions, the transmission of knowledge, value and skills of a culture, then we should be able to define the philosophy of education by a combination of both definitions.

Firstly, let us examine the historical basis of educational philosophy. We may have observed that in one sense, the philosophy of education is an ancient subject because there were thinkers in bygone ages who theorized about education. The great philosophers of all times have also been great educators. Educational movements which some of the former initiated, were really the expression of their philosophical beliefs. Socrates, who took delight in "pricking bubbles" and who rebelled against traditional ways of thinking, was one of greatest of teachers; he is the originator of the "Socratic method" of teaching, by questioning and examining. Plato, the great philosopher, was an outstanding educational thinker. His inquiry into the nature of justice in "The Republic", is a remarkable treatise on education, at once comprehensive in its content and universal in its application.

The writings of Aristotle offer an interesting example of the intimate connection between philosophy, educations and politics. One can discover a close connection between empiricism in philosophy and encyclopaedism in education, in Comenius, who was an exponent of the latter John Locke had a passion for truth and sanity in thought, as a philosopher, and he advocated education as a means for realizing these virtues. Rousseau's anti-social philosophy, and his negative or natural education, that he advocated for Emile, Frobel's idealistic philosophy and his concept of the Kindergarten, Dewey's pragmatism and the emergence of the project method, are other examples indicating the close relationship between philosophy and education. Ross remarks appropriately, that the inevitable tendency for a philosopher to turn educator is as manifest today, as at any former time. Examples of such thinkers as H.G. Wells, Bertrand Russell, A.N. Whitehead, Alduous Huxley, Skinner and others, who in the light of their views about reality, knowledge and values, advocate a system of education, further, illustrate the relationship between philosophy and education.

It is not implied that teachers must first be philosophers. It is suggested that basic understanding of philosophical themes on the part of all teachers regarding ancient and contemporary philosophies might provide some ideas which teachers may find helpful. The purpose of this chapter is to provide the prospective teacher with an introduction to the major as well as contemporary philosophies to the extent that it may be useful in developing educational programmes.

Goals and Ends

Since there is a fundamental connection between philosophy and education, we shall now try to discover what form this connection takes with reference to the different aspects of educations; how does philosophy affect the formulation of aims in education, the choice of studies, methods of instruction and the problem of discipline?

Every system of education must have an aim, for only an aim or goal can give direction to the educative process, and make education meaningful. The objective in education has a reference to the meaning of life. The meaning of life to an individual is determined by the philosophy held by the individual at a certain time. Thus goals of education depend upon the philosophy that prevails in a society. In ancient Sparta, the ideal was that life ought to be lived with discipline and rigour, and that the country's honour had to be vindicated; hence the aim of the Spartan system of education was to prepare citizens to be solders and patriots. On the other hand, the Athenian system of education aimed at the cultural development of each individual, in conformity with the Athenian philosophy of that era. Rousseau learnt much from nature after receiving many rebuffs from society. In due course, he developed a philosophy that was naturalistic, negative and antisocial. He believed man's instincts, primitive emotions and unsophisticated impulsive judgements were more trustworthy and reliable in guiding one's conduct, rather than the standards advocated by society.

Hence, the system of education advocated by Rousseau proclaims "leave the child alone", so that he can receive education freely from nature and then develop according to his own inner power, in freedom and without artificial restrictions being imposed on him. Mahatma Gandhi's scheme of Basic Education was an expression of his philosophy—the need for unity in India through a common language, the necessity of education for the masses, the economic absurdities of the then prevailing exclusive educational system, all led to the advocating of a scheme, which would meet urgent demands of pre-independent India, and of the unsatisfactory plight of the masses in those times.

The needs of post-independent India led to the serious reconsideration of the purpose and objectives of education and led to the set up of the Mudaliar Commission on Secondary Education in 1952-53. The goals of education at the secondary stage were to emphasise the development of personality, development of the ideals of democratic citizenship, training in vocational efficiency and emphasis on leadership qualities.

Again in 1964-66, the Kothari Commission formulated other goals for education in schools which were to increase productivity, to bring about social and national integration, to accelerate the process of modernization and the cultivation of social, moral and spiritual values.

The failure in implementing many of the above goals in education, again in 1985, led the then Prime Minister Rajiv Gandhi to make a statement to the nation declaring that a new education policy would be made so as to "prepare Indians for the 21st Century. Education must promote national cohesion and the work ethic. The grandeur of our freedom struggle and its significance for national integration have to be brought home to every student. I would strongly emphasise education's organic link with the productive forces of Society." Accordingly a document entitled the "Challenge of Education" was prepared and this was incorporated into a Rensed National Policy on Education in 1986.

Later, in 1990, with a change in the Government, the Ramamurthi Report examined the National Policy on Education of 1986, and outlined certain values for education, emphasising that a sound knowledge base is necessary in schools. It also stresses the need to provide opportunities to acquiring skills by students—basic life skills, communication, computation, social and manual skills. Nature of values for development of character in a social, cultural and national context are to be provided. Education is also to play an interventionist and catalytic role for promotion of national cohesion and unity.

Effect on Syllabus

It is in the area of curriculum planning that philosophy in education reflects itself. The goals and objectives of any educational effort can only be implemented through a curriculum which translates them into subjects, units of instruction, themes and topics which enter the classroom. They are to be reflected into the reading, the instruction and the activities of pupils under the guidance and direction of the teacher.

Philosophy also plays a role in the methods of teaching and instruction. If self-learning is the goal, and a democratic atmosphere aimed at the teacher's role is to promote these by providing situations for their achievement. The teaching-learning process assumes a different role, according to the philosophy of education being upheld.

Whenever a nation's culture has been based on its religious tradition, education has not been a separate branch of activity. It has been a part of the total life, with its social beliefs about God, Man and the Universe. The teacher has been a part of this religious tradition and has imparted knowledge and skills, transmitted the cultural heritage and social traditions to the young in the society. The teacher has had a place in society in keeping with the tradition of learning and religion. Hence, for this reason, we do not find in ancient cultures, of any country, particularly in the East, special books on the subject of education. Rather, the teacher has had search for the principles of education and the philosophy behind teaching, in the sacred books. Such sacred texts in India, were the Vedas; they were a poetic expression of the reaction of people, the wonder and mystery of life. The Upanishads attempted to emphasize the significance of the self within man, while in the Bhagawad Gita the emphasis was on the joyful fulfilment of Dharma.

However, in the Western world, after printing was invented, education was secularized. Each man could interpret the scriptures, as he liked. Education and religion have been separated gradually from the sixteenth century onwards, in the western world. In the orient today, there is a marked tendency towards complete separation of education and religion. In spite of this, in all countries, there are still some schools where education and religion go hand in hand. But governments and states often do not want to aid these systems of education in any way.

The teacher, from the nineteenth century onwards; has had to search elsewhere for the meanings, purposes and goals of education, and their underlying philosophies. A study of the philosophies of education as propounded by great leaders of thought, will help the teacher greatly. The teacher faces problematic situations in the classroom-discipline, underachievement of students, poor attendance, and many others. A knowledge of the philosophies of education will help him to formulate his own philosophy and beliefs, and these can influence his choices and actions. His individual philosophy, based on a study of the philosophies of educators, may help him to determine the manner in which he will handle these problems.

This does not imply that teachers must first be philosophers. It is suggested that a basic understanding of philosophical themes on the part of all teachers regarding ancient and temporary philosophical systems of thought, might provide some guidance to teachers. They could use some of these ideas in classroom situations. The purpose of the next chapters on the philosophies of education, will provide the teacher with an introduction to ancient and contemporary philosophy, to the extent that they may prove helpful in education.

2

Essential Elements

One of the basic truths in education is that all discussions ultimately end in telling how learning can be made more efficient. Good teaching always focuses on effective teaching which means effective learning. Learning is not a unitary activity. It has at least three components: (i) acquisition of knowledge or information or understanding of principles, concepts, etc., (ii) retention of what is acquired, and (iii) recall or reproduction of what is acquired or understood. Hence, when we speak of learning, it refers to these three components put together as a single unit. In the same way when we discuss factors that influence learning we have to take into account all the factors that affect acquisition of material, retention of material and recall of material. Efficiency of learning, from this point of view means accuracy, speed and amount of material learned, retained and reproduced.

The factors that affect these variables of learning may be classified as those which pertain to :

1. The learner
2. The material to be learned
3. The method of teaching and learning

Each of these group of factors is discussed in detail as follows:

Pertaining to the Learner : The learner is the kingpin in the whole process of learning. It is he who has to make active efforts to learn. It is, therefore, the first requisite that he must have the capacity, abilities and entering behaviours needed for learning the proposed material. This factor is known as readiness on the part of the learner.

Readiness as a Factor of Learning: A person is ready to learn something when he has achieved sufficient physiological maturation and experiential background. For example, it is physiologically impossible for a child of 3-4 months to learn to walk or to learn to speak words, or to learn to read. Similarly, a non-science student can not be made to learn Einstein's theory of relativity. A youth of 10 years normally is not ready to study subjects such as calculus, Sankhya philosophy, romanticism in literature, etc. Learning and understanding of these tasks requires suitable experiential background which a child of ten is not expected to have. Exceptions may be there, but on an average certain level of physiological maturation and experiential background are essentially required for learning corresponding tasks.

If a child is incapable of learning to read at six and a half when children, normally, begin to read, he may face a year or two of failure and eventually may develop a mind-set against reading which will make it difficult for him to learn to read at any age.

Readiness for learning includes not only the physiological maturation, mental growth, but also such factors as interest and motivation. It is said that a child may achieve necessary coordination to perform a particular physical task at the age of 12, but if he begins trying at an earlier age he may significantly accelerate the development of the necessary coordination with the result that he may be able to perform the task at the age of ten. But, there is a limitation of this earlier training and this varies from individual to individual. Studies, however, indicate that not much can be gained by starting youngsters on a particular learning task earlier than readiness normally permits. If started at the proper level of maturation, children learn more speedily and quickly and catch up with those who started earlier.

De Cecco and William Crawford (1977) say that the student can not acquire new performance learning of which depends on other performance which he has not learned. To quote them "learning builds on learning in the way success builds on success", (p. 48). This they call entering behaviours, "behaviours the student must have acquired before he can acquire particular new terminal behaviour".

Thus, readiness is the most important factor that influences learning. Ausubel (1959) defines readiness as "the adequacy of the student's existing capacity in relation to some instructional objective." Robert Gagne and his associates (1962) talk of "learning sets" which means more or less the same as readiness. They define learning sets as the capabilities the student possesses at any given stage in the learning of a given task. In slightly a different language Jenson (1965) also emphasized the importance of readiness principle when he said, that a students performance on any given task will be a product of the levels of his learning abilities and the degree to which the task involves these abilities.

Motivation: Child's level of motivation is another important factor that influences learning. Learning is a kind of behaviour; and behaviour does not just occur. It is caused by some need and is oriented toward a goal. In other words behaviour is purposive. If the child sees purpose in his act of learning he will willingly strive to achieve this. The importance of this factor has been comprehensively discussed in the literature of psychology and has been widely accepted by teachers too.

Learning Set: This factor of learning emphasizes that there should be a "proper set for learning". It means several things; for example, learner's good study habits, his mental preparedness and cognitive awareness of the task to be learned. De Cecco and Crawford (1977) describe two kinds of learning sets - (a) learning to learn and (b) learning set and structures By learning to learn they mean progressive improvement in performance as a result of previously learned mode of working through learning of related tasks. It may be considered as the "general mode of attack" available to the student for learning various tasks. Learning set and structure as defined by Gagne means the most basic and general capabilities that the student requires for learning.

Clausmeier and Goodwin (1966, p.456) hold that giving short instructions to students before starting to teach may generate a kind of learning set. Instructions including information about purpose of learning, abilities required, relationship with other relevant knowledge already acquired, outcomes of learning, etc., may comprise a learning set, a predisposition to learn. Presenting advance organizers to the students may also contribute to establishing a learning set.

Concept of Material

The kind of material to be learned also influences students' learning. Ausubel (1963) has emphasized that meaningful material can be learned and retained better. If the material to be learned is organized in a systematic logical sequence it would be more easily learned. Ausubel's Advanced Organizers Theory comprehensively describes' the sequence. It proceeds from the most generalized idea to, less and less generalized one. If information and knowledge to be learned are organized in such a way that they consist, largely, of the mastery of simple concepts followed by the organization of these into larger systems of concepts and generalization or principles about facts and concepts, this becomes more meaningful to the students and is learned more efficiently.

Meaningfulness of the material has two aspects: the relatedness of the parts of the material and the ability of the individual to incorporate new material into his cognitive structure. Meaningful material is recalled better. Advance organizers have on learning a facilitating effect. Well structured material is easily learned.

Different Mechanisms

Quite a number of factors that affect efficiency of learning pertain to methods of learning and teaching. These are described as follows :

Practice as a Factor of Learning: This is the same as Thorndike's Law of Exercise which said that learning is merely repeating an act a number of times, and, thus, improving the performance. But, this is true only when the learner is motivated to learn. "Practice makes a man perfect" is only a half truth. Practice is a necessary condition for learning, but it is not a sufficient condition. Practice in the absence of learner's intention and will is of little avail. Yet, it is a fact that improvement in performance can not take place in the absence of practice. It is, therefore, necessary to encourage practice in order to promote a greater degree of understanding, retention and transfer. However, certain considerations should be kept in mind in this connection as follows :

(a) Practice should take place in meaningful setting. Most effective type of practice is that in which the learner uses his previous learning in dealing with more advanced work, such as mathematics.

(b) Practice should not be of monotonous type. If it is meaningless, uninteresting and disliked by the learner, it may lead to development of negative attitudes toward the subject or the task as the case be.

Distributed Practice vs. Massed Practice: Distribution of practice periods is another factor that affects efficiency of learning. This can not be a general rule that distributed practice, i.e., broken into a series of relatively short periods is always the better approach to learning. It depends on the nature of the learner and the nature of the material to be learned whether distributed practice or massed practice will be more effective. Research (Kingsley and Garry, 1957) has shown some advantage in the spaced practice periods in case of long term retention. But, in case of immediate recall not much difference is found between the two methods. In general, short practice periods over a certain length of time produce maximum efficiency in learning (Starch, 1927). In case of distributed practice of short periods learner's motivation is high, concentration is better and fatigue, is also absent. There is, however, no conclusive evidence as to the optimal distribution of lessons. The teacher must decide for himself how long a period is more productive of learning for a group of learners.

Part Versus Whole Method of Learning: Whether a unit of the material should be learned as a whole or in parts is also an important consideration in learning. Earlier the whole method was considered superior. But, recent studies have not supported this view. Research in this area has not been conclusive. Hence, the principle should be that whatever the learner can grasp clearly and meaningfully whether it is a chapter, a paragraph or a sentence that must be the best for him, the optimum unit of learning for him is to learn at one time. He should study it as a whole provided he perceives that as meaningful and useful from his point of view. But, in case of nonsense material the part method is found to be as effective as the whole method. Even in this case the learner will be more benefited if he gets an overview of the material and structures the field by relating the parts to one another and also to the whole field.

Concept of Over-learning

Over-learning (i.e., additional practice) means learning something over and over again for an indefinite time. A person can learn something well enough to make a perfect score immediately after learning; he then has continuous practice for a long time on the same material. This is over-learning the material which results into more stable and permanent retention of the material learned. It has been found that over-learning does contribute to better retention. Hence, it is considered a factor of more efficient learning. Over-learning is measured in terms of the percentage of additional practice spent after initial mastery. Krueger (1929) showed that practice carried on after the material is learnt and mastery is achieved first time is of great value in learning as, in that case, retention is more durable. Over-learning is a kind of massed practice. It is learning beyond mastery.

Over-learning is, generally, used and is more effective in case of learning meaningless material. When the material is sufficiently meaningful it is unnecessary. It is, particularly, more fruitful in case of learning tables, vocabulary, spellings, etc., i.e. the content which is of discrete nature, and can not be structured. Over-learning reaches a point of diminishing return when it goes much beyond the first mastery level. At this point additional practice increases retention only slightly and the effort surpasses the gain (Krueger, 1929).

The Assessment

It means giving some time for revision, recall or test after having learned the material. It may take several forms. It may be in the form of a test to just check how much and what has been learnt. It may be in the form of just making a hurried revision or restudying the material. It may be in the form of mentally summarising the whole material. It may be any form, but the fact is that it helps retention. Each form, however has its special advantage. It is more useful to have a recall test immediately after learning the material. It may be the form of a test or just in the form of a point-wise summary - at this stage rereading or restudy of the material is less valuable in comparison to recall test. Restudying is, however, more useful when sufficient time (say 2-3 weeks) has passed after having learned the material, as held by Sones and Stroud (1940).

The Organisation

Of all the factors that affect learning, particularly memory and retention, meaningful structure is perhaps the most important to be kept in mind. There is much less forgetting when the material is sufficiently meaningful and well-structured. If it is not well structured but is quite meaningful, even then it may be remembered, but only in proportion to its meaning (McGeoch and Iron, 1952). As a general rule meaningful material is remembered for longer period of time. Much of the factual material is forgotten after a year or so, but very little is forgotten in case of conceptual material.

Meaningfulness consists of relations between facts, generalizations, rules, principles, etc., for which the learner sees some use. Solitary facts, too, are meaningless. McDougall (1959) said that mere learning of any kind of organizing principle, in itself, contributes to retention of learned material.

Stephens (1956) says that in case of meaningful material there may be no forgetting whatever, nonsense material is headed for extinction before the last syllable is uttered.

3

Educational Philosophy

Diverse Standpoints

There are three important aspects of human life and development that philosophy is concerned with. They are:

Ontology: This is concerned with the theory of being. It is concerned with the problem/nature of ultimate reality of Me and the end of life. This branch of philosophy is also related to metaphysics which deals with questions beyond physical reality such as who am I? What is the purpose of life? What is God? What is the design of God? and so on.

Epistemology: This is concerned with the theory of knowledge. The aim of knowledge is to find the 'truth'. How can we discern the truth from falsehood? Theory of knowledge deals with various methods of drawing the truth. We shall discuss this branch of philosophy in detail at a later stage.

Axiology: This is concerned with the theory of values. Ethics, aesthetics and logic are the three normative sciences that deal with intrinsic values. Ethics is concerned with moral behaviour or conduct of man. Aesthetics deals with the appreciation of beauty. Logical analysis which deals with reasoning, is of two types—

induction and deduction. Axiology that is, theory of values or nature of values.

Idea of Knowledge

There are three terms which are interrelated—information, knowledge and wisdom. Information is related to bare facts which form data. It can be quantitative or qualitative or both. Knowledge is a meaningful structure of facts into some relationship. It reflects truth about reality. From Indian point of view, it is named as Vidya which involves—facts about reality and cognitive (mental) changes as well. There is mental growth in the process. Wisdom is the outcome of the process of realisation of reality related to life, universe and relationship between the two. It is based both on information and knowledge. Wisdom is the culmination of human experience and realisation in life.

There are certain questions related to knowledge which need thinking and reflection. They are given below:

(i) Can human knowledge acquire real knowledge?

(ii) To what extent can man acquire the knowledge of the supreme?

(iii) What is truth?

(iv) What is falsehood?

(v) In what manner, the truth can be differentiated from falsehood?

(vi) What is the evidence of knowledge?

(vii) What is doubt?

(viii) What are the sources of knowledge?

(ix) What are the types of knowledge?

(x) What are the theories of knowledge?

These questions are discussed under appropriate places in the ensuring paragraphs. But all these questions have direct bearing on discovery of truth, manufacturing of new knowledge human understanding and construction of curriculum and methods of teaching in education.

The Organs

Theory of knowledge attempts to define knowledge and explain its specific characteristics. The dictionary meaning of knowledge refers to assured belief; that which is known; information, instruction; enlightenment; learning; practical skill.

The nature of knowledge can also be understood with the help of its characteristics which are given below:

(i) Knowledge is a means to reach truth.

(ii) Thought is the raw material for knowledge.

(iii) Language is the vehicle of knowledge.

(iv) Meaning of words, terms, concepts form the foundation of knowledge.

(v) Knowledge is certain.

(vi) It is verifiable.

(vii) Its structure is based on facts and values. Knowledge is a structure of information into a meaningful whole. It is well organised system of facts giving meaning to it.

Diverse Sorts

General Types of Knowledge : Based on nature and criteria of knowledge, we can understand its types. Broadly speaking knowledge is categorised into the following types:

(a) a priori, and

(b) empirical

A priori knowledge is obtained by simply thinking. Its chief exemplifications are to be found in 'logic' and 'mathematics'. In order to see that 5 + 7 = 12, we do not need to take five things and seven things, put them together, and then count the total number. We can know what the total number will be simply by thinking. Propositions, maxims and postulates belong to a priori knowledge.

Unlike a priori knowledge, we obtain empirical knowledge by observation of external world (sense-perception) and of ourselves (introspection). This is based on sensations or sensory awareness. Five senses which are the gateways of knowledge, help to know our surroundings and individual self. All scientific knowledge derived through senses and observations belong to empirical knowledge.

According to Indian view, knowledge is of two types:

(a) para vidya

(b) apara vidya

Para vidya is related to physical world (external nature). It can be derived through five senses and reasoning. Apara Vidya is related to other worldliness, spiritual in nature. It is most elevated part of human nature. It is related to self, soul, spirit and God and their relationship.

Specific Types of Knowledge : Specific types of knowledge are determined through 'source' as criterion. The nature of source of knowledge leads to a type of it. Following are the specific types of knowledge:

Authoritative: This knowledge emanates from an authority or a specialist. All research based knowledge can be authoritative knowledge.

Empirical (Perceptual) Knowledge: Knowledge drawn through senses, observations is named as empirical knowledge.

Rational Knowledge: Knowledge drawn from reason is known as rational knowledge. Reasoning and critical thinking paves the way to rational knowledge.

Scientific Knowledge: That knowledge which is gained through observation and experimentation is known as scientific knowledge. It can be verified and tested by others. Here both empirical and rational knowledge are involved. They help in bringing out scientific knowledge.

Pragmatic Knowledge: The knowledge which is useful and of utility is known as pragmatic knowledge. This knowledge is personalised, relativistic. And it is based on observation, experience and experimentation. This knowledge is instrumental in one's adjustment.

Intuitive Knowledge: That knowledge which is subjective and spontaneous in nature is known as intuitive. It is neither related to senses nor related to reason, nor related to personal experience which can be repeated nor it is scientifically verified.

Revealed Knowledge: That knowledge which comes from a divine source and is communicated through man, is known as revealed knowledge. The knowledge contained in scriptures or religious books like Gita, Koran, Bible, Guru Granth Sahib and others is revealed knowledge. This knowledge is classical and universal in nature. It is not modifiable or subject to change.

Chief Sources

Knowledge is drawn from a variety of sources in human experience. Source of knowledge is related to either human self or cognitive process or external agent. Let us briefly discuss different sources of knowledge.

Revelation: This knowledge is conveyed to man by an external and more powerful agent like God or super-power. Knowledge contained in vedas or world scriptures (religious/philosophical books) is revealed knowledge. Some super-natural or divine power conveys knowledge to man. Man is the receiver of knowledge. This type of knowledge is accepted as universal knowledge. It is not limited to time and space. It holds good at all times and at all places.

Authority: This type of knowledge comes from an authority or a specialist in a particular field of knowledge. A philosopher, scientist, economist, psychologist, etc. are different examples related to special field of study or knowledge. Whatever is said or written by an expert or specialist is accepted as final and of a standard. A teacher for a learner is an authority. Learner accepts teacher as a great source of knowledge.

Intuition: This type of knowledge is spontaneous and sudden. There is no involvement either of the senses or the mind. A flash of message is experienced or listened by a person. That special experience is realised by man. It comes true. It is said to be revealed but to certain persons having purity of heart and mind. Or all persons at different point of time experience this.

Reason: This refers to mind. The function of mind is to imagine, think, reason out. Reasoning is a mental process in which one draws out inferences or results. To enable a person to reason out there are certain well tried techniques like induction and deduction. Induction is based on inductive thinking that is drawing out a fact or generalising an experience based on different examples (from examples to generalisation) whereas deduction is the reverse of it. Here one moves from generalisation to particular examples (from generalisation to examples). Law of gravitation is generalised while observing fall of all things towards earth. This is an example of inductive reasoning. Solving particular sum based on algebraic formulae is an example of deductive reasoning.

Senses: Knowledge is drawn through five senses. In this regard, senses are the sources of knowledge. All scientific knowledge or empirical (based on senses) is drawn through observation and experiences related to senses. The knowledge drawn through senses is immediate, first hand, real and concrete in nature. We believe when we see with our eyes or hear with our ears, or taste with our tongue or smoothness/roughness with our skin or smell with our nose. More are senses involved in the process, more comprehensive would be the knowledge.

Experimentation: Man draws knowledge while making experiments either under controlled situation (laboratory) or otherwise. This knowledge is verifiable. One can verify or validate facts of knowledge through making experiment. Experiment can be repeated in order to check the reliability of facts. Therefore experimentation is a way or mode of drawing out knowledge. This technique can be availed in physical sciences and other social sciences. These days knowledge is becoming double after every 3/4 years especially in sciences. So there is an explosion of knowledge since the technique of experimentation has been instrumental for drawing new knowledge.

Cardinal Wisdom

Different schools of philosophy like Naturalism, Idealism and Pragmatism paved different ways to discover truth. They have enabled us to form new concepts, terms, ideas, thoughts leading to new structures of knowledge. Most popular theories of truth are as:

Correspondence Theory: This theory is based on the assumption that our ideas and thoughts have certain external objects or reality with which they correspond. Without external reality, ideas or thoughts do not have then existence. Therefore, every concrete object does have an idea or a thought about it. There is specific relationship between the two identities i.e. object and idea or thought.

Characteristics of this theory are listed below:

— Correspondence is a matter of external relations.

— Truth is objective and specific fact having external basis.

— Relation is preexistent to the search for it.

— Observer/subject does not add or subtract anything of his own.

— Truth is researchable or verifiable at any point of time.

— Truth exists in relation to object only. Schools of Naturalism and Realism are based on the theory of correspondence in respect of truth and knowledge.

Coherence Theory: This theory is based on the assumption that ideas or thoughts are interrelated and consistent. There is cohesiveness, logical connection and relatedness in ideas. Hence truth and knowledge are coherent in nature. It is believed that criterion of truth is more than correspondence to external reality as in the case of correspondence theory.

Characteristics of coherence theory are listed below:

— Coherence theory is a statement of test of truth.

— Consistency is the quality of this theory.

— There is logical interrelation between facts revealing the truth.

— There is hierarchy and structure resulting to a form of truth.

School of Idealism and constructionism are based on the theory of coherence in respect of truth and knowledge.

Instrumental Theory or Pragmatic Theory of Truth: This theory is based on the assumption of utility and usefulness. That knowledge is true which enables a person to know about the situation and adjust with it. This personal adjustment is the main criterion.

Characteristics of this theory are listed below:

— Truth is revealed through one's personal experience.

— Truth has no relationship with external objective reality.

— Experience is personal.

— Experience acts/works as an instrument for personal adjustment.

School of Pragmatism or Instrumentalism or Experimentalism is based on instrumental theory in respect of truth and knowledge.

Theories of truth and knowledge work as foundation to work out a scheme of acquiring knowledge. A theory is an approach as how to receive it, how to process it, how to assimilate it as part of human experience and how to make it part of curriculum at institutional level for imparting knowledge.

Wisdom's Pavement

Knowledge is acquired at three stages of human experience while involving one aspect or component which predominates at that stage. These stages are:

(i) Sensory knowledge based on senses.

(ii) Rational knowledge based on reasoning and logical thinking.

(iii) Spiritual knowledge based on divine wisdom revelation and intuition.

Senses are the primary means to receive knowledge. This knowledge is known as perceptual or empirical. One draws knowledge through concrete objects or natural phenomena. It leads to formation of impressions, perceptions and sensory awareness about physical world.

Rational knowledge is of higher level than that of sensory knowledge. Here mind being at the centre-stage, rational thinking and reasoning are the means to attain this knowledge. Formation of ideas and attainment of concepts are the building material for critical thinking and awareness.

Spiritual knowledge is of highest order than the first two, that is, sensory and rational knowledge. Here spirit is at the centre—stage and self-knowledge, self-awareness, self- transformation and self-realization are the end points. Divine wisdom is based on spiritual consciousness and awareness of man.

Methods of acquiring knowledge are worked out at three levels as per the stage of development and evolution of human experience. Besides instruction in classroom can be designed and programmed as per the nature and the level of knowledge by teachers and curriculum framers.

Growing Consciousness

Based on senses, reason and spirit for attaining knowledge, philosophers and educationists have brought out specific methods. We discuss below these methods of acquiring knowledge:

Appeal to Authority: The knowledge which is attained while having confidence in authority or a specialist in a particular field of knowledge, is known as authoritative knowledge. This method of acquiring knowledge is related to the special fields of knowledge and the specialists working in those fields. That body of knowledge is accepted as true knowledge. One believes and has faith in it. In critical situations with regard to right knowledge, we refer to it.

Appeal to Senses: In this case, senses are the main sources of knowledge. One's awareness about immediate surroundings and of self takes place through senses. In this method, the intake of knowledge can be coloured by environmental factors and physical state of the body. Therefore the reliability of knowledge in this method, depends upon certain extrinsic/external factors, originating from the environment.

Appeal to Observation and Related Processes: In this case, there are four sub-processes of attaining knowledge. These sub-processes which enable us to acquire knowledge are:

— *Observation*—it can be external or internal.

— It can also be natural observation or with the help of scientific instruments.

— *Explanation*—here facts of knowledge are elaborated in a logical manner. Knowledge is accepted in a cohesive order.

— *Prediction*—this process is related to the principle of cause and effect relationship. Consequences are fore told or predicted while conceptualising the causal factors. Both cause and effect need to be understood in a specific relationship.

— *Control*—in an experiments, the element of control plays a vital role. There are certain factors or variables which a scientist supposed to be controlled. In this case the ensuing results are precisely and accurately filtered out because of effective control on factors or variables.

All the four sub-processes contribute to draw a systematic body of facts or knowledge. They are mostly followed in natural, behavioural and social sciences.

Inductive and Deductive Methods: In case of inductive method one starts with particular cases or examples. And he tries to arrive at certain conclusion which is known as generalisation. This further leads to formulate a law or principle. Whereas in case of deductive method, one starts with generalisation or rule and comes to particular examples. Therefore knowledge is gathered both inductively and deductively. These methods are more applicable in teaching of logic, mathematics and sciences.

Institution: The elements which help to attain knowledge in intuitive method are preparation, incubation, inspiration and illumination. Each element is contributive to reach a significant knowledge. These elements bring a structural change in cognition (mental faculties).

Concentration and Meditation: Concentration is an activity of mind in which mental energy is focussed with the help of physical aid like candle light flame or object. In case of meditation, one concentrates for a longer time on any idea or image or Mantra. Both concentration and meditation are the foundation of attaining knowledge. They empower the individual to conceptualise, infer and make link of the facts of knowledge in leading to a meaningful whole.

Problem Solving: The steps involved in the process of problem solving lead to a solution. This solution of a problem becomes part of knowledge. All the solutions of such problems or learnings form a significant part of knowledge. Therefore problem solving is an effective tool to acquire new knowledge.

The Impact

A variety of methods of instruction have been worked out in education and they are put to practice while taking into cognizance the level and stage of child's experience. Such methods of instruction have corresponding relationship with specific type, source and method of acquiring knowledge. These methods are discussed below:

Methods of Instruction Related to Senses: Playway methods at early stage of schooling are developed on multiple sensory involvement. Child gathers knowledge of surrounding world through his five senses. He makes a structure of truth in the background of his personal awareness.

Interacting with outside world and objects in the form of physical activities, modes of play and types of works, enable the child to draw knowledge. Maxims of instruction like concrete to abstract, hold good to draw concepts and understandings.

Methods Related to Reason: There are certain methods of instruction which seem to help the learner to draw knowledge and form concepts. These methods empower the mind. New ideas are reasoned out through inductive, deductive and other logical approaches. Ideas, thoughts and new awareness are made while introducing certain ways and techniques based on reasoning and reflective thinking.

Intellectual involvement, discussions, debates, brain storming, quiz, mental teasers, reflections are some of the examples of this category.

Methods Related to Spirit: Spirit/soul is the third level of human experience. Apart from sense and reason, there is another level or stage where spirit is involved. Knowledge related to spirit and divinity is realised through certain methods along with the growth of senses and mind. One is in a position to gather knowledge related to self and his inner being. This is the highest stage of one's experience and knowledge. Here intuition, revelations and illuminations work very effectively. A teacher should often take the learner to this stage of experience during his teaching.

Silent sitting, meditation, reading philosophical books and scriptures, devotional music, poems, classical and folk dances, discourses on how to live life, are some of the ways to reach spiritual wisdom and knowledge. Perhaps this is the end of education in educational institutions which needs to be practised.

Consequent Problems

Now-a-days there is an explosion of knowledge due to unprecedented advancements in the fields of science and technology. These advancements have resulted into making a successful trip even to the moon. Old ideas are gradually changing giving place to new ones. Values and traditions are in the process of transformation. New knowledge has been discovered in each subject. Man's mind is disturbed with the question whether he should teach the new knowledge or the old. Should we teach the old for helping the student to learn the new? How should we present the old and new knowledge in an interconnected manner? What type of knowledge should be imparted at a particular stage? How should the knowledge given at the various stages of education be made as one connected whole? What methods should be adopted to facilitate the achievement of the objectives of teaching? Under such a situation only that person can successfully give solutions to these issues who is thoroughly conversant with the knowledge we want to impart. This ever increasing store of knowledge has created following problems for education:

1. What should we teach?
2. What is the purpose of teaching?
3. When should we teach?
4. How should we teach?

Different Rules and Regulations

Structure of Knowledge : In the methods of teaching today one finds emphasis on acquainting the student with the structure of knowledge and not to impart informations. This means that the student should be helped to grasp the structure of subject in such a way as to enable him to understand things related to it in a meaningful context. The student has to be taught how things are related. If he understands the interrelationship between things, he will be able to grasp many other relevant things in a meaningful manner.

Readiness for Learning : Today it is believed that any subject may be taught at any stage of education. The basic idea is that the fundamental principles of any subject may be taught in some form to a child of any age group. Many scientists, technicians and machinists could be produced in U.S.S.R. through the theory of learning by conditioned response. This could be possible by creating a readiness in the individual for learning. Thus, education in U.S.S.R. may be as an example of readiness for learning.

Use of Intuitive Analytical Method : Intuition is the method through which one reaches a relevant conclusion without analysing the situation. After reaching the conclusion one verifies it by analysis. Training should be given in hunches for developing intuition. Intuition is important in intellectual work, as well as in daily work. When a person tries to think intuitively and reach a possible conclusion, this habit refers to his intuitive ability. He at once grasps the intricacies of a situation and is able to go ahead in his chosen sphere of activity. Several great scientists and great persons base their thinking process on intuition in their respective fields. Intuition may be received in any mental activity higher or lower. The difference being only of the degree and not of the kind. Hence, training should be given in intuition in every school.

Motivation : In order to enable the student to learn, he must be motivated to learn. This motive may be a desire to learn or to win some reward or to get promotion to another higher class. The external incentives, like reward and promotion is not always helpful in stimulating the child to learn. One should depend upon the principles of child psychology, teaching methods and reorganizing the curriculum in an integrated manner for creating motivation in the child.

Use of Teaching Aids : A number of teaching aids have been developed these days. In order to be more effective, the teacher is now expected to select a proper teaching aid and use it relevantly. As there are so many aids to teach, the teacher naturally feels a problem of selecting the right one out of many before him.

Structure of Knowledge : A man studies not only for self-pleasure but also to benefit himself in such a way that he may use the earned knowledge in future for his betterment. In the process of learning he may acquire many such skills by virtue of which he may do many identical things later. In the same way through his studies he learnt many things and acquire many attitudes. These learnt things and attitudes are used later in various situations of life. The main purpose of various methods of education is to help the students to acquire certain useful principles of work, desirable attitudes and modes of good behaviour according to the accepted social norms. This will be achieved only when he acquires a grip over the structure of knowledge. Therefore, the major emphasis should be on helping the student to enter into the basic structural elements of the subject placed before him to learn. This creates the following two main problems before the teacher:

(i) How to reorganize the curriculum of the basic subjects in such a manner as to help the student to acquire the basic ideas effectively in order to develop the desired attitudes which may work as propellers of good behaviour.

(ii) The second problem is how to tailor the curriculum to suit each and every stage of education.

In order to solve in the above problems, the experts in the various subjects should sit together and reorganize the curriculum for the primary and secondary levels. These experts should be helped by experienced teachers of various primary and secondary classes. Experienced authors, film-producers and other experts may also be consulted in this work. Such a procedure has been followed in many advanced countries in the reorganising of the curriculum in mathematics, natural sciences, social sciences and literature.

When the general principles of a subject are learnt by a student he should be able to arrange the learnt things in a systematic and meaningful manner in his mind so that he may use the same when an occasion arises.

Readiness to Learning : It is assumed that any subject may be taught to any child at any stage of his development. There are three following bases of this assumption:

The Process of Intellectual Development of the Child : In his process of development the child has his own characteristic way of viewing the world. He understands the world in his own way. Hence, a subject should be taught to the child according to his point of view. The teacher has not to teach a subject to the child according to the adult point of view. According to the demands of the development of the child, the subject-matter may be made more inclusive and comprehensive gradually. At first the child is better able to understand concrete things through the help of concrete things or concrete examples. This is able to comprehend abstract ideas. At first the child absorbs only those ideas which are presented before him through some concrete instances.

The Psychology of Learning : There are three mental processes during the course of learning: (a) acquisition of knowledge or ideas, (b) transformation of the learnt knowledge of ideas in which the learner tries to arrange the learnt things in his mind in his own way. In this transformation he analyses the inherent points and introduces such changes in the same way which may be helpful to him later, (c) evaluation about whether the transformation made is such as to fulfil teaching purpose. All these three processes, acquisition, transformation and evaluation are involved in learning of any subject.

The Notion of Spiral Curriculum : In the spiral curriculum the contents of a certain subject-matter is arranged in such a logical and challenging manner that the learner is propelled to learn further about the subject once learnt. In this process even a small child is taught such things which will be suitable even for an adult to learn. Thus, through the spiral curriculum the child is helped to absorb many such basic and structural ideas which are challenging even to an adult. Therefore, those problems, principles, ideas and values should be incorporated in the spiral curriculum which the society consider suitable for adults to imbibe. As the problems, ideas and values prevailing in society are undergoing constant transformation the spiral curriculum should be continually changed and modified according to explicit or implicit demands of the society.

Intuitional Method : When one is working on a problem for a long time thinking about its solution, all of a sudden he gets the solution, though he has yet to provide a proof for it. This method of finding a sudden solution is a result of intuitional thinking. Hence, it is called intuitional method. In analytical thinking one proceeds step by step and he is conscious of this step all the time. The operations and informations involved in the analytical thinking are deliberately chosen and decided upon. It may also involve deductive reasoning. In contrast to this procedure of analytical thinking, the intuitive thinking is not well-defined. It implies implicit perception of the total problem. The answer arrived at by intuitive thinking may be right or wrong, but the thinker cannot justify his conclusion immediately. Intuitive thinking is possible only if the thinker is familiar with the domain of knowledge and its structure.

Due to this familiarity with the domain and structure of knowledge the thinker is able to leap about, skip steps and employ short cuts. Through intuitive thinking an individual may get a correct solution which he can never obtain by analytical method. But once the solution is obtained through intuition, the same must be checked and verified through analysis, induction and deduction. An intuitive thinker may discover or invent problems, but it is analysis that gives proper form to these problems. But unfortunately the formalism of the school atmosphere does not recognise the importance of intuition. As a result intuition appears to be devalued in the school. Hence, the teacher in the school must devise methods for developing intuitive thinking in his students. For this the curriculum has to be carefully reorganized.

How to Develop Intuitive Thinking: After giving an answer through his intuition, the teacher should subject his answer to critical analysis to be made by his students. This procedure shall encourage the students to do their own intuitive thinking at times.

It will energise the students and will bring life in the monotonous atmosphere of the class. The teacher must not analyse everything for his students rather the analysis should be made by the students themselves. One should remember that the emphasis in teaching or helping the students to grasp the structure or connectedness of knowledge will immensely facilitate intuitive thinking because the comprehension of structure will help the student to increase his effectiveness in grasping problems intuitively. Self-confidence and courage should be developed because effective intuitive thinking may be developed in the student on the basis of these traits. For the development of intuitive thinking the intuitive thinker must never feel shy if he makes mistakes in his intuitive answers. On the contrary, he should be willing to make honest mistakes in his endeavour to find out solutions to problems.

Motivation for Learning : Today every human society is exposed to continual changes. After the World War II, these changes have been revolutionary. The various countries are afraid of each other. There is an arms race. The world is divided in aligned and non-aligned groups, big and small powers, developed, developing and underdeveloped countries. The politicians categorise the human race into three major groups—first world, second world and third world. Each country of the world is facing political, cultural or social crises. There has been the impact of automatic machines, new sources of energy and space investigations. Never was the human society so much mechanised. Never was it so near to annihilation which is dependent on the calculation of some super power. This state of affairs has revolutionized the very concept of the school offerings.

People no more interested only in intellectual, cultural and physical activities in schools. They are now emphasising the teaching of science and technical subjects. Students offer these subjects, because these assure them positions in some technical establishments. More brilliant students are encouraged to offer science or technical subject whether or not he has an aptitude for the same. This trend has brought in many students who are not deserving on intrinsic merits study science and technical subjects. Many students are being neglected. The children whose growth is delayed or who are not able to complete their formal education because of adverse circumstances are totally neglected. One finds a new current of pursuit of excellence which has divided children into two classes—brilliant and dull. In every country there is a search of science talent and there is a test for it on in all country basis. National scholarships are being awarded to able students in science and technical subjects. This has led to the neglect of the studies of humanities and social sciences. It appears that a day will come, when there will be dearth of learned persons and really efficient teachers in these areas. Hence, the cultural traditions appear to be exposed to great harm. Thus, it is necessary to reorganise the curriculum of humanities, social sciences and literature in the same manner in which it is being done for science and technical subjects.

Necessary reforms should be introduced in the examination system so that one may be able to classify students of various abilities on a scientific basis. If sciences and technical subjects are to be saved from unhealthy competitive spirit and over-importance, the Government must pay the same attention to the studies of humanities and social sciences. Incentive for learning should be made more comprehensive. Incentives should be energised by making the ability the basis of deservingness. Education should be saved from the ill effects of unhealthy competition.

Aids of Teaching : Today one should find a number of aids to teaching and learning. Some of these enrich the students' experiences. Some help them to understand the basic structure of the curriculum. The various aids to teaching may be grouped into the following four categories:

(i) Devices of Vicarious Experiences;
(ii) Model Devices;
(iii) Dramatizing Devices; and
(iv) Automatizing Devices.

Devices of Vicarious Experiences : These include films, television, microphotographic films, filmstrips, sound recording and the like which are ordinarily employed. Through these devices students are generally given such matters which are outside the prescribed courses. They are given experience pertaining to certain events directly. These devices enrich the experiences of the students and they also bring life in the educational procedure.

Model Devices : Through these the student grasps the fundamentals of an event or a certain context. These modes are generally shown as laboratory exercises. Certain wooden blocks have been devised for this purpose. Pictures and charts are also used for helping students to understand the basic structure.

Dramatizing Devices : These devices help the student in identifying a certain idea or phenomenon more closely. Some historical event or the life pattern of some great men may be dramatised. In the process of teaching the teacher himself may dramatise certain aspects of the subject-matter or may read out certain portions of the text-book in a dramatic tone. This may bring life in the class-room. It may also help the student to grasp the essentials in a better way.

Automatising Devices : These include machines to aid in teaching. Through these machines certain problems are presented in a systematic manner. Alternative answers are also associated with the problems. The student is required to select the correct answer. With the selection the machine begins to respond. If the selected answer is correct, the machine moves on further and presents another problem or exercise. The exercises for the machines are so arranged that the student encounters both easy and difficult ones. So if he fails in case of difficult exercises, in an easier exercise he succeeds immediately. Therefore, he is not discouraged.

4

Learning Procedure

In its biological nature it is the capacity to be found in plasticity of the nervous system which is due to the changes occurring in the formation of bonds and connections. Learning is the superstructure of our personality and characterised upon the basis of natural inherited organism by coming in contact with the world. Thus, learning is life and life is learning. Every experience is learning. Woodruff says that the process of learning is the vehicle by which the individual is changed from a bundle of potentiality to an active organism with ideas, habits, skills and other personality characteristics.

In the whole process of learning, the need arises, goal is set up, adjustment begins, changes in behaviour take place and stabilize. Further, learning involves problem solving i.e., understanding and discovering relations between different contents in a situation. Here, one may argue that why should one learn? To answer it, it is sufficient to note that learning is an activity aroused by the personal and social demands. And, hence it is the demand of the individual himself; it is the demand of the society which makes him feel to learn. But, the individual may learn things both desirable and undesirable. The task of education, here, should be to enable the individual to learn the desirable and eliminate the undesirable. It is thus said that learning is a process of improvement.

Incessant Process

Learning at all stages is a continuous process involving progressive organization of human behaviour resulting from an interaction with the environment. A few defining characteristics of learning may be mentioned as under

All Living is Learning i.e., the individual is in active relation with his environment. He constantly is interacting with it and is constantly learning.

Learning Results in the Change in Behaviour **:** We note a change in the persons response to the light. It is a change of behaviour influenced by previous behaviour. It is the outcome of an activity that leaves a more or less permanent effect on later activity.

Learning is an Adjustment **:** Most learning in children consists in modifying, adapting and changing their original behaviour in order to adjust to life's situations. Thus, they acquire new forms of behaviour.

Learning Comes about as a Result of Practice **:** This characteristic eliminates sources of change such as illness and maturation. Potent effects of motivation on behaviour are worth considering here.

Learning is Universal **:** Every creature that lives learns. Man learns most. Human children have the longest period of immaturity and helplessness and hence the longer period for opportunity for learning. The human nervous system is very complex, so are human reactions and so are human acquisitions.

Learning is a Relatively Permanent Change **:** After a rat wakes up from his nap he still remembers the path to the food. Even if you have not been on a bicycle for years, in just a few minutes' practice you can be quite proficient again. This is due to change that was acquired and persisted.

Learning is Growth **:** It is never-ending growth. At each stage the learner acquires new ideas and skills which add to his growth. Each learning forms the basis of a fresh endeavour; and thus the constant urge of newer and higher ideals of work and achievement is progressively fulfilled.

Learning is not Directly Observable : The only way to study learning is through some observable behaviour. Actually, we cannot observe learning; the performance, and the consequences of performance.

Learning is not confined to human-beings only; animals also learn in a similar fashion. The juggler makes the monkey to learn so many tricks. Dogs are trained to catch thieves, elephants are taught to perform circus tricks, pigeons learn to play pingpong. Dolphin fish are noted playing net ball or passing through a ring. Hayes trained chimpanzees to perform acts as dusting, washing dishes, sharpening pencil, painting furniture etc. The only difference in animal learning and human learning is in the quality and extent of learning because all learning depends upon the physical and mental structure.

Different Theories

Various theories of learning have been advanced to explain the nature of learning process. And, all these can be broadly classified into two categories

(1) Connectionist or Behaviourist or Mechanicalistic or Associative or S-R theories.

(2) Cognitive or Gestalt or Purposive or Organismic or Field Theories.

S-R Theories : Generally, a student of psychology understands the paradigm S-R, which means that stimulus is connected with and leads to response. Stimulus is any change in external environment which excites nervous system and brings a response. Thus, response is the end product of S-R chain. Certain responses follow certain stimuli. Learning is a matter of connection between S and R. What we learn are habits and tendencies. The theory explains that the learner solves his problems by assembling his past experiences and responds to the new problem either according to elements common to the old and new situation or according to some aspects of the new situation which are similar to the old situation. If there is no similarity we indulge in trial and error behaviour. When these circumstances are studied and put together in some logical form, we have a theory. Within this broad category, the following three theories will be discussed in detail along with some others too.

(a) Pavlov's Classical Conditioning Theory.

(b) Thorndike's Trial and Error Theory.

(c) Skinner's Operant Conditioning Theory.

Cognitive Theories : This theory points out that even with the appropriate past experience, the organism may not solve the problem, if it is presented one way and he will solve it if it is presented in another way, because there is a spontaneous reactions to the contemporary structuring of the field which is not necessarily dependent upon the previous experiences. The supporters of this theory believe in 'intervening process' or 'intervening variable', as there is no such variable present in S-R theory according to the connectionist view point. As regards the nature of this 'intervening variable' the human being is believed to have a mind that controls behaviour to some extent. So we think, we know, we are conscious, we have purpose, we imagine, we believe, we will. Whereas, according to the connectionists, the human organism works only on S-R pattern like a highly complex machine; the will, the purpose, the intention, have no place here. The field theorist takes these processes into consideration and makes 'cognition' a significant aspect of his theory.

They look upon the learner as a dynamic energy system set into an environment, that is, in turn, a complex of other energy systems. Both the learner and the environment are dynamic and not passive. They both act and react in field. Within this broad category the following two theories will be discussed in detail along with some others too.

(a) Gestalt or Insight Learning Theory.

(b) Kurt-Lewin's Field Theory.

Theory of Classical Conditioning

This is learning from the behaviouristic viewpoint. According to this viewpoint learning is "formation of conditioned reflexes" or "acquisition of involuntary anticipatory adjustment" or "a habit formation" so that behaviour may become automatic. By "anticipatory adjustment" he means "organic behaviour" which is "not complete" but "with a gap in the whole equilibrium pattern"; for example, hunger in which saliva gastric juice, function of the stomach etc., are the organic behaviours with a gap and so incomplete. It becomes complete when the object of hunger is obtained. Importance of anticipatory adjustment is very great for three reasons. Firstly, it is the foundation of all voluntary behaviour and secondly, it is the active desire that sets the goal and makes the organism strive. Thirdly, it determines "the mind-set" or "organic pattern of readiness." Unless this organic pattern takes place within, no real learning can appear. If we can control this anticipatory adjustment we can also control learning. This controlled learning is the conditioned learning. In this the thing to be learnt is termed as, the stimulus,' and this is then followed by a satisfying stimulus. This combination is repeated again and again and ultimately the learning of the 'cue-stimulus' is established. This is conditioned learning.

Conditioned learning is also accompanied by a generalization of the experience. For example, a child whose fear is conditioned to a white rat also begins to fear a rabbit, cotton wool, a white fur coat and other similar objects. When the same process is repeated again and again for a long time, after the conditioning has taken place, it produces adverse effects. The conditioned S-R becomes extinguished. For example, repeated exposure of the rat may gradually reduce the fear after it has been conditioned.

Conditioned learning actually means responding normally to a natural response and then to an unnatural situation or stimulus, even in the absence of the natural stimulus. We have watering of the mouth seeing a 'Gulab Jamun' or a child feels watering of the mouth when he sees or smells food and not by hearing a cell. But it is the common experience that the ringing of the recess bell leads to watering of the mouth. This teaming of watering of the Mouth on hearing the bell is conditioned learning. It is established when repeatedly the recess bell is followed by sonic refreshments, meals or lunch during recess and bell and food are associated in quick succession. Much of the learning is by conditioning. Fear, anger and many such reactions are aroused by unnatural, irrelevant or unusual stimuli. The approaching peon of the boss, for example. aroused nervousness and fear though the peon is harmless and innocent. But that peon almost always brought an unpleasant message, letters or news from the boss's office and so the person is conditioned to the approaching of this peon which leads to rousing of fear and nervousness. Similarly, if two girls have been seen together a number of times; seeing one makes you think of the other. These are all illustrations of associative connections. This idea of association has been the basis of the conditioned response theory according to which learning consists in building up of new associative bonds between a stimulus and a response. According to Guilford "The most simple interpretation of this phenomenon is that when two stimuli are presented repeatedly together, the new one first, then the original, effective one the new one also becomes effective."

Proofs based on Experiment

The Russian Psychologist Ivan Pavlov experimented for long on dogs to study how the stimuli and responses are associated with different types of the stimuli of bell-different colours or lights and established conditioned response of salivation in the dog. In his experiment, he took a dog, kept him in a room and repeatedly gave the ringing of the bell as a stimulus soon followed by food (piece of meat) which led to salivation. Bell and food were presented in a sequence over a number of times (about seven days) and at every trial there was salivation, because there was food seen or smelt soon alter the ringing of the bell. A stage reached when ringing of the bell led to normal salivation even when there was no food supplied. Neurologically it could be explained that the stimulus bell followed by food led to the response of salivation in this planner.

This process is that by making the nerves carrying the stimulus of the food which leads to the response of salivation, come closer and closer with every trial to the nerves carrying the stimulus of the bell reaching a stage where there is an overlapping of the nerves carrying the stimulus of food with the nerves carrying the stimulus of the bell. In other words, a stage is reached when the bell meant food giving rise to the response of salivation. Such establishment of the nervous connections is the conditioned reflex. Here sight of food' was termed as UCS, 'the ringing of the bell' as CS and the 'salivation' in response to the ringing of the bell was termed as CR.

A schematic plan of the procedure is as under

Before Training (conditioning).

1. Bell (CS) ⟶ (Head turning, cocking of ears)

Training

2. Bell (CS) and Meat Powder (UCS) ⟶ Salivation (UCR)

After Training

3. Bell (CS) ⟶ Salivation (CR)

In a similar manner. Watson, performed an experiment in which a rabbit was shown to a baby followed immediately by a loud bang which made the baby shriek with fear as the sudden and loud bang becomes fearful due to the bombardment of the sound waves on his delicate eardrum and auditory nerves. In the repeated presentation of the rabbit followed by the loud banging, a stage reached when the baby shrieked the moment the rabbit was shown even when there was no banging.

This is learning by conditioning. The baby learnt to shriek at the sight of the rabbit which was quite harmless and quite incapable of instilling any fear. But with the association of banging, which is certainly shocking and arousing fear, the baby learned to react in the fearful manner at the sight of the innocent and harmless rabbit. Watson further experimented with the same baby when at last instead of being afraid, the child was made to be happy on seeing the rabbit.

It was reversing the conditioning or what was called reconditioning. It was done by giving a chocolate or a candy to the child when the rabbit was shown. After some trials when the rabbit was followed by candy, the rabbit and candy sequence established the connection between rabbit and the enjoyment of candy-as a pleasant experience. A stage reached when instead of being afraid, the baby began to play with the rabbit and was very happy to see it because the rabbit was the harbinger of the pleasant feelings of enjoying the candy. This situation of the natural response to an unnatural stimulus with the help of natural stimulus is the process of conditioning.

Similarly, a sleeping infant is frightened by the falling pillow but as it is dark when the pillow fell, the fear is conditioned to the dark and he learns to avoid dark places. The mother feeds the infant after placing him in a certain position on the bed but he starts feeling the pleasure of being fed as he sees her making the bed. All these illustrations throw light on the process of conditioning.

Principles : The success of the theory depends upon the following principles

1. Time Principle: It means that there should not be a wide gap of time between the cue stimulus and the satisfying stimulus. The longer the interval between the two, the less effective the association. Normally the CS (Bell) is presented before the UCS (food). When UCS is presented before the CS, some learning may take place, but it is not as effective as when the CS is presented before the UCS. It is for this reason that reward and punishment should be given immediately.
2. Principle of Intensity: It means that the satisfying stimulus should be of sufficient intensity, otherwise, it cannot produce the desirable organic behaviour. .
3. Principle of Consistency: It means that the same process should be repeated in the same way without any change for several days.
4. The Situational Principle: It means that the situation or the surrounding in which learning is to take place should be such as there may not be in it chances of distraction.
5. Principle of Repetition: It means that repetition is necessary for reinforcement and fixation of learned response.
6. Principle of Inhibition: Inhibition should not be allowed i.e., there should not be allowed any factor or situation that inhibits learning. Pavolv's students often found that

having set up a conditioned response in a dog they did not exhibit it to Pavlov because his presence in the room inhibited it. Likewise, we see student-teachers failing to deliver a very well planned and prepared lesson in the presence of the supervisor.

Educational Implications : Many things of the school-subjects are learnt more adequately through this process. Reading, writing, spelling or habits, etc., are learnt more effectively through the process of conditioning. Direct method of teaching English is just a process of conditioning. We learn many things in a better way through this process, and that is perhaps the reason why language is more efficiently learnt by living in the society in which it is spoken. Teaching through visual aids also implies the same principle.

Discipline may also be caused through conditioning. Good sentiments, good habits, virtues and ideals etc., which are the components of discipline are effectively learnt through the process of conditioning, and they are learnt surely in a society in which they are actually lived and manifested.

Class room procedures are often far removed from the natural procedures required for the process of conditioning. Languages are not taught as they ought to be in connection with many vivid and widely different experiences. If the regulations, commands and virtues are followed by the friendly behaviour and the most sympathetic attitude of the teacher, he can bring about a compliant emotional tone in the class that no amount of punishment can accomplish. But uniformity of procedure is essential. Voluntary action may be controlled through reasoning, punishment and reward but if its involuntary basis is neglected it will not endure. In conditioning, involuntary responses are controlled through the cue stimuli.

Many of our fears and phobias may be traced back to some kind of conditioning. When things and objects associate with an unpleasant experience and a sort of generalization is made, phobias appear. Such fears and phobias can be removed by deconditioning. Dislike for a teacher or certain school subjects can also be helped to be overcome through reconditioning by associating pleasant stimuli with them.

Moreover, in experimental psychology the theory of conditioned reflex occupies an important place and it has revolutionised child learning. Before the advent of this theory the knowledge of learning process was vague. It is not a psychological truism that the child's learning consists in the establishment of conditioned reflexes leading to formation of permanent habits. The intelligent learner can establish conditioned reflexes with facility while the idiot cannot. Lastly, this theory brings learning under the teacher's control making desired learning conditioned by situations created or regulated by the experimenter himself.

"Different kinds of habits based on training, education and discipline are nothing but a long chain of conditioned reflex."

...Pavlov.

Criticism : In spite of the above merits, the conditioned reflex theory of learning is open to serious defects. It is in the first place, a mechanical theory overlooking the learner's interest, attention and other higher mental processes. For this reason this theory many a time does not work. Learning depends largely upon learner's will, interest and attention. Further, not all stimuli can be conditioned by unconditioned ones. For example, the child's natural love for the mother cannot, normally, be conditioned by the unconditioned stimulus of seeing somebody else, whom he naturally hates. Secondly, the theory of conditioning lays emphasis on repetition of stimulus and response to strengthen connection between them. But Dunlop demonstrated that the occurrence of a response is the probability that it will occur again when there is the same stimulus.

Dunlop had the habit of typing 'the' as 'hte'. He was able to mend his habit by consciously typing 'the' as 'hte' thousands of times. Thus, the probability of occurrence of response (typing 'hte') was lessened when same stimulus (typing 'the') was provided. This law is opposed to theory that repetition strengthens connection. We can conclude from these two conflicting positions that it is not the occurrence of the response which determines the probability of its occurrence, but pleasant and unpleasant nature of the response. Thirdly, the theory is not put forward as an explanation of learning; it merely states the conditions of learning, the condition that must be present if learning is to occur A certain amount of frequency, or duration of time is required to permit the effective factors to operate. The space of time separating the two stimuli or responses to be connected must not be too great for the backward or forward spread of association. Finally, the theory has been considerably elaborated into ascending orders of conditioning to explain the higher thought and reasoning processes and even voluntary activity. At this point most psychologists demur. While conditioning gives a plausible account of the conditions of specific learnings, particularly those involving emotional reactions, its adequacy in the case of complex thought processes is widely questioned. To the educator, in particular, it is of no apparent value in describing higher learning.

Theory of Guthrie

E.R. Guthrie (1886-1959) of Washington University in line with the thinking of Skinner and Thorndike, though with some differences in approach particularly with regard to the purpose or motivation, developed his own theory of learning similar to J.B. Watson. But he rejected the law of frequency developed by Watson. Guthrie, as a matter of fact, elaborated Watson's views of behaviour in general and of learning in particular. He conducted a series of experiments on cats in puzzle boxes. He proved that for establishing connection between S-R only one trial was enough with the conditioned stimulus of full strength; but practice is useful because it helps to knit S-R bond together to form the larger units of behaviour that we call acts.

Guthrie in his book '*Psychology of Learning*' says that learning can occur in the absence of reward only by sheer contiguity and the theory could be called the Contiguity Theory. For Guthrie, contiguity, which is temporal in nature is of situation or stimulus and the response. According to this theory temporal contiguity between a stimulus and a response is the basic condition of learning. When every time a response occurs in strict contiguity with the constellation of stimuli, it becomes associated completely in all or none fashion. If the stimulus pattern remains unchanged and a second response is caused, complete unlearning of the 1st S-R connection and complete learning of 2nd S-R connection occurs.

The rat learns to trace the maze when one response becomes stimulus or reminds of the next step which in turn becomes the stimulus for the next move. To him learning is automatic with all or none response and frequency is not so necessary. Learning may be sudden and even a frequency of one is sufficient.

Guthrie considers that a child learns what he does. Whatever he perceives becomes a stimulus for the response that occurs at the same time. Whenever the stimulus reappears, he does what he did the last time. Guthrie developed no separate concept of motivation; for him stimuli are motives. Stimulation may be from within or without which arouses the learner and causes him to respond in many ways. The teacher should not teach when the students are absorbed in their own affairs or when the teacher is not able to attract the attention of the students. Guthrie stresses that the organism responds to various stimuli by contraction of muscles and secretion of glands. These specific responses are called movements. According to Guthrie, an act is a series of movements associated together by the law of contiguity. We can explain it with the help of walking which requires a number of movements of muscles and senses which combined together make an act. Guthrie rejected the theory of Thorndike saying that he was concerned with acts, not with movements.

In order to test the theory of Guthrie, two noteworthy experiments are described as below :

Experiment 1: Guthrie and Horton conducted the first experiment in 1946 on cats in a puzzle box to prove that learning is a process of association and of nothing else. The experiment was a simple one. A cat was kept in a box with a small pole in the midst of the box as a release mechanism. The touching of the pole from any side and in any manner opened the door. The cat could come out of the box and eat the food put outside the cage. The cat found the solution immediately and whenever put in the box, the cat repeated its previous behaviour. He concluded that what any animal would do at any moment was based on a record of what he did the first time in the past. In a similar fashion Guthrie noticed in teaching children to read printed word. The child looks at the symbol and while looking he speaks. When the child notices these symbols in future, he tends to say them correctly because of stimulus-response (S-R) connection. The principle of association by contiguity is important to analyse emotional responses of human beings in daily life. The emotional responses of school children are very significant in the teaching-learning process.

Experiment 2: Vocks conducted the second experiment in 1954 to prove the theoretical concept of Guthrie. He used a bell as a conditioned stimulus (CS) and eye blink as the conditioned response (CR). He found that the subjects acquired conditioned response. A typical subject might show no conditioning in the first six trials and then on the seventh trial showed the conditioned response in full strength. Here it is essential to mention that according to contiguity, forgetting is simply to do something else. We forget not by disuse but by other learning. It believes in interference theory of forgetting. Guthrie was quite hopeful of the possibilities of transfer knowledge from one situation to another by way of giving practice in that specific area of knowledge or by providing practice in wide variety of situations that are generally like the situation in which performance is expected in future. Also, Guthrie did not believe that, goal or purpose determines activity in any future sense.

"A stimulus pattern that is acting at the time of a response, if it recurs, tends to produce that response." ....Guthrie.

Principles : Guthrie developed several fundamental principles of learning.

The first and most important of them is the Principle of conditioning. He attempted to reduce all principles to this basic principle.

The second principle of learning is the inhibitory conditioning which means that responses are inhibited if any other response occurs in between the original stimulus-response.

The third principle, which deals with delayed conditioning in his opinion, is not conditioning at all.

The fourth principle is that improvement in performance is the result of practice. Guthrie believed that conditioning takes place after a single trial. The emphasis on practice to strengthen stimulus-response connection is for the purpose of enlistment of increasing numbers of stimuli as conditioners and not for strengthening of individual connections.

The fifth principle is a basic law of learning which is known as the contiguity principle. According to this principle a combination of stimulus which has accompanied a movement, will on its recurrence tend to be followed by that movement. In other words, we may say that when two psychological processes occur together in time or in immediate succession, the probability increases that an associative connection between them will develop.

Critical Appraisal : Guthrie was the most leading advocate of stimulus-response theory of association by contiguity. He rejected the law of frequency developed by Watson in favour of a principle of posterity which emphasized that only the last response in the series which was connected to the stimulus is important. Guthrie also rejected the theory of Thorndike saying that he was concerned with acts, not with movements. He explained his position on learning saying "our position is that what is associated is a stimulus and response. It would be perhaps more exact to say what is more associated is some stimulation of sense organs and a corresponding muscular contraction or glandular secretion.

By calling them associated we mean that the stimulation has become the occasion for the response because of a past association of the two. Thus, we see that Guthrie's system was the simplest one. He emphasized the importance of the overt stimulus and overt response. There is no place for annoyers or satisfiers and reinforcement in his theory of learning. Guthrie's system, even being the simplest one, could not generate research. It was due to the reason that he had no research scholars who could carry on research on his proposed model. The other reason was that when his theory of learning was formulated, it stood outside the main stream of behaviour theory of that period.

In the meantime Tolman and Hull developed well-organized system introducing the concept of intervening variables. They attributed importance to the concept of motivation. But, Guthrie developed no separate concept of motivation. For him stimuli are motives; for example, when feeling of fear is generalized in the mind of the student about the various things and school situations including subject matter and teacher, the student will be compelled to repel from all these odd circumstances, and, if, on the other hand, a teacher makes the students feel good, then it means that he is making the students to like school and enjoy learning.

Guthrie's theory had an anachronistic quality when it first appeared in 1935. It was based on the principles of Pavlov and Watson. He explained behaviour in terms of stimulus-response connections excluding completely the concept of reinforcement. His analysis of extinction, punishment, habit breaking and other phenomenon had considerable impact on theory of education. His theory provided theoretical model for later workers. Behaviour therapists apply his methods of breaking habits in correcting deviant behaviour in children.

Briefly speaking, keeping all these points of view in mind we can say that though, no one point of view can explain fully the complex phenomenon of learning, and also, no point of view is also useless or wrong, yet, in fact, undoubtedly, the theory is a major contribution to the understanding of the various aspects of learning.

Theory of Trial and Error

Edward Lee Thorndike (1874-1949) is generally considered to have been the foremost educational psychologist not only of the United States but of the world. He contributed profusely to research and theory in the field of learning and genetic psychology, testing and social psychology. Thorndike first stated the elements of his theory of learning in 1913 saying that connections are formed in the nervous system between stimuli and response. These connections formed are illustrated by the symbol S-R Another word used to describe these connections is the word bond' and hence, this theory is sometimes called a 'Bond Theory of Learning'. Thorndike has written. "Learning is connecting. The mind is man's connection system."

According to Thorndike learning takes place by trial and error. Some people call it "learning by selection of the successful variant". Accordingly when no readymade solution of a problem is available to the learner, he adopts the method of Trial and Error. He first, tries one solution. If it does not help him, he rejects it. "Then, he tries another, and so on. In this way he eliminates errors or irrelevant responses which do not serve the purpose and finally discovers the correct solution. Thus, in Trial and Error method, the learner makes random activities and finally reaches the goal accidentally. Here, one thing should be remembered that in Trial and Error also, there are often systematic and relevant responses. Activities are not wholly random. All these activities though apparently random, are suggested to him by the situation and the learner proceeds on accordingly. The stages through which the learner has to pass are Goal, Block (hindrances), Random Movements or Multiple Response, Chance-success, Selection and Fixation.

When and how the connection is accomplished was stated first in the following three laws :

Law of Readiness: First Primary law of learning, according to him is the 'Law of Readiness' or the 'Law of Action Tendency', which means that learning takes place when an action tendency is aroused through preparatory adjustment, set or attitude. Readiness means a preparation for action. If one is not prepared to learn, learning cannot be automatically instilled in him; for example, unless the typist in order to learn typing, prepares himself to start, he would not make much progress in a lethargic and unprepared manner.

Law of Exercise: The second law of learning is the 'Law of Exercise' which means that drill or practice helps in increasing efficiency and durability of learning and according to Thorndike's S-R Bond Theory, the connections are strengthened with trial or practice and the connections are weakened when trial or practice is discontinued. The law of exercise, therefore, is also understood as the 'law of use and disuse' in which case connections or bonds made in the brain cortex are weakened or loosened. Many examples of this are found in case of human learning. Learning to drive a motorcar, typewriting, singing or memorizing a poem or a mathematical tables, and music etc., need exercise and repetition of various movements and actions many times.

Law of Effect: The third law is the 'Law of Effect' according to which the trial or steps leading to satisfaction stamps in the bond or connection. Satisfying states lead to consolidation and strengthening of the connection, whereas dissatisfaction, annoyance or pain lead to the weakening or stamping out of the connections. In fact, the law of effect signifies that if the responses satisfy the subject, they are learnt and selected, while those which are not satisfying are eliminated. Teaching, therefore, must be pleasing. The educator must obey the Rings and interests of his pupils. In other words, greater the satisfaction, stronger will be the motive to learn. Thus, intensity is an important condition of the law of effect.

Besides these three basic laws, Thorndike also refers to five subordinate laws which further help to explain the learning process. These are :

Law of Multiple Response: According to it the organism varies or changes its responses till an appropriate behaviour is hit upon. Without varying the responses, the correct response for the solution might never be elicited. If the individual wants to solve a puzzle, he is to try in different ways rather than mechanically persisting in the same way. Thorndike's cat in the puzzle box moved about and tried many ways to come out, till finally it hit the latch with her paw which opened the door and it jumped out.

The Law of Set or Attitude: Learning is guided by a total set or attitude of the organism, which determines not only what the person will do but what will satisfy or annoy him. For instance, unless the cricketer sets himself to make a century, he will not be able to score more runs. A student, similarly, unless he sets to get first position and has the attitude of being at the top, would while away the time and would not learn much. Hence, learning is affected more in the individual if he is set to learn more or to excel.

Prepotency of Elements: According to this law, the learner reacts selectively to the important or essential in the situation and neglects the other features or elements which may be irrelevant or non-essential. The ability to deal with the essential or the relevant part of the situation, makes analytical and insightful learning possible. In this law of prepotency of elements, Thorndike is really anticipating insight in learning which was more emphasised by the Gestaltists.

Law of Response by Analogy: According to this law, the individual makes use of old experiences or acquisitions while learning a new situation. There is a tendency to utilise common elements in the new situation as existed in a similar past situation. The learning of driving a car, for instance, is facilitated by the earlier acquired skill of driving a motor cycle or even riding a bicycle, because the perspective of maintaining a balance and controlling the handle helps in steering the car.

The Law of Associative Shifting: According to this law we may get any response of which a learner is capable, associated with any other situation to which he is sensitive. Thorndike illustrated this by the act of teaching a cat to stand up at a command. A fish was dangled before the cat while he said 'stand up'. After a number of trials by presenting the fish after uttering the command 'stand up', he later ousted the fish and the over all command of 'stand up' was found sufficient to evoke the response in the cat by standing up on her hind legs.

Experimental Evidence : Various experiments have been performed on men as well as animals to study this method. Thorndike made several experiments on rats and cats. Two important experiments are mentioned here.

Expt. 1 : Thorndike's most widely quoted experiment was with the cat placed in a puzzle box. The hungry cat was put in the puzzle box and a fish, as an incentive, was put outside the cage a little beyond its reach. The box was designed in such a way that the door of the cage could be released by some simple act like depressing a lever inside the cage. At first, the cat made a great deal of varied attempts to reach the food in a trial and error fashion such as jumping up and down, clawing at the bars, scratching the cage, walking around, trying to push the bars, pawing and shaking movable parts of the cage etc., but all attempts proved in vain. Ultimately by chance her paw fell on the loop of the rope and the door opened.

The cat jumped out immediately and ate the fish. When next day, the cat was put in the box again, this time she took less time in coming out and in the subsequent trials the time decreased further so much so that the stage reached when the cat came out soon after being put inside by directly striking the latch with her paw without any random movement. This is how she learnt to reach its goal.

Expt. 2 : (Experiment with Human Subjects): Gopalaswamy demonstrated trial and error in human beings through Mirror-Drawing Experiment. This is a classical experiment in the psychology of learning. In this experiment the subject is asked to trace a star-shaped drawing, not looking at it directly, but as it is reflected in a mirror. The subject's hand movements are visible in the mirror only and not directly. The experimenter observes the movements of the hands and thus, records the time of tracing in successive trials and the number of errors committed in each trial. In first six trials the subject traces the star with the right hand and then in the next six trials he traces it by the left hand. Two graphs-the Time Curve and the Error Curve are then drawn, which show the general characteristics of trial and error learning. In the original experiment Gopalaswamy arranged his apparatus so that a record was automatically made of all the movements of the styles of the subject as it traced out the pattern. In this way the successive times of teachings and a record of errors were obtained.

Gopalaswamy analysed the errors into two groups-lower level errors and higher level errors. Those errors which did not involve any novel process on the part of the subject in tracing the star were lower-level errors and those which involved higher process of mind at the perceptual and conceptual level were higher-level errors. He discovered that improvement in the higher-level responses correlated highly with intelligence and that the improvement in the responses of the lower-level errors did not show much correlation with intelligence.

Educational Implications : Thorndike's theory of Trial and Error and his three basic laws of learning have direct educational implications. The law of readiness lays emphasis on motivation while the law of exercise compels us to accept a well known fact 'Practice maketh a man perfect' and the third one i.e., law of effect opens fairly a large scope to discuss the role of reward and punishment as an incentive in the child's learning.

The significant aspect of this theory is that to master a complex or elaborate task practice is essential. It is not possible to handle each difficult situation in a single trial, no matter what the degree of motivation or reward is. One cannot cram the entire constitution of India in one reading even if the reward is a crore of rupees or the threat is to be shot dead otherwise. Each task initially seems to be difficult and fatiguing but as practice continues, it becomes smoother and requires less effort. Finally, we say that habit or S-R is established. An expert driver, for instance, goes on driving, listening to the radio and talking to his friend sitting by. In the light of class room teaching blundering is a natural phenomenon associated with student learning. But, the teacher should not regard this as a symptom of inefficient teaching because this is the way the pupils learn. He should not be at all worried when blundering appears. Insights will emerge as the blundering progresses from simpler associations to higher units. There is no royal road to success.

Actually, we learn by doing. The teacher's duty should be, therefore, to arrange situations in which the student has a chance to discover for himself what is significant. The blundering must be directed and methods that are wholly futile must be eliminated. But at the same time the teacher must exercise constant restraint in his supervision. The child who can work mathematical problem-when the teacher's promptings keep him on the right path is still a long-way from learning anything about mathematics.

Finally, though the theory is not widely accepted for its educational significance, yet, there are certain subjects such as mathematics, tables of mathematics, memorising poetry, rules of grammar etc., in which learning by Trial and Error can not be avoided. All reasoning subjects afford the greatest opportunity for the application of the Trial and Error method.

Critical Appraisal : The theory has been criticised by various psychologists on the following grounds. Firstly, the theory is mechanical, for it leaves no room for an end or purpose in any sense whatsoever. On the contrary psychologist McDougall maintained that even the behaviour of the amoeba or the paramecia consists in learning to face novel conditions to serve some unknown purpose. Even repeated trials are of no avail if the tendency to learn is not there. Again, if the tendency is there, even one trial may be fruitful. McDougall and Woodworth insist on readiness for reaching a goal in learning and Lloyd Morgan lays stress on persistence with varied efforts till the goal of learning is achieved. The hungry cat confined in the puzzle box with food in front of it goes on persistently trying various means until it gets out of it and has food. So its trials are not blind and mechanical. In fact, they are guided by perceptual attention and feelings of pleasure and pain. Yet, Thorndike pays no attention to these higher order mental processes. Secondly, in course of repeated trials the number of errors are not corrected of themselves or mechanically. The effects of Trial and Error depend to a great extent upon the psychophysical state of animal making them. In the absence of any purpose in view the animal is so puzzled, rather than enlightened by the errors committed, that it goes on blindly repeating them without end. Thirdly, Thorndike assumes that learning consists only in the association of several separate movements. But learning is a whole process related to a whole situation.

The hungry cat confined in a puzzle-box with food placed near it does not perceive the situation in a piecemeal fashion but as a whole. Finally, the laws of learning formulated by Thorndike appear to be unjustified. For instance, the law of effect seems to be inconsistent with his mechanical point of view. Satisfaction in or the sense of being rewarded by success and dissatisfaction in or the sense of being punished by failure seem to ascribe higher mental processes to animals like cats and rats than are psychologically ascribable to them. Or, it violates Lloyd Morgan's law. Similarly, the law of exercise has been severely criticised on the grounds that it does not regard other factors like motives, interests, special training etc.

Mechanical repetition without motive, interest, significance or understanding does not make anyone learn anything and remember it. One rupee-currency note passes hundred times through the hands of a person, but hardly anyone is able to tell the size, the colour and other details of it. This shows that repetition without motive, interest or understanding is of no avail.

Reinforcement Theory of Hull

C.L. Hull an American was professor of psychology at Yale

University. His theory is a stimulus-response theory; but he built a new system combining the law of effect with the concept of conditioning under the concept of reinforcement. His views have been applied to more complex learning by Miller, Dollard and Mowrer. His system of behaviour is studied under S-R reinforcement theories. His system is deductive, mathematical and testable. Hull's theory of teaming holds that association between S-R is ṅot enough for learning. He is of the opinion that some kind of reward or other reinforcement is necessary in order to establish the stimulus as signal. Hull was highly impressed by Pavlov and his experiments. The way Hull explained the meaning of learning is known as systematic behaviour theory. It is also named as Refined theory or Precise theory as it elaborates beautifully the formula S-R.

Its Principle: Hull's theory is also named as Drive Reduction Theory which was explained by him in 1915 in his well known book, *'Principles of Behaviour'*. In the same book Hull explained this theory under the name of 'Reinforcement theory', which explains learning in terms of the change in behaviour which occurs under such conditions as of reward or effect as called by Thorndike. Complex learning, according to him, involves conditioning principles, although simple learning and complex learning do not seem to differ in the essential principles or laws. Animal learning and human learning both involve the same principles, though factors like language and meaning may complicate the study of learning in some ways. Hull as a mechanistic psychologist, avoiding recourse to consciousness and as a follower of Watson, worked for the fulfilment of the behaviouristic programme, as proposed by Watson. According to him behaviour or learning are more or less synonymous. The central concept in this theory is that habits are mostly formed by conditioning. Complex learning according to him, is derived step by step from simple learning and the law of effect or of reinforcement was at the roots of Hull's system.

Emphasizing the importance of drives in the theory Hull believed that these drives impel the individual to respond to certain cues which determine when he will respond, where he will respond and which response he will make. The cue value of a stimulus depends upon its distinctiveness and drive value on its strength. The responses made to cues in the presence of drives will be learnt if they are rewarded. The gradients of effect or reward are what Hull called the gradients of reinforcement and what Thorndike called the spread of effect. The cue-responses sequence is increased in the neighbourhood of the reward which means that nearer the reward the greater is the strengthening of bonds. This is the main difference between Guthrie's and Hull's theory. According to Guthrie association occurs when the cues and responses are together but according to Hull the association between cue and response is regulated by their relationship with drive and reward. In brief, according to Hull a stimulus (S), impinges on the organism.

This results in a neural impulse which leads to a reaction (R). For this to occur, however, there has to be drive (D). Drive is a state of, tension resulting from a need. If the response or reactions (R) reduces the tension or drive (D), we have a condition of reinforcement. This reinforcement brings about an organization in the nervous system which is known as a habit or learning. In Hull's system, for understanding learning; the sequence is drive-cue-response-reward leading to further reinforcement making repetition easier and this leads to learning. Here we see that a factor of drive is also based on a need which is even more important than what was thought by Thorndike or Guthrie. Hull stated his theory in the form of sixteen postulates or general rules.

Basic Concepts : Some of the basic concepts involved in the theory are as under :

Stimulus: For Hull, responses are conditioned to the neural aftereffects of stimuli rather than to the stimuli themselves. The effective stimulus, in learning, is the trace in the nervous system caused by the environmental objects. According to Hull, the stimuli in the object would give rise to stimulus traces in the organism. The first we might designate S and the second s. Learning involves S and not the s.

Response: Hull was of the opinion that we may distinguish between tendency within the person to make a response and the actual response itself. If we designate the overt responses R we can refer to the preexisting neural activities which initiate the response as r. These internal response tendencies are not observable but inferred from behaviour. Symbolically the learned association of S and R is represented as SHR where H represents habit. Changes in SHR constitute learning in Hull's system.

Need : It is the lack of something which is experienced by the organism. It then tries to perform that activity which culminates in the satisfaction of the need. Thus needs are associated with goals. In human beings, needs are relatively permanent tendencies which seek their satisfaction in achieving certain specific goals. When a need arises, the organism acts in order to reduce the need. Sometimes. Hull's theory of learning is called need reduction theory.

Drive: Word drive is usually used when there is a feeling of mental tension or restlessness on account of our bodily needs. A drive is a tendency of shifts in physiological balance tissue, tension-sensitivity to stimuli of a certain class and response in any of variety of ways that are related to the attainment of a certain goal. In other words, it is a general condition of deprivation in the organism. It is a common denominator of all primary motivations whether due to food, water, sex or any other cause.

Reinforcement: The term reinforcement means strengthening the tendency of a response to be repeated. When an organism responds to a stimulus and that response is reinforced, it is very probable that the same response will be repeated the next time if that stimulus occurs. Reinforcement according to Hull is like Thorndike's reward. In a way, it is a stimulus which has the ability to alter the probabilities of certain R following certain S. When a response is reinforced, this means that it has been followed by one of a certain class of stimuli. Hull postulated that reinforcing stimuli were those which reduced stimuli associated with the drives.

There are few concepts related to reinforcement which are discussed in brief as follows :

(a) *Primary Reinforcement:* A conditioned response is possible only if the child or animal has a need or a primary drive and the law of effect operates when that need or drive is satisfied or reduced. Psychologists agree that the reduction in the strength of primary drive or need is a reinforcing factor. The law of primary reinforcement may be stated in a simple form: a stimulus S is presented, it is followed by a response R and if this S-R bond helps in reducing the tension, there will be an increased tendency for that bond to be repeated. Activities which reduce tension are reinforcing.

(b) *Extinction* : When there is no primary reinforcement, with repetition the stimulus response connection will grow weaker till it finally disappears. This process is known as extinction. Occasionally the extinguished response will return spontaneously after a rest period. The ringing of the bell may lead the dog to salivate after some days during which it did not so respond to it, but the response is weak.

(c) *Gradient of Reinforcement* : Several experiments have been made with the time interval between the conditioned stimulus and the response, and they indicate that with the increase in time interval the response follows less frequently. If the interval is more than 30 seconds conditioning is negligible. This reduction in the frequency or strength of conditioning is called the gradient of reinforcement. In some experiments it was demonstrated that reinforcement did not work if it was delayed by 5 seconds and was maximum if it was delayed only by half a second. The dog would not salivate oil, the ringing of the bell if there was an interval of more than 30 seconds between the presentation of food and the ringing of the bell.

(d) *Secondary Reinforcement* : Hull puts forward the theory of secondary reinforcement to account for learning where there is a longer interval of time between the reinforced response and need reduction. All our needs are not primary. The need for food is primary but the need for money which can buy food is secondary. Secondary needs are acquired, and though they do not by themselves reduce any need, they are associated with things which help to reduce need. Money is a secondary reinforcer, its need-reduction power is remote but it is closely and consistently associated with need reduction. This is secondary reinforcement.

(e) *Stimulus Generalization :* If a child is bitten by a non-barking dog the sound of the word dog, its sight or smell will make the child shrink in fear though these stimuli did not function in the original situation. In a study described by Watson an eleven-month-old boy who was conditioned to fear a rat, later on showed fear in the presence of a rabbit, a dog, a fur coat, cotton and wool. The fear was aroused by the similarity of these stimuli- their woolliness or furriness. If a bell leads to salivation, any sound of higher or lower pitch resembling it will also lead to that. This Hull calls stimulus generalization, and it is responsible for many of the confusion and mistakes of children in both life and learning.

Theory of Operant Conditioning

B.F. Skinner is a very staunch behaviourist. He was the professor of psychology at Harvard University. His theory of operant conditioning also known as instrumental conditioning is nothing but only an extension of S-R Bond theory of Thorndike, Watson and Pavlov. Skinner, considers man like a machine or an automation with no personality and no inner free will and is only a tool of the environment. His psychology is of engineering type and lays emphasis on application of psychological principles to actual life situations. Man is neutral and passive. His basic thesis is that an organism tends to do in future what it was doing at the time of reinforcement which meant that by reinforcing at each step, one could make the organism to do what one wishes it to do. In operant conditioning, the important stimulus is the one, immediately following the response and not the preceding one. Any response which leads to reinforcement is thereby strengthened. If the occurrence of an operant is followed by presentation of reinforcing stimulus, the strength increases. Hence, carefully stated, an operant is a class of responses of which a specific response is an instance or member. A rat presses a lever and gets food, so the rat will be more likely to press the lever again. What is changed is the future probability of the response made. The operant is a class of behaviour rather than the response at a particular instance. It is not correct to say that an operant reinforcement strengthened the response which preceded it. The response has already occurred and can not be changed. What has been changed is the probability of that class of responses that will occur in the future. Since each reinforcement builds up reserve of responses, a pigeon may continue to raise its head, or rat to press the lever several times even after food has ceased to appear.

The law of operant conditioning is that if the occurrence of an operant is followed by presentation of a reinforcing stimulus, its future probability of occurrence will increase.

In the words of Skinner

"Operant conditioning is the learning process whereby a response is made more probable or more frequent and operant is strengthened i.e., reinforced"

Classical and Operant Conditioning: There are some basic differences between classical and operant conditioning which are mentioned as below :

(1) C.C. was developed by Russian scientist, Pavlov and is called Pavlovian or type-1 learning while operant conditioning was developed by B.F. Skinner and is called Skinnerian or type-2 learning.

(2) In classical conditioning the CR and UR are the same while in operant conditioning they are different. For instance, in case of operant conditioning pressing the lever is different from eating the food.

(3) In classical conditioning there is pairing of UCS and CS, while in operant conditioning there is no pairing of UCS and CS.

(4) In classical conditioning there is definite bond between UCS and CS, while in operant conditioning the tendency to respond in a specific manner is developed.

(5) Classical conditioning is controlled by autonomic nervous system, while operant conditioning is controlled by central nervous system in the organism.

(6) Classical conditioning may be represented in the S-R form, while operant conditioning is R-S form.

(7) In C.C. the association between S-R is on the basis of law of contiguity, while in O.C. association between S-R is on the basis of law of effect.

(8) In C.C. reinforcement comes first, while in O.C. reinforcement is provided after the response is made by the organism.

(9) In C.C. stress is laid on time control, while in O.C. stress is laid on motivation and reward.

(10) In C.C. the essence of learning is stimulus substitution, while in O.C. the essence of learning is response modification.

(11) C.C. is stimulus oriented, while O.C. is response oriented.

(12) Classical conditioning is restricted to the animal learning only, while operant conditioning may be useful for animal and human learning both.

Experimental Evidence : Operant conditioning has come into considerable prominence in recent years as a result of Skinner's success in training animals and more recently in shaping academic behaviour through programmed instruction. He performed many experiments on rats, cats, dogs, pigeons, etc. Below are mentioned few important ones.

Exp. 1 : In an experiment a hungry pigeon was kept in a Skinner box. The pigeon had to raise his head to a particular height and peck at a particular spot in order to get his food. In actual experiment, the pigeon was first rewarded with a food pellet when it approached a disc, then only when it nodded toward it and eventually only when it actually pecked it. By certain repetitions it learnt to do so quickly and automatically. Skinner called such behaviour of learning to peck or to press a lever or bar to get the reward as operant conditioning. Operant means effective or active and this term indicates that the organism is operating upon the environment. Here, the process of operant conditioning is the change in frequency with which the head is lifted to a given height. The reinforcer is food and the reinforcement is the process of food presentation, when the response is emitted (the head is raised to a particular height and a particular spot it pecked). The operant is the height to which the head must be raised. By judiciously rewarding the spontaneous action of birds, Skinner has shaped the behaviour of birds in many ways. Some pigeons have been taught, for example, to peck a bell back and forth across a table, to play ping-pong and to peck out tunes on a xylophone.

Exp. 2 : In a similar experiment Skinner put a hungry rat into his box. The box was equipped with a bar and food tray. The bar could be depressed. Occasionally, the rat would wander over and push the bar down. After a while Skinner would reinforce this action by permitting a food pellet to fall into the tray when the bar was depressed by the rat. Skinner, further modified his experiment. Food pellets would, now, be supplied under certain conditions when the bar was pushed down, for instance, when a tone was sounded but not under other conditions. The experiment involves all the basic principles of classical conditioning, as, the rat learned to press the bar more frequently, when the behaviour was reinforced by a food pellet. If it was not reinforced, extinction occurred. For a while the rat generalised and pushed the bar down at the same rate when the tone was sounded. Eventually after enough time it discriminated and pushed the bar only when the tone was sounded. Although the experiment seems similar to Pavlov's experiment as regards dog and the rat, Skinner's rats are more active as they operated on the bar. It is thus, that Skinner called this operant conditioning as instrumental since the behaviour of the organism is instrumental in accomplishing the purpose.

Exp. 3 : In 1950, a man of 70 who had lost his speech at the age of 50 years could not be cured by psychoanalysis and was later subjected to operant conditioning. Kessorla treated him. The subject was supplied food and Kessorla herself sat aside, watching the subject. The man looked and looked again at the food but could not speak. The woman did not pay any attention to him nor looked at in support. The man just moved his lips and did not perform any activity. The woman took away the food. Next day, when the food was supplied again, the subject made greater efforts with the speech apparatus. At this moment, the woman put some food before him. As a result of the experiment in about 25 days, 75%

of his speech was restored. As the man, was 70 years old his 100% speech could not be restored. Operant conditioning technique (OCT) is often used to modify the behaviour in many cases in mental hospitals. Later on this techniques proved of great importance in the field of education also.

Its Principles : To repeat any desired activity or to make a desired behaviour permanent Skinner has suggested a schedule of reinforcement. On account of these schedules any desired behaviour can be made fixed or permanent. The behaviour which suits us is repeated again and again. The individual who performs desired behaviour in his first attempts is provided incentives so that he repeats the same behaviour again and again. Such incentives may be provided through schedules of reinforcement.

As regards schedules of reinforcement Skinner has suggested' the following schedules of reinforcement.

Fixed Ratio Schedule: Fixed Ratio Reinforcement is given when the frequency of reinforcement depends on the rate at which responses are given i.e., the pallet of food is delivered after each fourth, eighth, twelveth responses. Higher ratio should be approached gradually.

Variable Ratio Schedule: In a variable ratio schedule the reinforcer is presented after different number of responses on different occasions. Sometimes the difference amounts to one or sometimes two. Thus, the digit goes on changing as one, four, seven, nine etc.

Fixed Interval Schedule: On a fixed-interval schedule, a fixed interval of time has to elapse before the reinforcer can be presented i.e., every 2 minutes or 4 minutes. This is also known as periodic reinforcement. So, interval reinforcement depends simply on the passage of time. Shorter intervals yield more rapid response rates than the longer ones.

Variable Interval Schedule: When the interval between reinforcement is randomly varied it is known as a variable interval schedule. In this situation the subject is reinforced on a time interval basis but the interval of time is indefinite. Sometimes the subject is reinforced a couple of times very close together and sometimes a considerable amount of time is allowed to elapse.

Educational Implications : Skinner's operant conditioning theory is of great importance in teaching-learning situations. A few situations have been discussed in detail as under :

Conditioning Study Behaviour : For Professor Skinner, "Teaching is the arrangement of contingencies of reinforcement which expedite learning. He is convinced that operant conditioning, so effectual when applied to animal, promises equal success when used in schools." Further more, he thinks that the most effective control of human learning requires instrumental aid. He is appalled at the present inefficient practices in schools and recommends a procedure whereby they can be corrected. He thinks that, when teachers have taught successfully, they always have arranged effective contingencies of reinforcement, but they are more likely to do this if they understand what is it that they are doing. Hence, if the teachers want that students should learn something, they should reinforce such behaviours of students as coming well prepared in the class, sitting in the library and participating actively in school programmes through a variety of incentives such as prize, medal, praise, smile, affectionate petting on the back or even by giving higher marks in the examination.

Conditioning and Class Room Behaviour : In order to change the behaviour of the pupils in the class room and to bring about desired change in their behaviours, conditioning is of immense importance. If a child's experiences in a certain classroom, while studying a certain subject with a particular teacher are predominantly unpleasant, the unpleasantness becomes conditioned to the teacher, the subject and the classroom. If this is repeated, the child will develop a dislike for the subject as well as for the teacher. Hence, to check all these, suitable behavioural contingencies may be used. An atmosphere of recognition, acceptance, affection and esteem may help the child in approaching the teacher and the subject with good will. For instance, if a student is not serious in his studies, the teacher can control this behaviour by using negative reinforcement such as showing his negligence to other student or by criticising him in front of the whole class. On the other hand, a student who is serious in his studies should be provided positive incentives such as prize, medal, praise, smile etc.

Managing Problem Behaviour : Generally, students perform a variety of behaviours that seems undesired and problematic from social conduct point of view. Hence, to alter them success may be achieved through the process of operant conditioning. Operant conditioning has established as an important behaviour therapy technique in the recent years. In this regard Albert Bandura's views are of great significance. But, one has to admit here that instead of making use of negative contingencies such as punishment, a teacher must make use of positive contingencies such as praise, appropriate encouragement for better learning prospects.

Dealing with Anxieties : Students develop many fears, anxieties, prejudices, attitudes as well as perceptual discomforts through conditioning. When we see that a train or a car stops whenever there is a red light, we interpret the red light as a sign to stop. In wartime, when a siren is blown in a particular way, we interpret it as a signal for air raid. A child who has received a painful injection from a doctor, may develop an aversion to or fear of any doctor. Such are examples of conditioned anxiety in the human being. Anxiety is a generalized fear response. To break such habits or fears extinction process of conditioning may be helpful. For this, the subject should be kept repeatedly in the situation that causes fear in him and he may be treated by controlling fear producing response. The technique is known as desensitization. In this technique firstly we provide a very weak form of conditioned stimulus and then gradually the strength of stimulus is increased.

Conditioning and Cognitive Processes : Feedback or knowledge of progress is another fore of reinforcement. The concept may be utilized in controlling the cognitive behaviours of the students. Programmed instruction and Teaching Machines are based on this principle. As regards knowledge of progress much longer lapse of time between behaviour and its reinforcement should not be allowed. To make effective use of operant conditioning principle the technique of programmed instruction is best suited.

Shaping Complex Behaviour : To control complex behaviours which exist in the form of a chain of small behaviours, the extended form of conditioning, known as shaping technique may be employed. In this technique the smallest behaviour of an individual at the very initial stage is controlled. Then gradually the next order of chain of behaviour is controlled or conditioned on the basis of different contingencies. In schools the technique is widely accepted for its use to control students' behaviour. Skinner said that "Teaching spelling is mainly a process of shaping complex form of behaviour. In other subjects, for example, arithmetic responses must be brought under the control of appropriate stimuli."

Theory of Gestalt

Max Wertheimer is generally considered to be the founding father of Gestalt Psychology. The other pioneers in this field were Kohler, Koffka and Wolfgang. 'Gestalt' is a German word whose equivalent in English is 'form' or 'pattern' or 'configuration'. Max Wertheimer has explained the term 'Gestalt' saying that the whole is greater than the parts. For example a flower is just not a total of sepals, petals, calyx, corolla, colour, honey and fragrance but some thing more than that. The total of the parts is not equal to the whole. This is known as Gestalt viewpoint. According to this view "learning is the organisation and re-organisation of behaviour which arises from the interaction of a maturing organism with its environment. It is the bringing about, through this interaction, of new forms of perception, imagination, motor coordination and other organic behaviour." Sudden appearance of the solution is an essential characteristic of insightful learning. A sudden coherent pattern of solution appears at once. The individual does not perform random activities, but he perceives the situation as a whole, and intuitionally reaches the goal through awakened insight by continuous, definite and seemingly purposive reactions. Insight is the perception of a relationship between at least three factors, an agent, a goal and intervening conditions or obstacles. Insight is often called as the 'Aha' experience, the flash of understanding which comes to us all of a sudden. Insight when it occurs, is characteristically accompanied by an 'I have got it ! exclamation', the eyes light up, knit brows unravel and fingers snap.

The Gestaltians tend to place far more emphasis on the intrinsic organising capacity in the brain of the individual, and they emphasize the dynamic interactions of the elements in the entire perceptual field. Gestalt theory of learning essentially consists in problem-solving by understanding the relative position of the elements in entire perspective of situation. When a problem arises, it tends to disturb the equilibrium of the organism who seeks a balance. Actually, Gestalt psychology began with the work of German Psychologists who were studying the nature of perception. We are all now well aware that the 'moving picture' is not a moving picture at all but it is a series of still pictures. The reality of still pictures as flashed on the 'movie screen" becomes our perception of moving pictures. The focal point of this theory is the fact that when two optical stimuli are perceived by the human eye in quick succession the reaction is one of simultaneous patterning. Wertheimer called this the phi-phenomenon.

Principles : The Gestaltians have mentioned some laws involved in learning. The age at which memory begins is determined chiefly by development of a sufficient number of association fibres to bring about recall. There are different modes of connection or association among percepts and ideas. Suggestive forces work according to certain laws given as under :

(a) *Law of Similarity :* Makes the individual to grasp things which are similar. They are picked out as it were from the total context. Similar ideas and experiences get associated together. An object reminds another object which resembles it e.g.. seeing a man and remembering an intimate friend by some resemblance in his personal appearance, though never seen together in the past. A photo reminds us of the person it represents.

(b) *Law of Proximity:* Makes things proximate or near together to be picked up first and learned as to how near these are among the more distant things. In other words, perceptual groups are favoured according to the nearness of their respective parts. Items tend to form groups if they are spaced together. It states that objects which are close in time and space tend to form a gestalt.

(c) *Law of Closure:* It states that our perceptual patterns always tend to be simple, regular and complete with no loose ends. The gaps are closed by the perceiver.

(d) *Law of Continuity:* Makes the individual to grasp things which are joined together in a string or along the line which constituting a whole are grasped together than the disconnected disjointed or scattered. In other words, experiences which occur together either simultaneously or in close succession tend towards reviving one another e.g. the perception of a ripe mango suggests the idea of its sweet taste and flavour because they are perceived together in the past or the idea of inkpot suggests the idea of pen.

(e) *Law of Contrast:* A perception or an idea tends to suggest its contrary opposite. For instance, adversity reminds a person of his days of prosperity. Similarly, the heat of summer suggests the cold of winter. In these laws of learning is brought out the Gestalt point of view that the organizational capacity of the brain makes to grasp the whole, in priority with the parts.

Educational Significance : Gestalt psychology's contribution to education lies in its concepts of the organization of stimuli and or insight. The world of the classroom in which the child is living, learning is not just a body of discrete stimuli nor are his responses to it those of trial and error adaptations. The world is organized; it has meaning. The child can react with understanding, he has insight. Arithmetic is not isolated fact but a system of numbers. History is not names and dates but the sweep of events through time, with one thing leading to or following another. Learning is meaningful. So say the educators and so says Gestalt psychology.

Gestalt psychologists suggest that the educators should conceive the problem of learning in more comprehensive terms. The teacher should organise the learning situations in such a way that significant relations emerge and understanding of the material results. The learning experiences should be so arranged that the learner discovers and generalises the relationship for himself. The subject matter should be organised into meaningful wholes. The concept of unit-planning is based on the same. The daily lesson plan is many a time fragmentary. It amounts to mere accumulation of facts, principles, concepts and skills. The student does not get a clear picture of the whole. A lesson of prose may be taught in four or five steps or periods. But, if the matter taught on the first day and the last day fails to establish relationship, students get confused. They do not see any, significance. It is thus said that whole is just not equal to its parts.

Briefly speaking this type of learning is very important in education because it discards memorizing type of learning. It does not consume much time and emphasizes meaningfulness, organization and interpretation of the lesson. Here, the individual is engaged in problem solving attitude. It encourages reasoning, develops thinking and trains imagination and creative activity of the child. Learning by insight can be cultivated. Thus, the teacher should emphasize it by encouraging. helping and guiding the child.

Critical Appraisal : As regards the criticism of the Insight Theory of Learning, it is worth mentioning that the theories of Trial and Error and of the Conditioned Reflex are not absolutely wrong. Insight, like a flash of lightning, as it occurs, does not totally discard trial and error behaviour. For instance, the chimpanzee who plucked banana joining two sticks altogether, does not do so instantaneously, but through trial and error by manipulating the two sticks repeatedly till Sultan reaches his goal.

The only difference in the two theories is that the latter is governed from the initial stage by the perception of the situation as a whole. Further, insight is hindsight and foresight as well. It does not lie merely in perceiving the present situation but involves also what proceeds and what succeeds it.

The controversy whether trial and error leads to insight or not is meaningless since the two concepts are of different nature. But, one has to admit here that Gestaltian view is subjective, less sophisticated and more useful in certain situations. It is wrong to say that every behaviour is the product of insight. For instance, many of our- day-to-day experiences are, the outcomes not of insight but of trial and error exercises. Again, the laws of perception, also known as laws of learning according to Gestaltians, are not very exhaustive and do not explain all types of learning.

Theory of Sign

Edward C. Tolman (1886-1559) developed a theory of learning by combining the advantages of stimulus-response theories and cognitive field theories: and thus his system stands in-between S-R Theories and cognitive field theories. His system, no doubt, is rooted in behaviourism but he was strongly opposed to S-R associationism. He criticised stimulus-response theory and trial and error theory both by saying that all learning is not a hit-and-miss affair. Neither it is aimless nor random. According to him, learning is not mechanical: it is purposive. Striving towards a goal is the heart of the learning process for example, if a hungry rat is placed in a maze it wanders about in right and wrong paths until it finally reaches the food spot. If these trials are repeated, the number of errors grows less and the rat takes less and less time to reach the goal.

According to the theories of connectionism and reinforcement the bond between the stimulus and- the response has been strengthened. Wrong response have been eliminated and correct responses learned. Tolman's explanation is that it is not a series of movements that is learned but signs. The learner perceives the nature of the situation, works on it, builds a cognitive structure or map of the environment. These perceptions are considered to have their correlations in the brain. The structure or the map provides guide or signs or stimuli with a meaning which decides what route the rat will take in the maze.

Tolman published his major work "Purposive Behaviour in Men and Animals" in 1932. His system is known as Purposive Behaviourism. He rejected molecular approach to behaviour developed by Watson and developed molar approach to behaviour which is goal-seeking and purposive. He was also influenced by Freud and McDougall in the development of principles of learning. Agreeing with Guthrie he thinks that there is temporal contiguity in terns of successive cognitions.

For example, in maze learning the cognition that one event leads to another is accompanied by a second cognition concerning the behaviour. Behaviour route must be followed if this sequence is to occur. In learning tying the shoe laces, for example, pulling the two ends of the lace in two hands serve as a cue to put one end round the other which suggests to pull the two apart. It leads to making half the knot which further serves as a cue to slip the one string under the other and pull them again, thus making the knot complete. Here the movement serves as a cue for the other till the knot is completed. There is simple temporal contiguity. In maze learning also one movement serves as a cue for the other and that in turn for the next, and so on. In short, to Tolman goal is a name for a recognised need which the individual seeks to satisfy by action which enables him to reach it as the goal.

This is a clear acceptance of the motivating forces or needs as the basis of learning. Here it is worth mentioning that even behaviourists depend upon some need to be at the base in conditioning. For example, satisfaction of hunger in the cat in the puzzle box or in the rat to learn to go through the maze or in the cat to stand on its hind legs is the basic need. If these animals were first fed and then made to do the work required they would not bother. The rat would sit silently or the cat would go to sleep instead of struggling to open the door. These needs are of course more physical in the case of animals and in case of human beings there are also psychological needs.

Tolman deals with patterns instead of reducing behaviour or activity into components. His concepts are similar to those of Gestalt but are more precise. His approach is holistic and concepts are larger and more comprehensive He agrees with Hull in stressing needs and their satisfaction but not through reinforcement or need reduction. He says that the response is learned in terms of the sign, and hence, the theory is named as Sign Gestalt.

Experimental Evidence : Several experiments have been conducted to test Tolman's theoretical system of behaviour.

Experiment 1 : In one of the experiments Macfarlane (1930) trained some rats to swim across a simple maze filled with water to reach the goal box. Assuming that the animals learned to reach the food, there remained the question of whether they had learned something cognitive about the maze or had learned a series of stimulus-response connections. To clarify this problem, he drained the water out of the maze. Rats were put into the maze so that they could run through, instead of swimming to reach the goal box. He found that the rats could reach the goal without committing any error. He, thus concluded that the animals learned the specific lay out of the maze acquiring a cognitive map of the maze.

***Experiment* 2 :** The experiments known as 'place learning experiments' were conducted in 1940. These experiments proved that the learner does not reach its goal in a fixed or set sequence of movements but, instead, changes his behaviour according to the variations in conditions. In one such experiment rats trained to follow a right-angled path from starting point of goal were blocked on the original path and a number of paths going in all directions were provided. It was observed that mostly they chose the diagonal path to the goal. Tolman guessed that rats developed a generalized orientation and could trace alternative routes to reach the goal.

In the similar experiment with slight modification the rats were trained on simple experimental apparatus of 'T' type maze (A) to get the food and then were tested on the inverse maze (B). It was found that the rats could easily learn the place.

Experiment 3: A new type of experiments known as 'Latent learning experiments' were conducted by Tolman himself at Berkley. In one such experiment Tolman and Honzik (1930) conducted experiments on rats. A group of rats was allowed to run through the mazes without giving food. Later on the food, as a reward, was introduced. In the course of experimentation it was observed that the rats who had the chance to explore the maze, learned much faster than those of group B who had not explored the maze. Tolman concluded that some latent learning took place as a result of exploration of the maze.

Experiment 4: During this experiment Tolman found that those rats whose efforts were rewarded learned to reach the goal sooner than those whose efforts were not rewarded, and their errors in the maze were reduced. But the unrewarded rats also improved and showed less errors when they were rewarded. If goal directed rats are observed at certain selected points in the maze they look about seeming to hesitate and seeking a cognitive guide or sign. If they are given an electric shock, when they are reaching the food spot they will avoid it. Tolman argues on this basis that cognitive guides or signs are selected because they are significant aspects of the situation.

Critical Evaluation : Tolman was an electic theorist. He collected various ideas from here and there but could not shape them into a systematic theory. Also, he never adhered to a single explanation of behaviour. Even then Tolman and his associates made significant contributions to learning which may be explained as follows :

1. Tolman's main contribution is that behaviour is docile and purposeful. He always emphasized that what is learned is an expectancy or the value of signs rather than stimulus response connections.
2. Tolman developed a cognitive framework for interpreting learning. He stood outside the main stream of behaviouristic psychology, but was influenced to a great extent by the psychologists who were in the mainstream of behaviourism. He was against Watson's simple S-R connectionism and mechanistic philosophy of life. He attempted to combine the advantages of two families of learning theory and succeeded to a certain extent.
3. Perception and observation are two important factors in Tolman's theory of learning. Tolman is of the view that many retarded children who fumble in the classroom and indulge in blind trial-and-error show that there is something wrong with their capacity to learn and they are not able to organize their mental activity. Thus, self-activity accounts for higher forms of human learning. Tolman recognizes that in all learning some intelligence is at work, that the learner is an active participant in learning, who organizes his perceptions and observations and gives meaning to them.
4. Tolman recognizes that motives arouse, direct and determine the learning behaviour and that responses learned in one situation are generalized and apply to related situations also, but he goes further to emphasize

that motivation or reinforcement improves performance only. Learning is not determined solely by an expectation of rewards. Though Tolman agrees with the importance of motivation but he warns also that strong motivation may interfere with progress in learning.

5. Educational procedures and practices attach great importance to purposes and meanings in class work and it appears that Tolman's views though not so well known, harmonize with them.
6. According to this theory cognitive process is the heart of learning. Therefore, a teacher should always bear in his mind that what he teaches to his students must be meaningful and related to real life situations.
7. According to this theory unsystematic and unplanned haphazard activities do not make any significant contribution to learning. Only intelligent behaviour seems to be responsible for learning. Therefore, the process of teaching and learning must not be a blind folded action.
8. According to this theory route is more important than the results. Therefore, a teacher must make use of proper and, effective methods in teaching. While solving numerical problems in science or mathematical problems it should be kept in mind that students choose a right approach rather than worrying about results. The same must be observed in practical work also.
9. In this theory special emphasis is laid upon goal or objective. Hence, before teaching something new to the students the teacher should announce well in advance the goal or objective related to content and also the means to achieve the same so that the students may take full interest in the teaching-learning process.
10. While imparting education to children due consideration should also be made regarding age and other experiences of the students.

11. If a student, while attempting a mathematical problem or learning some simple act, makes more irrelevant activities or trials and errors, then, according to this theory the teacher can conclude that the child is suffering from some sort of defects definitely. Either, he is a lazy fellow or a backward one.

In view of these points it is quite evident that the theory is of immense help as regards the elementary learning of the child, Briefly speaking, Tolman postulated a large number of laws of learning during his long career which vary with nature of learning situation and are concerned with conditioned reflex learning, trial and error and inventive learning.

5

Fundamental Issues

If one were to go to sleep in 1947 in India and wake up in 2001, he would not be able to recognize the educational scenario of India. At the time of independence the educational scene was very dismal. The British government designed the educational system in India only to produce clerks and middle level functionaries to support and sustain their own rule. India which gave scripts and literature to half of the world in ancient times remained a poor country with illiterate population.

The percentage of literacy at that time was only 14.0 and the total expenditure on education was only 57 crores of rupees. In the age group 6-11 only one child out of every three was on the school register while in the age group 11-14 one child out of every eleven was enrolled in the school. Rural population was thoroughly neglected and girls' education was only in name. It was with this scenario that we in India began our independence with high level of illiteracy and poor standards of education.

During the past fifty years the educational system in India has expanded beyond recognition. Today, the number of primary schools in India is more than six lakhs as against one and a half lakh in 1947. About 14 per cent of children in the age group

6-11 are served by primary schools located within a radius of one kilometer from the house of the child. Where the child is unable to go to school, the school goes to the child in the form of a non-formal education center. There are more than three lakh such centers in the country. Girls' education is free throughout the whole country upto class XII. The rate of literacy has gone up from 14 to 62.3 in 2001.

Yet, in spite of these achievements we are faced with a number of challenges and have miles to go before our targets are achieved. Eradication of illiteracy leading to total literacy is one of the most intricate problems which is alluding all our efforts. Universalization of elementary education to which we are constitutionally committed under article-45 and which was to have been achieved by 1960 is still miles away from our reach. While most recent surveys indicate that nearly 70 per cent children in the age group 6-14 are attending schools, the painful fact is that while the net enrolment rate at the primary stage continues to be 70 per cent, it has dipped to a shockingly lower 40-50 per cent at the upper primary level. According to 1991 census the number of illiterates in the country was 48.22 crores out of which 27.47 were females.

Educational Universalization

This is an approach to achieve total literacy in India which emphasizes that all children in the age group 6-14 must be brought to schools. For achieving this objective there must be provision of schooling facilities for all children, i.e., there must be a school within an easy reach of every child This means universalization of schooling facilities which should be ensured by the government. Another aspect of this is universalization of enrolment. This requires enrolling every child of age 6+ in class-1. This also implies restricting admission of a child of higher age group to class-1. Again, the scheme of universalization of elementary education requires that every child who is admitted to class-1 should continue upto the last stage of primary education. This is the problem of retention and checking drop-outs in the middle and ensure permanent literacy. Thus, universalization of elementary education is a three-pronged strategy : (i) universal enrolment, (ii) universal retention, and (iii) universal provision for schooling. In fact the task of universal education begins when children are enrolled in class-I. It is completed only when they are successfully retained till they complete class VIII.

The Hindrances

It is a fact that universalization of elementary education which was to be achieved by 1960 is our cherished goal even in 2002. Only about 50 per cent of all children and 40 per cent of girls in the age group 6-14 attend schools. The rest either do not go to the schools at all or drop out before they reach class V. This is a serious problem and should be treated as a crucial area for national development. The most challenging problems of universalization are:

Wastage: Wastage in elementary education is generally understood to connote the premature withdrawal of a child from the school before completing the last grade of the stage, i.e., grade VII or VIII. Wastage is also known as 'retardation' or 'grade repetition'. It is also defined as the retention of a pupil in a grade for more than one year due to unsatisfactory progress. A number of studies have been conducted to find out the incidence of wastage and stagnation. The figures vary from state to state, But the general picture reveals that wastage is very high at the lower primary stage- about 56 per cent for boys and 62 per cent in case of girls. At the higher primary stage it is much less about 24 per cent for boys and 34 per cent for girls. It is also reported that wastage is decreasing consistently although at a slow rate. Reduction of wastage and stagnation in class I is the most important element. There are a number of reasons of this stagnation and wastage. Stagnation means repetition of class by the student while wastage means drop-out, i.e., leaving the school before completing the primary courses.

The main problems of universalization of elementary education are (i) how to ensure cent per cent enrolment in grade-I, and (ii) how to check stagnation and wastage. The various factors that stand in the way of solving these problems are:

1. Uneven spread of education.
2. Low enrolment of girls.

3. Low enrolment of the scheduled caste, schedule tribes and backward sections of the society.
4. Apathy and poverty of the parents.
5. Lack of suitable reading and writing material for children.
6. Lack of qualified teachers.
7. Frequent transfer of teachers.
8. Lack of effective inspection and academic, guidance by the inspecting staff.
9. Failure to enforce compulsory attendance.
10. Lack of a suitable admission policy.
11. Conservative attitude of parents towards coeducation.
12. Inadequate building facilities for schools.
13. Financial insufficiency.
14. Population explosion.

The Education Commission (1964-66) gave the following reasons of large stagnation and wastage in class I :

1. Heterogeneity of the age composition of students. It means that children of different ages varying from 5 to 12 + are admitted while their age in case of all admitted to class I should be 6+ only.
2. The practice in some states is of making fresh admissions throughout the year.
3. Irregularity of attendance.
4. Lack of educational equipment in the school.
5. Over-crowded classes
6. Unsuitable curricula
7. Inability of the teachers to use play-way techniques which can assist in initiating the children pleasantly to school life.
8. A wrong system of examinations.

The commission also suggested remedy for some of these defects as follows:

1. The examination at the end of class I should be abolished.
2. Adoption of play-way method of teaching in class I.

Factors Responsible for Stagnation

The Commission divided these causes into three categories-educational, economic and social. The Commission observed that 30 per cent of wastage was due to educational factors such as : existence of incomplete schools which do not teach the full courses, dull character of most of the schools and their poor capacity to attract students and retain them, absence of ancillary services like school meals and school health services and failure of the parent or the child to see the advantage of attendance of school. The social factors which operate mainly in the case of girls play a minor role. They include betrothal or marriage and opposition to sending grown up girls to school, especially to mixed school or school without a woman teacher.

The Commission observed that 65 per cent of the wastage is due to poverty. After the age of 9 or 10 the child becomes an economic asset because he can work at home. This is specially true in case of girls who have to assist the over-worked mother at home. The child is, then, withdrawn from the school and he becomes a "wastage" case. The solution to this problem lay in the general economic improvement. Another solution may be part-time education.

Enrolment Problems

The Education Commission (1964-66) had estimated that after 1980-81 the enrolment at lower primary stage would decline due to anticipated effect of the fall in the birth rate and this decline was predicted to continue for a few more years. Then, it could be possible to concentrate resources to a greater extent on the development of higher primary stage. This did happen by 1985-86. But, the overall enrolment position could not be found to be satisfactory despite the apparent achievement in terms of gross enrolment as was observed in the Challenge of Education (p. 34).

Universalization of enrolment is still a big problem. For various reasons the number of non-enrolled children at the primary stage (Classes I to V) consists of children from the weaker sections of the society, such as scheduled castes, scheduled tribes, agricultural landless labourers and urban slum dwellers. Two-thirds of non-enrolled children are girls. Three-fourth of the non-enrolled children are in nine educationally backward states, namely.

Andhra Pradesh, Assam, Bihar, Jammu and Kashmir, Madhya Pradesh, Orissa, Rajasthan, Uttar Pradesh and West Bengal. Even in advanced states low enrolments were found in respect of girls, scheduled castes and scheduled tribes. In certain states very low enrolments of girls had become a problem. The reasons of this state of affairs have already been discussed.

Ministry of Education, government of India had taken special measures for checking wastage and stagnation and for increasing enrolments. These are:

Assistance for Non-formal Education: Run on 50-50 basis the entire administrative and academic expenditure is reimbursed by the center. The expenditure on non-formal centers is shared on 3: 5 ratio, i.e. for every three centers funded by the center, the cost of 5 centers is borne out of the state budget.

Financial assistance is also given to voluntary agencies in the nine educationally backward states for running non-formal educational centers. Grant is also given to any academic organization/institution in any state/union territory run by the government or under private auspices for experimental and innovative projects with replicable potential.

Paper Assistance for Non-formal Education: Under Central Commodity Assistance the central government gives to all states including union territories paper for use in the production of textbooks and instructional materials for non-formal education for elementary age group children. The paper is purchased by the Government of India with the cash assistance given by the Swedish Government.

Early Childhood Education: By way of broad basing universalization of elementary education, a programme of early childhood education has also been started. These pre-school programmes aim at enabling out of school children to attend schools, thus minimizing the non-enrolment of children. The central government gives grant to voluntary organizations for running such centers.

Education of the Disabled: Programmes for the education of nine groups of handicapped children have also been introduced as these children constitute a substantial section of non-enrolled population of children.

Qualitative Improvement: Programmes of qualitative improvement of elementary education have been started in the states under the central government initiative. Under this scheme innovative projects have been in operation to improve the school curriculum. These programmes are being assisted by the UNICEF and are implemented in conjunction with the states and the Union Territories. These projects include various kinds of activities such as :

(1) nutrition, health education and environmental sanitation.

(2) curriculum renewal

(3) community education and participation

(4) comprehensive access to primary education,

(5) early childhood education,

(6) non-formal education programmes for women and girls.

Launched as a pilot project in 1976, the project on Nutrition, Health Education and Environment Sanitation was implemented till 1980. Curricular material on nutrition, health and sanitation habits for primary schools has been developed. It is intended to reach the community through teachers and children in regard to these aspects of elementary education.

Primary education curriculum renewal aims at a qualitative adjustment of the curriculum to the life-styles of the children and to the socio-economic opportunities available in the areas of the project schools. Developmental Activities in Community Education Project launched along with Primary Education Curriculum Renewal aims at developing non-formal educational programmes for various target groups particularly for out of school children and adults so that the educational activities could meet the needs of those who are partly or totally deprived of any education. Comprehensive Access to Primary Education (CAPE) had been taken up for implementation in 29 states with a view to decentralizing the curriculum according to the needs and life situations, of out of school children. Under the project relevance based learning material was developed which may be used in the network of non-formal learning centers.

Early childhood education project aims at developing new capacity for the training of pre-school educators, extension of research and developing activities and development of model pre-school centers. Non-formal Education Programmes for Women aims, among other activities, at introducing a substantial component of maternity and child care training in the programmes of adult education.

6

Effect of Education

Philosophy is related to all concepts of education, directly or indirectly. In fact, Philosophy and education are the two sides of the same coin. They present different views of the same thing. In other words one is implied in the other. Sir John Adams said education is the dynamic side of philosophy, the practical means of realizing ideals of life. Philosophy is the contemplative side and education is the active side of the same coin. Following is an account of some philosophies as they perceive and describe various aspects of education such as (i) aims of education, (ii) methods of education, (iii) curriculum of education, (iv) place of the child in education, (v) place of the teacher in education, etc.

Impact of Education on Idealism

The fundamental proposition of idealism is that the mental or spiritual is more real and more important than the material. To the idealists reality is spiritual rather than material. This view of the idealists influences their educational thought. The aims and methods of education are particularly described to be different from what other philosophies consider them to be. In fact, idealism has contributed more to the aims and objectives of education.

Idealism and Aims of Education : The idealists consider education as a man-making process. In their scheme of education man is assigned the central position. All of them stress the dignity of man and the distinctiveness of his nature. They accept the doctrine of evolution of man, but assert that the biological account of man is inadequate and incomplete.

They hold that realization of ultimate values lies at the heart of the universe; man must become a moral being knowing what is good and what is evil. Man possesses a spiritual nature which enables him to apprehend moral values. Man's true environment consists of universal values realization of which should be the ultimate goal of evolution. Man's spiritual nature is not something added to him; it is the essence of his being.

Hence, the goal of education must be self-realization for all. This constitutes, according to idealists, a philosophical charter of universal education.

The idealists like Plato said that one fundamental aim of education is to enable the mankind through its culture to enter more and more into the spiritual realm, to enlarge the boundaries of the spiritual realm.

Education must help the individual to attain self-realization through development of cultural values which guard man against any possible misunderstanding of self-realization as an isolated or self-sufficient attitude of the individual. Man's higher or spiritual nature, according to them, is essentially social, as social is an expression of man's rational or spiritual and hence, of universal nature. The individual can realize his full potentialities only as a member of the human family. Thus, it follows that education should make efforts on children's social development and cultural development. Education for self-realization does full justice to the social aim.

The idealists asserted that spiritual values are eternal and unchanging. Hence, this is one of the tasks of education to foster these values through educative process.

Plato said that the function of education is to help individuals in their exploration of the ultimate, universal values so that the truth of the universe may give power to their life.

The idealist hold that education must be religious, moral, intellectual and aesthetic. None of these aspects can be neglected if a harmoniously balanced personality is desired to be developed. They also say that physical development also can not be ignored.

Development of personality is the most prized aim of education according to the idealists. It is, defined by them as culmination in self-realization. It is, to them, the end of ends, the goal of goals, realization of the absolute idea. In the words of Rusk it means enhancement or enrichment of personality characterized by the embodiment of universal values. 'To some of the idealists self-realization means development of divine qualities which are inherent in human beings but dormant at the time of his birth. Unfolding of these dormant qualities is the aim of education.

Development of will power essential for self-realization is also said to be the aim of education according to idealists. Home has given eight points for the realization of this ideal. These include:

(i) training of the will indirectly through activity rather than idea,

(ii) the object lesson method according to time and context,

(iii) self-suggestion, knowledge and practice,

(iv) proper discipline,

(v) providing knowledge of facts concerning nature and society,

(vi) development of moral character by ethical instruction,

(vii) freedom to make choice in most of the matters concerning the individual.

Another aspect of idealistic conception of education is the synthesis between nature and human beings. Education must aim at achieving an understanding of nature in human beings and educating them to achieve harmony with it. It is, as held by idealists, the essence of human nature to work towards a rational unity in himself. Education must lead the educand nearer reality, and towards his utmost possible perfection, "fine roses".

Great importance is attached to child's cultural development and preservation of social heritage. The individual should make his own contribution also to this. Education must enable the child to do so. For achieving this education must provide the child with cultural environment created by religion, morality, art, literature, mathematics science, etc. Teaching of humanities is more emphasized for this purpose. Plato said that moral principles had eternal validity and hence, education must help children develop qualities like rightness, justice, courage, and so on which were considered of permanent nature. Idealism places more emphasis upon more universal objects of education. Ross says that the function of education is to help us in our exploration of the ultimate universal values so that the truth of the universe may become our truth and give power to our life.

Idealism and the Method : Idealists suggest that the method of education must be oriented to achieving the complete development of all the innate abilities of the child and to train him for self realization. Specific methods suggested are

Instruction: It is the most important tool to impart information. But, it does not mean, as held by idealists, a tool for stuffing the child's mind with junk material. It implies modification and refinement of child's mind. It has to be, therefore, supplemented by sympathetic guidance. Idealists stress that training of all kinds must be provided in the school.

Activity: Like naturalists and the pragmatists, idealists also recommend activity based teaching learning. The child must learn through doing. Lectures must be followed by questioning by students. But, more important than this is the creative activity. The creative activity has to be natural, continuous and progressive. This helps in child's approaching nearer to self-realization as through this child's innate tendencies are manifested. The instruction has to be active.

Experience: The child's own experience should be, as far as possible, the basis of his education. The task of the teacher is not to stuff his own experience in the educand's mind but to provide the child some insight through his own experience. Teacher's guidance must help the child to get rid of his frustrated and repressed tendencies. Independence and freedom is an essential prerequisite for experience.

Idealism and Curriculum : The determinants of what should be taught in the schools, according to idealists, are the spiritual development of the child and the preservation and creation of cultural heritage of the human race. Hence, they said that curriculum has to be man-centered not child-centered, ideals and values-centered not freedom-centered, character and morality-centered not expediency centered. Ideals for children should be the objective of curriculum transaction as asserted by Socrates, "Not man but reason is the measure of all things; not individuality but universality, not percepts but concepts and ideals are the norms for all human experience including that of children."

Idealism approaches the problem of curriculum from the domain of ideas rather than from the child and his present or future activities. To them present experience of the child is not very important. What is more important is the experience of the human race as a whole. Hence, the curriculum must reflect the civilization, the capitalized experience of the race which gives two broad divisions of the curriculum (a) science ad (b) humanities. T.P. Nunn (1923) said that a nation's schools should consolidate its spiritual strength, maintain its historic continuity, secure its past achievement and guarantee its future. To achieve this, the idealists stress that the curriculum must reflect those activities that are of greatest and most permanent significance in the wider world, and which are the grand expression of the human spirit. These activities are of two kinds- (a) those that safeguard the conditions and maintain the standards of individual and social life such as the care of health and body, manner, social life, morals and religion, and (b) creative activities. Hence, the curriculum must comprise (i) literature, (ii) art including music, (iii) handicrafts, (iv) science including mathematics, and (v) history.

From psychological point of view the idealists held a belief that the curriculum should reflect (a) what man knows, and (b) what man does or strives to do. Looking from this point of view the idealists curriculum should represent major modes of man's thinking enshrined in language and literature, science, mathematics, history and geography which constitute traditional intellectual studies. In addition to this art, poetry and music which represent man's modes of feelings should also be included in the scheme of studies. Representatives of what man does or strives to do such as major crafts should also form part of the curriculum.

Role of Teachers

The idealists attach much more importance to the role of the teacher in organizing education for the pupils. They consider educator and the educand two essential parts of an organic plan. They assign to the teacher the most important responsibility of creating a specific kind of environment for the desired development of the pupils. The teacher, as they say, must provide appropriate guidance to pupils, so that they may progress towards perfection and a well-rounded ideal personality. The teacher in the scheme of the idealists, is like a gardener who 'by his art' sees to it that both his cabbages and his roses achieve the finest form possible." The teacher by his efforts must help the pupils, who are developing according to the laws of their respective natures, to attain levels that would otherwise be denied to them.

Ross (p. 12.2) says that the relation between the educator and the educand is such that both of them work out in the process of education, their own salvation achieving self-realization by interaction with one another. Quoting Eucken Ross (p. 124) says that the educator can help the pupil towards true self-realization by regarding him not as "a particular and exclusively individual being" but as "a being in whom a new and universal life seems to emerge".

Idealism and the Discipline : Just contrary to naturalism and pragmatism idealists stress the value of discipline as part of the educative process. However, this does not mean that pupils' freedom and liberty are not important to them. Freedom to follow any and every inclination of action is, certainly, not acceptable to them. Such freedom to the idealists is license, not true freedom. On the other hand, true freedom is "discipline" which means denying himself this kind of freedom one "becomes master in his own house" "achieving the higher freedom to follow the light that is in him, unhampered by the chains of his lower nature. Self-realization is the only freedom worthy of the name. That man is free who is conscious of himself as the author of the law which he obeys" (Ross, p. 170). Thus, discipline not the freedom is the cry of the idealists. Ross (p. 171) further says, "if the educand is to succeed in realizing his spiritual possibilities, he must submit to a process of discipline which will enable him to apprehend the great values of life that are stressed by idealists." Almost all idealists emphasize that the child should be taught to discipline himself and to contribute to the disciplined behaviour of others. Pupils' learning to be self-disciplined is an important educational value for the idealists. Punishment and strict external control to enforce discipline are not advocated. Idealists, on the other hand, recommend influence and impressions left on pupils by the teachers, parents and members of society, to be the most practical methods for this purpose. They emphasize that, for achieving this purpose, the educators themselves should be disciplined; in their own behaviour they must present the highest ideal of self-discipline. They stress that the entire natural, social and spiritual environment in which the child lives should be so fashioned that it should encourage the desire for self-discipline in the child.

Impact of Education on Naturalism

As a philosophy naturalism has influenced the aims and objectives of education apart from discussing and describing its methods, curriculum, and a few other aspects of education. In the field of education, naturalism is neither the positivism of the physical world, nor mechanical positivism or even biological naturalism. It is entirely a different concept which seeks to base education on the experience of the child; and thus is a repudiation of all textbooks teaching. It adopts a scientific posture and seeks to base all education on psychology. Its motto is 'follow nature". Jean Jacques Rousseau (1712-1778) was the most important naturalistic philosopher of education. Another widely known such philosopher was Herbert Spencer (1820-1903) who published his book *Education* in 1861. This book is an excellent exposition of naturalism in education. Like Rousseau he also criticised the methods and curriculum of schools of his times. Rousseau's *negative education is* one concept which is sometimes very much misunderstood. Hence, before discussing other aspects of education, this concept is discussed in the following section:

Gloom Aspects

Rousseau said that the first education of the child ought to be purely negative. This he described as not teaching any virtue, value or do's or truth but shielding the heart of the child from vices and mind from errors. In other words it would mean imparting no education, no information of any kind to the child in the very early years of life. He said, "In childhood the aim of education is not to utilize time but to loose it". Elsewhere he said, "A 12-year old child should know nothing. Attention should be paid to the child only, not to knowledge."

The emphasis in negative education of Rousseau was on strengthening the sense organs and the power of reasoning. Rousseau said, "Nature wants that the child should remain a child before he becomes an adult." Rousseau criticised the system of education of his times saying that it was barbarous as it sacrificed child's present in favour of his uncertain future: It was trying to make the child an adult. He called this education of his times positive education. By negative education he would mean changing the old sequence of positive education by allowing the child to grow in his own way, own way of seeing, thinking and experiencing; and, thus, saving the child from groaning under the dead weight of the old imposed meaningless education. Explaining his new system of education Rousseau said, "give me a 12-year old child who does not know anything. By 15 years of age I will teach him so much as other children read in 15 years of early life."

Thus, negative education is self education. It is the education of sense organs and body. It is negative in the sense that it was a negation of the old system of teaching-learning, negation of classroom learning, negation of teacher's teaching in formal ways, negation of teaching morals and values. About morals Rousseau said that if you are all the time teaching morals to the child you will make him a fool; if you are all the time giving instruction, then child's mind will become useless. Whatever the child learns in the playground is four times more useful than what he learns in the classroom.

Naturalism and Aims of Education : Different philosophers have expressed and, emphasized different aims and objectives of education. Even among the different forms of naturalism, variations are found with regard to educational goals. Mechanical naturalism suggests that education should aim at the efficiency and perfection of the human being. This, however, is not the representative view of naturalism as a whole. Biological naturalism stresses proper adaptation or adjustment of the child to environment. Herbert Spencer described education to be a preparation and a training for complete life. As described by Ross the aim of education according to naturalism seems to be the present and future happiness, pleasure and happiness that are lasting and permanent are more worthwhile in the long run. But, McDougall denied the truth of this hedonistic view of aims of education. According to McDougall the aim of education is the sublimation of the energies of the propensities, the redirection, coordination and harmonious working of the native impulses. As described by McDougall education should enable the individual to attain the goals set for him by nature in ways that have individual and social value.

Naturalists also believe that education should prepare the pupils, equip them and through them the nation for the struggle for existence and survival. From another point of view, education is seen as the process of adjustment to environment, enabling the individual to be in harmony with and well adapted to his surroundings. Health of body and mind both is stressed and the ideal is a well adjusted happy being with no discontent. Bernard Shaw, another naturalist saw education as man's deliberate effort on accelerating the pace of evolution itself. To him the aim of education is the preservation, the handing on and the enhancement of racial gains from one generation to another.

Stagewise aims of education as stressed by Rousseau are:

(1) During the first five years the aim of education should be child's bodily development, development and strengthening of every part of the body. The child should grow up healthy and strong through complete liberty.

(2) During childhood from 5th to 12th year the education should aim at developing child's sense organs through experience and observation.

(3) During adolescence from 12th to 15th year the child is

ready for systematic education. At this stage education should aim at the development of adolescent's personality through hard work, guidance and study. The adolescent should be given knowledge of various kinds.

(4) The youth (15-20 yrs) as pointed out by Rousseau, should be taught moral and social qualities. The aim of education of the youth should be bodily, sensory, mental, social and moral development of the individual.

The aims of education according to Herbert Spencer another naturalistic philosopher of 19th century were as follows

1. Self-preservation, i.e., preservation of body and mind.
2. Earning a living, i.e., education in all the sciences.
3. Establishing family and upbringing of children
4. Citizenship development
5. Use of leisure time devoted to study and practice of painting, music , sculpture, poetry and also recreation.
6. Moral development

The naturalists of nineteenth and twentieth century, however, believed that education should achieve a synthesis and adjustment between the individual and the society, between man and nature.

Naturalism and Curriculum : What should be taught in the school is the matter to which not all naturalists have the same answer. To have an all-embracing glimpse one has to extract a common factor from various views presented by several naturalists. The extreme form of naturalism emphasizes the present experience, activities and interests of the child himself. So, they say, it is these which should determine the content of the curriculum. Their motto is "knowledge for the sake of knowledge."

The latest naturalistic movement in educational theory and practice had been expounded by A.S. Neill in a series of books. He tried to make *Summerhill* a residential school, the happiest school in the world, a place where the child's curriculum is dominated by play to the extent that if the child wishes he can play all the day, where teaching-learning matters little, books are of little value and examinations are hated. The school's curriculum consists of creative arts and activities having pottery room, wood and metal shop where children make whatever they want.

As a system of philosophy, naturalism has been exceptionally susceptible to the development of science. The naturalists attach greater importance to evolutionary theory, empirical teaching and scientific analysis. They recommended physical and social sciences to be taught at every level of education. They also said that language and mathematics being the tools for the learning of science should also be taught. The naturalists recommended that history should also be taught.

Yet, there are found differences and contradictions among the views of the naturalists with regard to the curriculum theory. For example, Comenius wanted the educand to study every subject without making selection, while Locke said every educand should not be required to learn every subject for reasons of individual differences. He emphasized that curriculum should be modified to suit the needs of the individuals. Similarly, Herbert Spencer wanted science to be the nucleus of the curriculum. The arts subjects were given, by him, secondary place in the curriculum. T.H. Huxley, another naturalist attached greater importance to cultural aspects of life in comparison to science. Thus, it is very difficult to say what exactly the curriculum of the naturalism was. In fact, all eyes of the naturalists were fixed on the child and his freedom. About other aspects of education they only cursorily glanced.

Naturalism and Methods of Education : The naturalists conception of education was that it is the *Child* himself rather than the educator, the school, the book or the curriculum that occupies the central position. Stanley Hall calls this the paidocentric attitude which is said to be the keynote of 20th century movement and is essentially naturalistic. Naturalistic conception of education is based on psychology.

As regard the method of teaching, the naturalists stressed the direct experience of things. As Rousseau said, "give your scholar no verbal lessons; he should be taught by experience alone." "Things rather than words" was the slogan of the naturalists. They said that science should not be taught from readers or by "chalk and talk" lessons; it should rather be learnt by the pupil through his own work in the laboratory or wherever possible through a direct study of the natural phenomena. Similarly, geometry should be taught not by arguments and problems in the textbooks, but by means of actual survey of the school field, playground, etc. In the same way, geography should be taught through school journeys and actual excursions rather than taught from books and maps. Rights and duties of citizens should be taught not through talks but through the organization of the school as a free natural society where every pupil is encouraged to participate. Students' self-governments should be the methods for teaching these qualities. Thus, most important method of teaching according to naturalists is to leave the child free to learn from nature.

Authoritarianism in teaching, rote learning, book-learning, classroom learning, theoretical teaching were denounced by the naturalists. Child's own experience was considered the most comprehensive book from which the child should learn according to naturalists. Playway method of learning was very much emphasized by all naturalist philosophers. Artificiality of any kind was very much condemned by them. Informal atmosphere in the class and the school was considered important. Participation of children in extracurricular activities was emphasized. The naturalists had a conviction that, left to himself the child will himself evolve the method which suits him best.

Naturalism and Discipline : Almost all naturalist philosophers discarded the traditional concept of discipline, which was imposed on the child from outside. Particularly, they opposed the method of physical punishment for they believed that this generated undesirable conflicts and strain in the mind of the child. Rousseau said, "Freedom and not the power is the greatest good. If the child makes a mistake he will get his reward from nature itself and thus he will learn to distinguish between right and wrong through the consequences of his own actions. Thus, discipline through consequences of behaviour was emphasized. This, however, should not be understood to mean giving license of doing anything and every thing to the child. As hinted by Dewey it becomes necessary sometimes to scold the child, to caution him or even to punish him.

Naturalism and the Teacher **:** Least important is the position of the teacher in the scheme of Naturalistic education. He is barely tolerated. His interference with child's education is deprecated. He is forbidden to resort to any coercive or didactic method. He may not even seek to influence the child. As said by Ross (p. 94) "His place, if any, is behind the scenes, he is an observer of the child's development rather than a giver of information, ideas, ideals and will power or a moulder of character. These the child will forge for himself." The teacher's role according to naturalists, is that of the setter of the stage, the supplier of materials and opportunities, the provider of an ideal environment, the creator of conditions under which natural development of the child may take place. Influenced by naturalism, several systems such as Montessori System, Dalton Plan, Project Method, etc., developed and they all assigned to the teacher a similar status. In Froebel's Kindergarten system the teacher is considered to have the same position which a gardener has in the garden. His only function is to make sure that the plants grow according to their own nature and that their development is not hindered.

Contribution of Naturalism

Naturalism has made important contributions to education as follows:

Paidocentric Movement: This tendency, as highlighted by John Adams means that it is the child himself rather than the educator, the school, the book on the subjects of study that is in the foreground of the educational picture.

Emphasis upon Psychology: Naturalists' emphasis on child's natural development resulted into psychological studies of the child's nature. Concepts like child's nature, his adjustment to the environment, individual differences with regard to their nature, etc., brought psychology into prominence.

Freedom of the Child: It was emphasized that the child must be given freedom to choose and learn. No predetermined design of growing up should be imposed on him.

Direct Experience of Things: Learning through one's own experience, an important principle of teaching-learning in education was an outgrowth of naturalistic philosophy. Rousseau said, "give your scholar no verbal lesson; he should be taught by experience alone." .

Playway Method: This is an important contribution of the naturalists towards children's growth and learning. The principle emphasizes that young children be given enough opportunity to play. Through play activities children develop their creative and constructive powers.

Real Effects

The term pragmatism has been derived from the Greek word "Pragma" which means use. Thus, pragmatism means a philosophy which emphasizes usefulness of anything, use being the criterion of reality. It was born around 1878 and Charles Pierce was the person who, first, gave its clear-cut formulation. This is the doctrine that evaluates any assertion solely by its practical consequences, and its bearing on human interests. It has several forms. It is a philosophy which may be said to be corrective of naturalism and toned down idealism, a midway house between idealism and naturalism. Charles Sanders Pierce (1832-1914), William James (1842-1910), John Dewey (1859-1952) and Bertrand Russell (1872-1970) happen to be some of the eminent philosophers of pragmatism. According to emphasis there are four important forms of pragmatism- (1) Humanistic Pragmatism, (2) Experimental Pragmatism, (3) Nominalistic Pragmatism, (4) Biological Pragmatism.

Humanistic Pragmatism asserts that all truths are human truths; Satisfaction of human nature is the criterion of utility. Experimental Pragmatism said that truth is that which can be ascertained by experiment, and is useful in practice. According to nominalistic pragmatism the results of an experiment are always particular and concrete, never general and abstract. According to Biological Pragmatism, the ultimate aim of all knowledge is harmony of man with his environment. It further asserts that the school is a miniature society which prepares the child for future life.

Pragmatism and Aims of Education : The pragmatists do not accept development of eternal spiritual values, discovery of preexisting reality and universals and teaching of moral standards to pupils, as the aims of education which were the heart of the idealists' scheme of education. They assert that any effort on the part of the educator to prescribe specific goals or to decide the child's purposes for him stultifies true education. The aims of education as described by most pragmatists are the cultivation of a dynamic, adaptable mind which is resourceful and enterprising in all situations, one which is powerful enough to create values in an unknown future. The pragmatists accept growth or development of the child as the aim of education. But, the forms and standards of these are not preexisting, not permanent and fixed. They are to be discovered in future. All the aims of education, they say, must be concerned with the present and the future and must be subject to modification.

According to Dewey education as such has no aims; education is an abstract idea. Only persons have aims. And the aims of persons are indefinitely varied differing with different children, changing as children and their teachers grow. Stated aims do more harm than good unless they are taken only as suggestions. Thus, aims of education, for the pragmatists, are mere suggestions, not to be taken literally. Even these aims must possess three elements in order to be useful. These elements are: (i) based on educand's actions and needs, (ii) they must elicit educand's cooperation, (iii) they are specific and temporary, not permanent and general.

American pragmatism, however, is certainly not guilty of neglecting the social aspects of education, as it emphasizes that education must aim at realizing democratic values in life. It should instill in the educand a respect for democratic institutions. Kilpatrick said, "The classrooms must become living democracies; in a democracy it is self-directing personalities that we try to build; the kind that can carry forward life even more successfully in a developing world; and the progressive development of a better life for all men is the basis out of which morality and moral conduct arise". Thus, it may be concluded that the pragmatists favour the democratic ideals of education.

Pragmatism is emphatically humanistic. It also assumes, like Protagoras, the sophist that "man is the measure of all things" and emphasizes human purposes and the satisfaction of human wants rather than "one grand purpose towards which the universe is to move".

Pragmatism and Curriculum : The pragmatists favour that curriculum which satisfies the following criteria:

Utility Criterion: This criterion would mean that whatever is put in the curriculum, it should do good to the pupils, it should be of some utility, some use for the child. The knowledge that is provided to the child must help him in his later life in solving his problems and adjusting to his environment. "The school must store up experience that is to stand the child in good stead" (Ross, p.195). The curriculum must include the knowledge and skills that the child requires not only for his present life as a child, but also for his future life as an adult. In view of this criterion it was suggested that the curriculum for the young child of elementary school must include language, arithmetic, health and physical training, history, geography, domestics science for girls, agriculture for boys and training for some vocation.

Reality Criterion: The curriculum should be real, i.e., it should be concerned with the realities of child's nature and of life. Hence, its content should be selected from different activities of real life. The determining principle should be the natural interests of the child.

Child's Experience as the Criterion: This principle implies that the curriculum should be based on child's experience. It means that practical work should constitute an essential ingredient of the curriculum. Teaching through books should be supplemented by programmes which provide actual experience to the child.

Child's Interest as the Criterion: This criterion implies that while selecting material for constructing curriculum, child's own interests must be taken into account. Genetically, children have four kinds of interests-talking, searching or discovering, creative and artistic. Hence, the curriculum should include reading, counting, handicraft, painting, etc.

Purposiveness Criterion: The curriculum, according to pragmatist should be purposive. It means knowledge to be incorporated in the curriculum should be such as it must serve some purpose in the life of the child.

Integration Criterion: This criterion emphasizes that the different subjects should not be completely segregated from each other as knowledge is one single whole. This is an important criterion which has been much emphasized by the pragmatists. Knowledge contained under various subjects should be organized in the curriculum in an integrated manner as far as possible.

Pragmatism and the Method : Pragmatic methods of education are based on psychology and sociology subject to the conditions that they give adequate scope for active participation by the educand and also that the method adopted must be dynamic and changeable. The method suggested is the "project method' which is the most characteristic and valuable contribution of the pragmatists. This method focuses on the learning process which involves some practical problem to be solved by the child.

The project as defined by Stevenson as a "problematic act carried to completion in its natural setting". Thomas and Lang define it as "a voluntary undertaking which involves constructive effort or thought and eventuates into objective results." Educational projects may be of individual or social character. Social projects are a sort of "socialized activities" and they are preferred to individual projects. In case of very young children, projects may take the form of play such as playing the roles of the school teacher, or running a family or a post office, etc. At higher levels more complicated activities such as production of a play, or a concert involving elocution, music, literature, craft work, needle work, etc., may be organized in the form of projects. In all subjects such projects may be prepared. But, it is not like this that the whole of teaching may be done through projects. Nor projects can be suggested readymade from outside. It is educator's insight that is needed for successful selection and completion of the project. What is more important is not the project itself but the incidental learning that takes place as a by-product of the project method.

The great principle involved in project method of teaching is learning by doing, experience-based learning, one's own learning. Pragmatism offers more help in the methods than in the aims of education. The pragmatists assert that education is not so much teaching the child things he ought to know, as encouraging him to learn for himself through experimental creative activity. It is action which is emphasized by them rather than reflection. It was the belief of the pragmatists that true knowledge does not come from books; it, comes from child's own doing. The most general method of education according to pragmatists is putting the child into situation with which he wants to grapple and providing him, at the same time, with the means of dealing with them successfully.

Role of Educator

The pragmatists consider the role of the educator important unlike the naturalists who like him to banish from the scene. The educator has to be there in the capacity of an adviser and a guide of the pupils as well as a servant of society. His job is to create in the school an environment which may help in the development of the child's social personality and enable him to become a responsible democratic citizen. Dewey gives the educator so great an importance as he calls him God's representative on earth. But, unlike the idealists he has not to impose himself on pupils, Rather he has to see how best he can help the pupils to grow and develop naturally in conformity with their interests and potentialities. He has to identify most appropriate educational projects, motivate and guide students to carry them out, facilitate and provide essential materials needed for completing the projects. How efficiently, successfully and fruitfully the project method is used depends very much on educator's insight and wisdom. He has to be a model for the pupils.

Pragmatism and Discipline : What is discipline and how discipline should be enforced are discussed in detail by the pragmatists. They stress self-discipline instead of discipline as control and restraint from outside. True discipline comes from child's own inner striving. Strict control imposed by authorities, ultimately, does harm to the child. True discipline is the result of developed social consciousness of the educand. It is this social consciousness which prevents the child from indulging in anti-social activity. Pragmatists believe that freedom is the root of true discipline. Freedom and discipline are inseparable according to them. Self-discipline is the best discipline to them.

For developing self-discipline it is essential that the educand must understand and realize the importance of discipline. This realization emerges, according to the pragmatists, from educand's engagement and participation in those activities which lead to fulfilment of his social obligations. Through their participation in school activities the educand happens to develop such qualities as responsibility, inspiration, insight, cooperation, compassion, etc., which make him a good, responsible citizen. Blind obedience to rules is no discipline, they say. True discipline is responsible behaviour emerging from the sense of social responsibility. This developed sense leads the educand to be self-disciplined. Dewey maintained that discipline is not the sole function of child's personality; it is very much dependent upon the socio-psychological environment in which the child is placed. Hence, acquiring the habit of being self-disciplined is the consequence of environmental manipulation. School activities may generate the kind of environment needed. Free, happy and purposive activity of the pupil is likely to result in permanent attitudes, initiative and independence. Training in citizenship, character-formation, moral education come from school activities which, ultimately, lead to self-discipline on the part of the child.

Ross (p. 211) said that realism emerged as a reaction against curricula of studies which had become "bookish, sophisticated and abstruse". Realism is the theory that holds that the existence of objects is real. The main tenet of realism is that objects and their qualities are independent of and uninfluenced by the knower and the process of knowing or knowledge. There are four types of realism which are well known. These are: (1) Naive Realism, (2) Neo Realism, (3) Representationism, and (4) Critical Realism. The naive realism emphasises that the object is what it seems to be; its qualities are not affected by knowledge: objects are known directly and they are common for all. Neo Realism says that an object is what it is manifestly seen to be. The total object is not the subject of knowledge, but its aspects are and they are independent of knowledge. Representationism is Lock's theory and implies that objects have their representation in man's thought. Knowledge of the objects is direct in the case of simple thoughts, but indirect in the case of complex thought. Critical Realism was propounded in America at the end of the 19th century. It is critical in nature. This realism says that objects are not what they seem to be. When the object becomes an object of knowledge it is influenced by knowledge. Knowledge of objects may be direct as well as indirect. The relationship between the knower and the known is not direct but takes place through the medium of thought which is the subject matter or knowledge.

In educational theory two forms of realism, *social realism* and *sense realism* emerged after the enthusiasm of Renaissance had been over. The social realism opposed bookish studies and stressed the value of direct studies of men and things. They advocated tours and travels as methods of teaching-learning. Sense realism stressed observation and scientific study of natural phenomena maintaining that all knowledge comes from the senses.

Realism and Aims of Education : It was the oft-repeated cry of realism that education should be made to conform to the social and individual needs of the child so that he may lead a happy and contented life in future. Its primary purpose was to prepare the child for real life, to prepare the child for adult life. An implication of this broad objective was that education should be directed towards a particular calling in life. Thus, preparing pupils for a career in life was one of the most sought for aim of the realists. Besides this the realists asserted that education should impart to the pupils a training that aims at the development in the pupil of certain attributes, habits, skills, sentiments and attitudes of mind as well as the possession and use of knowledge. This should be the training which is suitable for every future occupation, not fit only for one particular calling. The realists emphasized that education should fit a man to perform justly, skillfully and magnanimously all the offices both private and public. In a way it may be concluded that the aim of education as advocated by the realists was to give all round training of the mental faculties. It was emphasized that the main function of education should be to develop the qualities, in the educand, of determination, reason and intelligence so that he may successfully solve the problems of life.

Thus, vocational aims, social development aims and personality development aims of education were mainly advocated and emphasized by the realists.

Realism and Curriculum : As mentioned earlier realism was a reaction against curricula consisting of studies that had become "bookish, sophisticated and abstruse". To escape from this state of affairs some realists, particularly, the sense realists advocated the study of natural phenomena of which the senses could give firsthand knowledge. This resulted into displacing literary, and linguistic work by scientific studies including studies of real things by inductive method. Spencer said that scientific studies are of much greater value than linguistic studies. He further said that the study of surrounding phenomena is more valuable than the study of grammar and lexicons irrespective of the fact whether it is intellectual, moral or religious training. Huxley also vehemently pleaded for incorporating into the school curricula "a complete and thorough scientific culture."

The other subjects constituting elements of curriculum were given a new treatment. History should incorporate contemporary events to be studied in the light of past events. The study of civics should be included in the curriculum. Literature should be taught as a criticism of life. Mathematics must aim at understanding of the world. Application must be emphasized in the case of study of science.

Realism and Educational Method : The social realists stressed the value of direct studies of men and things and hence, recommended that educational tours and travels which would give real experience of varied aspects of life should be an essential component of the curriculum. Sense realists also advocated study of natural phenomena through actual observation and study of real things by the inductive method. For teaching science, experimentation and application of knowledge were considered important. The realist supported fact-centered or knowledge-centered method of teaching. The inductive method of teaching emphasized teaching to begin with the parts and leading to the whole gradually. This is the same as the main "from part to whole " The realists said that knowledge should be analyzed into principles and principles into hypotheses: and facts should be analysed into propositions. Thus the method of teaching should be analytical and rational.

The realists also advocated that all teaching in the class and outside the class should be child-centered and purposeful. The realistic doctrine stressed that the teacher should think not only about his method of teaching but also about the value and significance of its content.

Impact of Education on Existentialism

All philosophies have grappled with the problem of existence. In that sense all philosophies can be said to be existentialists. Modern existentialism, however, is concerned unlike other philosophers more with the problem of becoming than with the problem of being, more with particulars than universals, more with existence than essence. Kierkegaard is said to be the father of existentialism. The problem before the modern existentialists is "how to become Authentic Being". They emphasize "Action" and "Choice", instead of usual emphasis on knowledge and explanation. "How", not "What" is their main concern.

The contemporary existentialists hold that mans' existence is real in the sense that he is unavoidably a participant in the affairs of the world outside: he can not stand alone: he interacts with man, things and events of the outside world. He can not keep himself away from this bondage and hence his most common despair is not to be able to "choose", not to be able "willingly to be himself'. More serious type of despair is that he has to choose to be another than himself. Hence, they advocate that the aim of man's life ought "to be that which one truly is". Sorer Kierkegaard was a staunch religious person and had great faith in God's existence. Later existentialists, however, did not consider God to be a necessity. Jean Paul Sartre, for example, said that human life has no purpose: existence is ultimate: man should be free to choose: through freedom to choose man becomes himself.

Following are the assumptions of existentialists: (1) center of existence is man, not the truth. (2) man is unique, being a composite of emotions, feelings, perceptions and thinking, (3) Man makes the universe meaningful. (4) man is not alone in the universe and, hence, the real living person is more important than anything else. (5) man is free capable of shaping his own life and choosing his own destiny.

The existentialists criticise idealism saying that there is nothing like universals and spiritual elements in life. Man's existence as it is and practical problems of life are more important. Truth is not God but existence. They criticized Naturalism also saying that man is completely free and can not be subjected to psycho-biochemical laws of causation operating universally as was advocated by the naturalists. They bitterly criticized scientific philosophy and developments saying that science has abrogated the value of man. It has dehumanized him. Scientific developments and technological progress leading to industrialization and urbanization have resulted into deprivation of man's freedom and a threat to his real existence. Everywhere man is found groaning under the weight of numerous constraints. He is not free: There is growing despair in the mind and heart of men. "Life is becoming like a raft on the open sea which is carried hither and thither without any definite direction." Man is the center of universe and nothing else is equal to it. Man can not be subjected to any law, rule or principle, be it a universal, natural or social or political. Any external encroachment upon man's freedom is unjustified.

The existentialist philosophy asserts that the most serious problem of modern highly complex life is not ideological, but practical, such as how to inspire in man a sense of responsibility and freedom, removing feelings of alienation from the world, society and the self of the man.

Existentialism and Aim of Education : The aim of education according to existentialists, is humanitarian and humanist, which means inner development of man, development of real consciousness, i.e., consciousness of real self. The individual must understand and realize what it means for him "to be", "to exist". Thus, to impart knowledge of self-existence is the fundamental aim of education.

The existentialists emphasize education of the whole man, i.e., development of all aspects of his inner self, his feelings, emotions, thinking, etc., realizing ultimately what he is, what his purpose of living is, i.e., what he has to become. Education should create an environment which is conducive to this kind of realization.

The existentialists want the schools to lay emphasis on subjective knowledge, i.e., inward thinking rather than objective knowledge, the knowledge of subjects. For this reason teaching-learning of literature and arts is emphasized. They want that development of materialistic interests should be discouraged and self-realization should be encouraged. They, particularly, favour religious and moral education.

Existentialism and Curriculum : Existentialism is averse to study of science subjects which impart objective knowledge because they think that this kind of objective knowledge displaces man away from his own self. Their belief is that science does not help in achieving inner peace and realization of real self. Yet, they do not expressly say that science should not be taught. They only say that along with study of sciences more emphasis should be on arts and literature, ethics and religion. Character and personality development as aims of education can not be achieved without having a synthesis of both sciences and other subjects. At the elementary stage, they say the three Rs. should be mastered. They also say that foreign language, logic, mathematics, and philosophy should be taught at higher level. They prefer liberal education to vocational education.

Existentialism and Discipline : The key idea of existentialism is the freedom of the child, complete freedom. But, this should not mean giving license to the child to do whatever he wants and is free to do. It only means that the child should not be so restricted as he is constrained to develop his inner self. The existentialists do not talk about discipline. They only talk about child's freedom to choose and grow in self-consciousness.

Existentialism and the Teacher : In the scheme of existentialists' scheme of education the teacher is given an important position to occupy. He is required not only to teach, but also to create an environment in the school which provides freedom to the child and, at the same time, stimulates his thinking. The whole purpose of existentialist education is realization of inner-self through his free existence. The teacher has an important role to play in this context. He has to guide and counsel the students to this effect apart from teaching the subject. Through the impact of his personality he has to make the students realize what his inner self is, what he has to become and how. This is the most delicate but very important role that the teacher has to play.

7

Social Relevance

In the late seventies, the Government at the Union level attempted major policy changes in some spheres of Public Policy except perhaps in foreign policy. In pursuance of its election manifesto, a radical realignment of priorities was attempted within the education. For the first time since independence, a National policy to educate illiterate adults was formulated to educate an estimated 100 million in the age group of 15-35 years. The target was fixed as 1983-84. The commitment of the government to adult education is reflected in Policy Statement on 'National Adult Education Programme' issued in 1978. It says "exclusion of a vast majority of the people from the process of education is a most disturbing aspect of educational and social planning. This has been uppermost in the consideration of the present government ever since it assumed office in March 1977".

Recognising the role of primary education in checking illiteracy, the policy statement says that "while determined efforts must be made to universalise elementary education up to the age of 14 years, educational facilities must be extended to adult population to remedy their educational deprivation and to enable them to develop their potentiality. Indeed, universalisation of elementary education and of adult literacy are mutually dependent".

Further, the policy statement says that "the government have resolved to wage a clearly conceived well planned and relentless struggle against illiteracy to enable masses to play an active role in social and cultural change".

Adult Education policy, thus, has been visualised as a major policy input to bring radical socio-economic and political changes. The report of the working group on adult education further confirms the government's intention on role of adult education as a 'change agent' when it says that : "Adult Education, looked upon as a method of human resource development, including literacy, functional development and creation of awareness among the poor regarding their inherent power to determine their destinies, should become the method in the new development process. It can contribute to the new development strategy in three significant ways : firstly, by making a substantial part of the work-force literate and better skilled ; secondly, by involvement of people in various developmental programmes which would make it possible to achieve optimum potential and minimize wastage ; and thirdly, by creation of awareness among the poor regarding the laws and policies of government, whereby, it would be possible to implement the strategy of redistributive justice".

Touching on the various aspects of the problem of illiteracy, the policy statement clearly stated that "a massive programme should be launched to cover the vast segment of population in the 15-35 age group as early as possible". The planners of this programme dwelt at length on the organizational aspects of the National Adult Education Programme.

The role of non-governmental and semi-government agencies in the implementation of this programme was particularly recognised.

In fact, the policy document makes it very clear that "Adult Education must cease to be a concern only of the educational authority. It should be an indispensable input in all (major) sectors of development, particularly where participation of the beneficiaries is crucial to the fulfillment of development objectives".' Further it was stated that "A prerequisite of an adult education movement is that all agencies; government, voluntary, private and public sector industry, institutes of formal education should lend strength to it". Thus, it can be seen that the policy planners rightly perceived the importance of non-governmental agencies (popularly known as NGO's) in the implementation of qualitative Public Policy like adult education.

A unique feature of the National Adult Education Programme is the special place given to voluntary agencies. The policy statement emphatically stated that "voluntary agencies have a special role to play and necessary steps shall have to be taken to secure their full involvement".

Thus the goal liquidating illiteracy in the country through a National Adult Education Programme is being planned and this programme was launched in 1978 throughout the country on Mahatma Gandhi's birth anniversary. It was planned to cover 100 million illiterates in the 15-35 age group within five years.

Top Body

It may be recalled that the National Adult Education Programme was started as a result of the initiative taken by the then Union Government which was elected to power in late 70's. The preliminary work relating to the programme began with the establishment of a National Board of Adult Education in 1977. The Chairman of the Board was Shri Morarji Desai who was the Prime Minister then. The composition of the board includes some ministers of Central Government, a Minister dealing with adult education from each of the regions of the country, heads of organizations such as University Grants Commission, Central Social Welfare Board, Khadi and Village Industries Corporation, Federation of Indian Chambers of Commerce and Industry, Indian Adult Education Association and a host of other non-officials and field workers.

The National Board of Adult Education has set up five committees to attend to specific tasks relating to adult education programme. These were :

1. The Committee on Preparatory action.
2. The Committee on Motivation.

3. Committee on Voluntary Agencies.
4. Committee on Post-literacy and follow-up.
5. Committee on Evaluation.

It was stated in one of the publications of the Ministry of Education and Social Welfare that "all important decisions taken by various committees are generally endorsed by the National Board of Adult Education".

The overall responsibility for the administration of the national adult education programme rests with the Ministry of Education (now rechristened as Ministry of Human Resource Development). It provides secretariat to the National Board of Adult Education. The Ministry also deals with the various inter-ministerial matters and is charged with the responsibility of overseeing the implementation of National Adult Education Programmes in various states. The schemes of assistance to voluntary agencies and Shramik Vidyapeeths under the Ministry directly sanctions grants and is thus administered by the Central Ministry.

The organisational chart drawn here gives a picture of the administrative framework of the National Adult Education Programme.

As can be observed from the chart, the programme is being planned to be implemented through a variety of governmental, semi-governmental and non-governmental agencies.

The administrative structure for the programme extends from the central to the field level (i.e. Adult Education Centre). At the Central level, as has already been discussed, the Ministry of Education and the Central Directorate of Adult Education are the overall in-charge of the programme management. The Ministry and the Directorate have a special responsibility for involvement of various organizations like voluntary agencies universities and colleges. The specific functions of the Directorate include: (a) arrangement of training programmes; (b) production of teaching/learning material; and (c) evaluation. These two agencies are also charged with the responsibility of involving other developmental ministries like Agriculture Rural development and other autonomous agencies in the programme. In 1987, the programme has been redesignated as National Literacy Mission and target year had been put off to the year 2020.

At the state level, the State Board of Adult Education (S B A E) is regarded as an apex body for entire state. It is usually chaired by the State's Chief Minister or the Education Minister. The main functions of the Board are: (a) to provide policy guidelines; (b) creating a favourable environment; and (c) reviewing the progress of the programme.

A Steering Committee to aid and advise the state board of Adult Education is also created with such functions like working out implementation strategies like location of centres, target of coverage as well as coordination of the programme besides involving other developmental departments. Further, this agency is also expected to take steps to involve government, semi-governmental and voluntary agencies and the implementation. Monitoring of the progress of the programme is yet another task entrusted to the Steering Committee.

The government's determination to give a place of precedence to Voluntary Agencies was reflected in the terms of reference of the Working Group on Adult Education for Medium Term Plan (1978-83). One of the term of reference to this committee was "to apportion the areas of responsibility among the centre, states and voluntary agencies."

Thus, the policy makers envisaged almost a primary role to voluntary agencies after the State Government's in the implementation of National Adult Education Programme. Delineating on implementation agencies, the 'Outline on National Adult Education Programme' states that "the programme which gives importance to flexibility and diversity in organization as well as its content can be best implemented through voluntary agencies." Noting that the involvement of voluntary agencies is not much then, the policy planners of National Adult Education Programme recommended several steps for increasing their participation in National Adult Education Programme which include: (1) to involve all voluntary agencies working at present in the field of adult education or having the potentiality to do so; and (2) to create circumstances for emergence of new agencies, particularly in areas where such agencies are few. Further, the programme planners of N A E P visualised partnership role to voluntary agencies along with the State Governments and recommended the association of the voluntary agencies at all decision making levels particularly in matters which affect the work of these agencies, like the procedures for applying grants.

The report of working group on Adult Education appointed for medium term plan 1978-83 also identified the areas where voluntary agencies' participation was relevant and necessary. The report says that "these agencies should organise field adult education programmes, including post-literacy and follow-up programmes . . . resource development particularly training, production of teaching and learning materials and evaluation." The report further says that "the all India voluntary organizations should be encouraged to organize orientation programmes for other voluntary agencies."

Commenting on the rigid procedures in government which may drive away the enthusiastic agencies from the programme, the working group recommended that "the government must also replace the mechanism which obstruct involvement of the voluntary agencies by enabling mechanisms." However, the group struck a note of caution regarding the selection of voluntary agencies in the implementation of N A E P and recommended that only those agencies should he selected for financial assistance which have potentiality to implement the programme.

The functional agency of the State Government for implementation of National Adult Education Programme is the Directorate of Adult Education, with specific tasks such as: (1) preparation of plans; (2) encouraging voluntary agencies to participate; (3) direction and overall supervision of government programmes; (4) overseeing and coordination of programmes taken up by various agencies other than the government; (5) selection and placement of personnel; and (6) monitoring and evaluation of the programme.

The next important agency in the Nation Adult Educational Programme is the State Resources Centre which is entrusted with such essential functions as: (1) preparation of teaching/ learning material; (2) organization of seminars; (3) development of methodological guidelines for curriculum preparation; and (4) training support to the programme, including post-literacy programmes, evaluation, research and publications.

Local Standards

At the district level, the major responsibility for the implementation of National Adult Education Programme is vested with the District Collector. He/She occupies this position as the Chairman of District adult education board/committee. The government projects are expected to be supervised by the District Collector who would organize, coordinate and supervise the implementation of National Adult Education Programme through all agencies—governmental, voluntary and other agencies at the district level. The Collector is assisted by the District Adult Education Officer, now styled as Dy. Director of Adult Education in Andhra Pradesh. The District Adult Education Officer/Deputy Director of Adult Education acts as member secretary of the District Adult Education Committee/Board which first of all scrutinises the proposals for starting Adult Education Programme in the district. All the government project officers and some representatives of voluntary agencies, Universities, Nehru Yuvak Kendras are members of this committee. The committee is also charged with an important responsibility of processing the applications of voluntary agencies for financial assistance and also to assess progress of their work periodically. Besides, the district adult education committee also monitors and evaluates the work of all agencies in their jurisdiction.

Scheme's Implementation

A key unit for planning and implementation of national adult education programme is a project which usually consists of about 300 adult education centres. It is headed by a Project Officer. He/She is assisted by an Assistant Project Officer. In Andhra Pradesh, the geographical area of a project generally is co-terminus with that of a block. (Block has been further divided into Mandals recently). A project in National Adult Education Programme framework is visualised as an autonomous unit with Project Officer vested with powers to run administration, to manage finances, appointment and training of instructors and supervisors (which was since passed on to State Resources Centre:) taking steps to prepare the teaching/learning materials and finally organize post-literacy and other follow up activities.

For every 30 Adult Education Centres in a project, a supervisor is appointed who is expected to assist the Project Officer in resource development particularly in training instructors. Besides these functions, the supervisors discharge such varied functions like liaison with development functionaries, Mahila Mandals, ensuring regular supply of teaching/learning materials and payment of honorarium to instructor, and in organizing post literacy operations.

At the Union Level

The critical unit of the administration in the organisational framework of National Adult Education Programme is the adult education centre under the charge of an instructor. The instructor's main functions, besides teaching, are: (a) Survey; (b) ensuring cooperation with village level developmental functionaries; (c) establishment of rapport with village elites and sending periodical reports about the progress of the programme.

Thus, it can be seen that a vast administrative machinery at various levels was created to Implement National Adult Education Programme. The National Board of Adult Education, The State Boards, Steering Committees, the Project Level Committees are expected to function as Coordinating bodies.

Instructor's Role

The policy planners of National Adult Education Programme have identified six categories of people as the, 'instructional cadre'. They include: (1) The School teachers; (2) Students; (3) Village youths; (4) Ex-serviceman and other retired personnel; (5) Field level government and other functionaries and (6) Voluntary social workers.

School teachers in particular were regarded as the catchment area to take up the job of instruction in adult education centres.

The students, as part of the National Service Scheme activities, were marked as another source.

The policy planners also gave a place to the village youth with some educational background in running the adult education centres. With an expectation that the retired people would be free and would accept a job which would yield a supplemental income to them, ex-servicemen and retired persons are identified as one of the sources for the teaching part of the programme. The village level workers and Gram Sevikas and voluntary social workers are yet another category who were identified for the job of instructors.

Source Development

The conceptual position spelt out in the policy statement implies creation and development of a resource base for National Adult Education Programme, the priority being given to diversified and need based learning material. The National Resource group consists of such agencies like the Central Directorate of Adult Education, various other agencies of Central Government and National level voluntary agencies.

The next important unit in resource development is the State Resources Centres (SRC's) which in cooperation with the National Resource Group and by continuous interaction with the field, are expected to attend to the task of resource development. Some of the important functions of the SRC's include: (a) development of competence in curriculum planning and development; (b) preparation of diversified teaching/ learning material to suit the learners' needs ; and (c) organization of training programmes to key level functionaries.

Fiscal Facets

An amount of Rs. 200 crores had been allocated to this programme in the draft sixth five year plan (1978-83)21 by the then Janata Government. To cover 65 million adult illiterates, the cost was estimated at about Rs. 686 crores. The following table gives the details of the year wise expenditure outlay for N A E P from 1978-1983. Recently, the Union government announced that a 'National Literacy Mission' (NLM) to educate about 80 million adult illiterates would be implemented from 1987-88. The cost of the programme was stated to be Rs. 550 crores. It has been calculated then that the cost for 'educating' an adult illiterate would be Rs. 60 per year. Since the programme planners expected that one third of the participants would dropout the cost per learner was worked out as Rs. 90/-.

It was also expected that some funds would be available in the form of contributions and the final cost per learner was put at Rs. 80/-. This estimate, however, does not include expenditure on administrative structure and other activities connected with the programme.

The Construction

An impressive administrative structure seemed to have been provided at national, state and district levels to implement the N A E P. A number of state governments have created separate directorate of Adult Education. The State government send their proposals to the Ministry for starting projects. The Central Directorate is also associated in scrutinising such proposals. A set of guidelines were formulated which facilitate easy scrutiny of the proposals. Projects sponsored and entirely funded by the Central Government are known as Rural Functional Literacy Programme's (R F L P), projects funded by states are known as 'State Adult Eduction Programme's (S A E P's). The Central Ministry of Education directly sanctions the grants to voluntary agencies for running adult education programme. The State Governments are expected to be informed about the sanction of grants sanctioned to voluntary agencies by the Government of India and the state directorates are supposed to supervise the implementation by the voluntary agencies.

However, like in any programme, we notice snags in the organisational design. In the earlier years of the programme some voluntary agencies got the financial sanction bypassing the State Governments, the Directorates of Adult Education and District Adult Education Committees using the political linkages they had with the power structure at the union level. Such situations gave rise to infiltration of undesirable elements into the programme.

Monitoring of N A E P is stated as an important component of programme management. Elaborate procedures have been evolved to monitor the progress.

It was stated in one of the handouts, released by the Central Directorate of Adult Education, that qualitative reporting is desirable rather than reporting of mere quantitative data. One of the aspects of the reporting procedure is a column relating to the achievement of learners in terms of the main objectives of the programme viz., literacy, functionality and social awareness. However, except in the year 1979-80 we do not find it in the annual report brought out by either the Ministry of Education or the Central Directorate of Adult Education in the subsequent years.

The States are not coming forward to take up the programme on the scale expected. For the last five years, the Central Government's share" is very much higher compared with the other agencies.

Coming to the personnel policies, most of the staff of State Directorates are brought on deputation. The discussions with some officials revealed that the staff lacked the required commitment that is so necessary for the success of the programme. The visits by them to the 'Centres' either under the R F L P, or S A E P or by Voluntary Agencies is routine and their reactions to the problems is passive. Thus, the personnel policy with regard to the State Directorates warrants reconsideration.

While about twelve Deputy Directors at the rate of one for every two districts are required for effective supervision of the programme, there are about four or five Deputy Directors which indicates absence of commitment on the part of the State of Andhra Pradesh. The supervisory recruitment policy was marked by ad-hocism and short-sightedness. It is to be noticed that there is a lot of gap between what policy planners visualised and what is actually happening now in the States. The point is that since the overall management of both centrally sponsored and other agencies programmes rests with the State Governments, the Education Department of the State and the Directorate of Adult Education needs to be properly equipped in terms of staff and other requirements.

Coming to the District level administrative framework, the much burdened District Collector is further loaded with the Chairmanship of the District Adult Education Committee in which besides District Education Officer and Deputy Director of Adult Education the voluntary agencies participating in the programme, are also members. Most of the District level Education Committees are inactive for one reason or the other. Curiously enough, the Andhra Pradesh State Government made the District Education Officer the Convenor of the District Adult Education Committee, while the field representative of the Directorate of Adult Education is just a member.

In this superior subordinate power relationship sometimes a junior District Educational Officer may act as a boss to the senior Deputy Director of Adult Education. The power conflict between them may have an adverse effect on the effectiveness of the programme.

As already pointed out, the National Board of Adult Education (N B A E) is not meeting regularly to give a higher and necessary policy direction. This has sometimes created vacuum in policy making. Even the meetings of State Boards of Adult Education and the State level Steering Committees are not held regularly as they are expected to. With the result, a clearly conceived policy on Adult Education is suffering from ad-hocism. The progress of the programme in terms of number of adult education centres opened from 1979-80 to 1983-84 for whole country can be gleaned from Table.

Data in Table presents the progress in terms of number of adult education centres opened and functioning in the country from 1979-80 to 1983-84. Reporting procedures seemed to have been modified since 1984-85. It was given to understand that the monitoring of the progress gradually became ineffective. The central directorate of adult education is not supplied information by its counterparts in the states.

We only find number of projects (each project consists of 300 ABC's) sanctioned by the Union Government. That is the reason why data is not up to date.

Total Number of Adult Education Centres Opened

Sl. No.	*Name of Scheme*	*1979-80*	*1980-81*	*1981-82*	*1982-83*	*1983-84*
1.	Rural Functional Literacy Programme	28,996 (35.56)	37,643 (41.44)	48,369 (52.55)	63,602 (49.55)	99,574 (59.01)
2.	State Adult Education Programme	19,644 (24.1)	38,178 (41.72)	37,352 (40.58)	59,840 (46.62)	59.015 (34.97)
3.	Voluntary Agencies	19,029 (23.34)	11,293 (12.34)	339 (36)	822 (64)	5,873 (3.48)
4.	Nehru Yuvak Kendras	7,129 (8.74)	1,514 (1.65)	4,884 (5.31)	1,519 (1.1835)	527 (0.3)
5.	Universities & Colleges	3,684 (3.91)	2,340 (2.56)	585 (.64)	899 (.69)	644 (0.381)
6.	Others	3,049 (3.74)	542 (.59)	516 (.50)	1,662 (1.3)	0837 (1.83)
	Total	81,531	91,510	92,045	1,28,344	1,68,720

From the table, it will be clear that the majority of centres are run under centrally sponsored functional literacy projects followed by the States. Contrary to the popular expectations and policy statements, the role of voluntary agencies in the programme appears to be declining.

This may be due to the mounting criticism against the participation of voluntary sector as it was alleged in Parliament and Press that some agencies are diverting funds earmarked for adult education to 'other' purposes. The Committee headed by Prof. D.S. Kothari appointed to review the National Adult Education Policy, however, gave a clean chit to voluntary agencies.

The role of Nehru Yuvak Kendras, Universities & Colleges and others also shows a decline. National Adult Education Policy appears to be almost under an eclipse for two years i.e., between 1980-81 and 81-82. The report of the review Committee on National Adult Education Policy had been withheld. The whole programme was in a state of suspended animation till 1982.

The New Education Policy—1986 mentions continuing priority to adult education. The document on 'Programme of Action' too delineates on various ways and means to stir activity on the adult education front. In 1987, the Union Government announced a National Literacy Mission to educate about 80 million adult illiterates in the age group of 15-35 years by 1995. Thirty million are proposed to be brought under the programme by 1990. It should be remembered that this is the second time the Government changed the target year.

Changes in the institutional framework are on cards. The Union Directorate of Adult Education is proposed to be converted into a National Resource Centre. A high power board seems to be in the offing to give a new thrust to the programme.

The process of implementation of National Adult Education Programme is attempted in the next chapter starting with an analysis of the instructional cadre.

8

Various Approaches

Theory of Hierarchy

Learning, undoubtedly, is the consequence of an interaction between the two groups of forces-internal (i.e., the individual's capacities) and the external, i.e., the environmental conditions. External conditions necessary for learning exist outside the learner in the environment. An individual's success in learning is, largely, the result of the effective interaction of these internal-external conditions. There are different theories that explain how these factors interacting with each other determine what and how much will be learned by an individual. This chapter discusses how Gagne explains learning and the learning events. The learning event comprises the learner, the stimulus situation and the learner's response.

Event based Learning

Gagne (1970) considers human learning as an activity which involves simultaneous operation of three components the learner, the stimulus (i.e., the learning situation) and the response. The learner represents internal conditions in the form of his previous learning or entering behaviour. The environment or the learning situation presents the stimulus or stimuli which interact with the learner's previous knowledge or his entering behaviours. The consequence of the interaction of these two internal external conditions of learning results into response which is a part of human behaviour. For example, "seeing the snake an individual runs away" is the event in which "running away" is the response resulting from the interaction between the stimulus, snake and individual's previous knowledge of the snake and of the fact that if the snake bites the man dies. Gagne has developed a whole theory of learning to explain the learning event. He explains how learning taken place, particularly, how an individual learns principles and generalizations. His theory is known as Hierarchy of Learning. Gagne's name is associated with the attainment of general principles in the same way as Ausubel's name is associated with meaningful learning. Ausubel emphasizes meaningfulness of the material to be learnt, the structure and organization of the material; Gagne emphasizes the process of learning, the sequence and chaining of responses involved in the process of learning.

Learning based on Hierarchy

Gagne's theory is most comprehensively described in his The Conditions of Learning (1970). He describes eight types of learning which, actually, are the stages, in the sequence of learning complex behaviour. According to Gagne learning of simple to complex behaviours is sequential activity. A higher level learning can not occur unless the learning at lower levels in the sequence has taken place. In fact, these learnings of Gagne's are types or classes of behaviour. Learning of one class or type of behaviour is contingent upon learning of the behaviour corresponding to the lower level. These eight types of learning, or conditions of learning or classes of behaviour from simple to complex are hierarchically linked to each other. He calls them conditions of learning for the reason that each one of these is necessary for learning the next higher level behaviour.

For example, mastery of a certain number of principles is a prerequisite for problem-solving. To master a Principle, it is essential, that the learner must have acquired related concepts. To have developed concepts, he must have learned multiple discriminations. And this, in turn, implies that ability to link words to things and words to each other, i.e., acquisition of verbal associations which themselves are based on combinations or chains of simpler S-R associations following conditioned responses or signal learning

Thus, the eight conditions of learning as described by Gagne are (from lowest to the highest)

Signal Learning: This is the most elementary behaviour learning, a kind of classical conditioning as referred to by Gagne. All learning begins with this elementary S-R unit of learning, the brick with which the wall is constructed. This kind of learning is involuntary, diffuse and emotional; for example, withdrawal of the hand from fire. Pavlov studied such learning in great detail. Stopping the vehicle immediately seeing the red light at the cross, salivation of the dog seeing the food, running away of the child seeing the dog, etc., are examples of sign learning. In these examples red light, food and dog are the stimuli or the signals in the language of Gagne. The conditioned responses are stopping the vehicle, salivation of the dog and running of the child.

Stimulus-Response Learning: This is learning of precise response to specific stimuli. The responses in signal learning are diffuse and emotional. But, in S-R learning they are fairly precise and are called, often, operants. This is used more profusely in acquiring verbal skills, as well as behavioural skills. For example, the child learns to say 'dog' when shown a picture of dog and asked to say 'dog' and is rewarded on correctly speaking 'dog'. Words of foreign language are learnt by adults mostly in this way.

Chaining: This is the stage where the person combines previously learned S-R associations together, thus, acquiring a new structure. Learning of this kind of response consists of a series of events which are, generally, not noticed. For example, a child who learns to say 'dog', then, learns to say 'dogs eat', 'dogs are in the street', and so on. In chain learning, each learned response gets linked to another response relating to the same object, thing or situation. According to Gagne' verbal learning is like skill learning in that it involves a chain of at least two links. The first link is the presentation of the object (S) and the observing of the object (R). In the second link the observing response results in certain internal stimuli which give rise to the verbal response - the utterance "dog", etc. At the most basic level according to Gagne verbal learning is just labelling behaviour, i.e., naming. Gagne' diagrams the simple act of naming as follows :

Ss ------------------> ~ s -----------------> R

(object) (response) (dog)

observing

The small 's' refers to internal stimulus.

The observing response enables the child to distinguish 'dog' from other objects and is acquired through operant conditioning. The second link connecting the internal stimulus to the actual utterance of the word 'dog' is also acquired through operant conditioning. Both these links are considered necessary entering behaviours for naming or labelling. More complex form of verbal learning consists of longer chains and verbal hierarchies.

Verbal Associations: This kind of learning is just the chaining of verbal units. In its simplest form it is verbal association in the activity of naming an object, which involves the chain of the links, as is explained in the previous section on chain learning. The observing response enables the child to identify the object that he sees and the internal stimulus (s) enables him to name the object. But, when he associates this object with some other quality or characteristic, this becomes association of three links. For example, when the child has learned to name the object 'dog' and, then, also learns to say 'black dog', he has learned a verbal association of three links.

Gagne' talks of one more kind of a common verbal association, the translation responses or verbal mediation, an internal link which helps the person associate, for example, an English word for Hindi word.

Discrimination Learning: This is the kind of learning in which the learner must learn to discriminate between different responses to different stimuli. For example, he must learn to distinguish between the new stimulus "pet dog" and the verbal chain he has already acquired. He must learn that "pet dog" is different from "dog", similarly, he must learn to distinguish between "street dog" and the "pet dog". When he is associating the word with the correct type of dog, what he is doing is discrimination. When there are several objects and names, linking the name with the same correct object and no other object illustrates discrimination learning.

Concept Learning: In concept learning the student's behaviour is not under the control of particular physical stimuli but of the abstract properties of each stimulus. In this kind of learning the individual responds to stimuli in terms of abstract characteristics like height, size, shape, colour, movement, position, number, etc., as opposed to concrete physical properties. For example, if given a series of numbers, he is able to select those which are odd as opposed to those which are even.

Rule Learning: This involves combining two or more concepts to explain an event, fact or a situation. A rule is the chain of the concepts. This takes the form "If x, then y" or "If it rains, I will be drenched". "If the dog is hungry, it will salivate if food is brought before him." It is said that knowledge is, largely, a hierarchy of rules; a system of rule within rules.

Problem-solving: In this kind of learning rules are used to achieve some goal. According to Gagne' problem-solving is learning of higher order rules in which case two or more lower order rules are combined and used for understanding the situation. It involves internal events such as thinking. Without the knowledge of rules which are necessary for solving the problem, success is not possible. For example, a student planning to qualify the competitive examination having been unsuccessful on the first occasion is solving a problem.

There are eight types of learning Gagne has described.

The Usages

Gagne explains how his theory can explain various kinds of learning.

Learning of Skills: According to Gagne a skilled performance involves a chain of motor responses. A skill has three important characteristics- (a) a chain of motor responses, (b) coordination of eye-hand movements, and (c) organization of chains into complex response patterns. Motor responses are muscular movements, movements of the fingers, arms, legs, toes, etc. Each motor movement is an individual S-R association. A number of such chains of movements coming together constitute a skill. They are to operate in series. Gagne (1970, p. 124) gives an example as follows of a novice driver's starting a car engine.

S (Start the engine)	R (looking forward and to the rear)
S (Sight of rear road)	R (testing for gear in neutral)
S (gear in neutral)	R (turning the key to activate starter)
S (Sound of motor catching)	R (release of key)
S (key released)	R (depressing the accelerator)

In the above R = motor responses or muscular movements. They are and must be performed in a sequence. In the same way S =internal muscular tension (kinesthetic stimulation), the feel of the matter. Gagne's work (1970) calls for the careful development of lower-order skills before these are called into play in more complex activities.

Transfer of Learning: Transfer of learning occurs when whatever is learned in one situation is used in a new or different situation. Gagne (1970) talks of two kinds of transfer - lateral and vertical. In lateral transfer the individual is able to perform a novel task of about the same level of complexity as that which he has learned. For example, a child having learned the meaning of some words in his class reads and understands then when he finds them in the advertisement on the T.V. screen: This is lateral transfer and is based on the acquisition of S-R associations. But, when a person is able to learn more advanced or more complex outcomes, this is vertical transfer which is based on previously learned verbal associations, rule learning and problem-solving. For example, having learned to add, subtract and multiply lays the foundation for performing long divisions. Any hierarchical organisation of knowledge follows a similar pattern. Subordinate concepts lay the basis for the subsequent learning of superordinate concepts.

For example, possessing the concept of subject and predicate is essential to learning the concept of sentence. Similarly, ability to read at one level permits learning to read at the next higher level. Gagne (1962) also said that verbalizing the method one is using while solving a problem also facilitates transfer by high school students.

Problem-solving: Gagne calls problem-solving, sometimes, as rule- learning also (1964, 1970). This is so as it combines two or more principles previously learned into a higher-order principle. To Gagne problem-solving represents acquisition of substantive knowledge. Gagne (1964) holds that problem-solving is different from other kinds of learning in that problem-solving has high generalisability or transferability. In problem-solving the single solution to a single problem is not important. Students' solving a type of problem (may include solving a number of problems instead of a single problem) should be encouraged.

Importance of Gagne's Hierarchy: The hierarchy has following implications which are important from the point of view of teaching: (1) While teaching a complex principle, the teacher should concentrate on the subordinate skills and should ensure that they have been mastered by the students. These subordinate or lower-level skills or learning constitute learner's entering behaviour necessary for learning new material. Ensuring these entering behaviour contributes to effective learning. Eustace (1969) found it helpful to begin with a noun as a specific name, and then to work up to the use of a noun as an abstract general concept, before teaching the role that noun plays in the sentence. This approach is most important in the teaching of a complex task in which there is considerable risk of failure.

Modern Theory

Education is said to be preparation for life. Whatever we learn in schools and colleges is useful only when we can apply the same in day-today life. All education is based upon the assumption that the knowledge, the skills and the methods of learning which are used in relation to definite school tasks will not only be available in the future but will be applied in some measure; at least to the solution of new problems as they arise in the life to come. Learning is the most fundamental problem of education. But, nothing is learnt for its own sake. Learning is a dynamic process and so what is learnt in one situation must be capable of being applied in future life's situations. It means what is learnt in one situation must have some transfer value. If we learn any given thing, does it necessarily follow that what was learned will automatically be applied when the need arises? Is the fact, that certain subject matter has the effect of exercising the student's intellect, of such prime importance as to justify the teaching of that subject more than other subjects? Does the manner in which information is acquired have anything to do with whether or not it will be used in new situations? These and other questions of educational and practical significance are such as must be considered in dealing with the general problem of transfer of training.

In brief, the problem of transfer of training raises the following questions. Can the forgetting tendency be minimized? Do abilities acquired in one situation help in another? Does the study of science develop scientific attitude in the student? Does study of one subject improve our mental process in general? Does participation in games develop a sense of fair play and good sportsmanship? Can we improve imagination, perception etc., by training one aspect only? Does the child who completes his assignment neatly also keep his room neat at home? Can we improve character and personality more broadly by practising one specific trait or virtue, such as honesty and originality? Does a student observe honesty in examination too, who is honest at his home? Does the study of English help a student to learn French or Russian? All such questions may not be answered in a very definite manner either in 'Yes' or 'No'. But, whatever the answers be, they all depend upon the operation of the psychological process known as transfer of training or transfer of learning.

The psychologists differ in responding to these questions. Previously the philosophers and scientists believed that there were several faculties independent of each other which resided in the mind of each individual such as memory, imagination, attention and reasoning, etc. The oldest psychologist R.M. Hutchins believed that each subject trains a particular faculty of the mind e.g., the teacher of algebra assumed that his pupils would apply their knowledge of algebra to the solution of problems in physics and chemistry, the teachers of social sciences assumed that their students would gain the ability to interpret the social problems more intelligently than others. A professor of mathematics would always say "mathematics and language are the meat and potatoes of the educational diet." But, on the other hand, the modern psychologists say that there are no faculties of the mind, but we do make use of the experience gained in one situation in another situation. Thus, transfer is possible, though it is not same for all individuals. Individuals differ in the capacity to make use of the past experience.

Briefly speaking, the process of carrying over knowledge, skills, understanding, attitudes and habits of thinking from one learning situation to another is called the transfer of training or transfer of learning. The fact that transfer of training does occur is rather self-evident. The fact is that learning through practice has a cumulative effect. Having learned to walk, the child transfers his skill in maintaining balance and in locomotion to the closely related task of running. When learning or the development of skill is sequential, it is obvious that transfer takes place. If this were not true formal schooling would be utterly impossible. Future learning depends upon past learning.

The whole concept of readiness is based on this premise. We do not learn independently of what we have experienced in the past. In learning anything new we bring to bear on the task as much of what we have previously learned as possible. In memorizing a poem, for example, we use coordinated eye movements and the ability to read that we have previously acquired. We also apply what we have learned about learning to the new poem to be memorized. The attitudes about poetry, and memorization that we have formed through learning are transferred to this new situation with either positive, neutral or deleterious effects.

Transfer is an all-important matter for those concerned with curriculum construction and for those concerned with aims and methods of instruction. Education for the future necessarily must be concerned with the applicability of the learning in the school to life situations beyond the formal classroom situation.

Transfer of training has been defined by various educationists and psychologists as under :

According to Bigee, "Transfer of learning occurs when a

person's learning in one situation influences his learning and performance in other situation."

According to Lovell, "Transfer of learning means the effect which some particular course of training has on learning or execution of a second performance. Such an effect may be of a helpful nature, or it may hinder."

Sorenson defines transfer as, "recognition, use and application to a given situation of knowledge, skills and habits that were learned in another situation.

According to Crow and Crow, "the carry-over of habits of thinking, feeling or working of knowledge or of skills from one learning area to another usually is referred to as transfer of training."

Transfer of Learning Concept

Modern researchers lead only to believe that there is the "possibility of general training in the sense of training for adaptability." This is only a little more than the new version of the old formal discipline theory. This is referred to as transfer of training.

Through recent researches on transfer of training, it has been discovered that "carry-over from one situation to another," is definite. Thus, transfer of training is concerned with the question whether or not the learning of a material A, aids, hinders or has no effect in the learning of another material B. Transfer of training assumes nothing about the faculties. It is concerned with how the organism meets the situation B, C, D, and so forth, after having had an experience in the situation A. Educationally, it is concerned with finding out how the organism can benefit to the largest degree from its experience in one situation, when it finds itself face to face with other situations. Thus, transfer of training means transfer of experience in one situation of learning to another situation of learning. When, that which is acquired in one situation, appears in another; we speak of transfer of training.

Experimental Evidences : Experimental investigation began with William Jame's experiment on memory training (1890). Between 1890 and 1940 about 211 experiments were performed.

Out of these; in 53 experiments 25% transfer took place (considerable); in 95 experiments 45% transfer took place (appreciable); in 16 about 8% (varying with conditions of learning), in 20 about 9%. (very little); in 9 only 4% (no transfer) and in 18 again 9%.

Thus, there can be little question about whether or not there is transfer. The problem of education is how to achieve the greatest amount of favourable gain in one situation as a consequence of experience in another.

Transfer problem studied with reference to school subjects is important from teaching point of view. Prof. Bridges took two groups of seventh grade pupils, equal in intelligence. One studied grammar and the other language and composition. The grammar group improved in the ability to see likeness and differences. He proved the positive transfer. Many other studies have been made. H.O. Rugg found that a course in descriptive geometry transfers 32% to another geometrical material, but only 7% to non-geometrical material. Hewins, a teacher showed that 34% transfer takes place between two kinds of botanical material, but only 5.4% between botanical and non-botanical. Thorndike and Rugger showed that study of Latin improved knowledge of English language. The degree of positive transfer was found to have varied from a very slight amount to 93%.

Transfer Theories

The revolt against the doctrine of formal discipline was now well under way, and the problem of transfer of training had become a legitimate topic for research. To explain how and why transfer takes place, psychologists have propounded various theories. These theories also describe what transfers from one situation to another. The theories are :

1. Theory of Formal Discipline
2. Theory of Identical Elements
3. Theory of Generalization
4. Theory of Ideals-of-Procedures
5. Configuration Theory

Theory of Formal Discipline : This theory is based on the theory of mental faculties. It is an old important theory of education that mental faculties can be developed uniformly as a whole by providing training in one subject. The word 'formal' means that it is form of the activity that is important in education and not the subject-matter itself or its content. If one wants to improve the reasoning one has merely to practise the forms of reasoning. Similarly, if one engages in activities of memorization, memory would be improved no matter what is memorised.

Formal discipline should not be confused with transfer of training. The modern psychologists do not accept the original theory of formal discipline. They believe in the transfer of training. Yet, the influence of formal discipline has not died even uptil now. Formal discipline seems to have been an outgrowth of the belief in the faculty theory of the mind. Two faculty theories of the mind are distinguished- general-faculty-theory and, organismic-unity-theory. In the 'general-faculty-theory' mind was considered to be composed of various powers or faculties, each working independently. Formal discipline theory meant that one study sharpens this or that faculty and the result transfers to another study. 'Organismic-unity-faculty-theory' is found to be stated in Greek literature. To the Greeks mind was unitary whole which expressed itself in the activities of judging, reasoning, remembering, etc. These powers or faculties were not considered as isolated from one another but were viewed only as distinct modes of activity of the same mind.

Modern psychology with its stress on neurophysiology to explain mental processes has discarded these faculties of the mind.

Thus, formal discipline simply means that the powers or the faculties of the mind may be trained or influenced by the study of special subject matter. In the middle of the 19th century Huxley and Spencer advocated the inclusion of natural sciences in the curriculum on the same ground.

Theory of Identical Elements : This theory propounded by Thorndike, suggests that transfer takes place to the extent to which there are identical elements in the old and new tasks. These identical elements may be in the form of content or technique. To quote the words of Thorndike himself, "Transfer occurs from one situation to another because the situations have identical components. The components may be in the form of skills, generalizations, information, procedures, principles or attitudes." Thorndike explains transfer by this theory. He says that transfer takes place when there are the same neural bonds in the two situations which happen because of identity of element. This is perceptual in nature, that is, the common elements must be perceived by the subject. In other words transfer depends on the common element and perception of the same by the learner.

Theory of Identical elements holds that because in two situations certain elements are common and they require the functioning of the same mental abilities, therefore, transfer takes place. The study of Sanskrit improves mastery over Hindi because of identical elements. Similarly, Anurag is a good player of cricket and Abhishek is a good player of hockey. Both make an effort to learn football. Abhishek will be at advantage because hockey is more similar to football than cricket. In case of rote memory, Identical elements theory is helpful. Some may like to extend it to embrace identities of substance or content or procedure, mood or attitude.

When it has been established that the amount of transfer depends upon the presence of common components, it is obviously essential to make the classroom teaching and other school activities similar to real life situations. Then and only then the transfer of knowledge, habits, accuracy and techniques of learning and problem-solving to the real life conditions will be large. This notion will help in removing the unreal and fantastic problems and impractical information.

The idea of identical elements as the sole means of securing transfer was not fully accepted when applied to education or when contrasted to the theory of mental discipline. Experiments conducted revealed small amount of transfer that actually took place and yielded information as to the positive or negative effect of transfer. These experiments also provided evidence for or against the theory of 'Identical components' and from that other theories were derived.

Ruger (1910), in his study of puzzle solving in adults found that training in a particular portion of a puzzle very often did not help in the solution of the puzzle as a whole. He felt that the mere presence of identical elements as such did not ensure transfer. His experiments yielded information, too, on problem of the possible negative effect of transfer. He found that when the principle of solution is the same but the details of the puzzle are different, the transfer effect may be negative and actually a detriment to the solution of the new puzzle.

A large number of experiments performed on transfer revealed that the amount of transfer in most situations was discouragingly small and that such transfer had in some cases an inhibitory rather than facilitative effect. Moreover, these findings served as bases for further theorizing.

Theory of Generalization : The theory of generalization was propounded by Charles Judd (1908). Generalization means process of attending to common features, principles or relationships in a variety of specific situations. According to this theory transfer takes place due to certain generalizations of experience in one situation, and it takes place to the extent to which one generalizes his experiences. Judd said, "When a pupil fully grasps a scientific generalization or when he gains a view of a wide range of relations, he acquires independence and breadth of intellectual power, and becomes capable of transferring training to situations that are different from those in which he was first trained. Transfer by generalization is transfer of principles.

Judd performed an experiment in which he tested the ability of students to hit a target with a dart placed under water. Some of the students had studied the principle of refraction of light, how the rays of light shift direction when passing from one medium to another and how this makes objects appear to be where they are not. The remaining students (controlled group) had not been given any such instruction. It was discovered that when the target was one foot below the surface of the water, there was no significant difference in the abilities of the two groups (controlled and experimental) but that when the target was raised to 4 inches instead of one foot of the water's surface, the students who had been taught refraction were able to adjust better than the others.

In another experiment M.C. Barlow tried to study the transfer of a technique through generalization (1937). Children were asked to interpret Aesop's Fables. One fable was the tale of a widow who doubled the amount of food she fed her hen, expecting two eggs a day. The best interpretation was that 'figures are not always facts.' Then the experimental group was given training through lessons in reasoning by induction, reasoning by analogy and reasoning by analysis, but the other group was given no such training. The trained group was found to have done sixty percent better than the other group.

In this theory, method of teaching or study is the most important factor. The content or the subject matter is of little significance. The function of training is to discipline, to develop a scientific attitude, training in observation, discrimination and reasoning which may transfer to real situations of life. This sounds well and seems to be possible if viewed from the standpoint of this theory.

Theory of Ideals: Ideals-of-Procedure is another theory formulated by W.C. Bagley. It is a special form of the generalization theory. It is generalization plus appreciation. Bagley holds that generalization itself will not tell the whole story. To be effective the generalization must be made emotionally toned so as to take the form of and rise to the level of an ideal. He conducted an experiment in which children were taught to be neat and tidy in a particular subject. But, this neatness and tidiness did not transfer itself to other tasks or subjects.

Such specific training does not go beyond the immediate field in which training is imparted. But, as Bagley suggests, if neatness is stressed in a general way as an ideal to be pursued, it may be transferred to the whole of life and learning. Ideals facilitate transfer. It is obvious that ideals involve generalization and are effective when learning situations have identical components.

In education, ideals have always been emphasized. One may feel that they have been overdone. We should not stress impossible or unrealistic ideals such as absolute obedience, preferring duty to death, self-sacrifice at all costs. Instead, if we emphasize ideals that are well within the reach of young people like love of learning, toleration, eagerness to minimize difference of opinion, putting one's best foot forward etc., one would have a better chance of transfer or realization from one situation to another.

The teacher can do well in this regard to emphasize transfer of an ideal to be achieved through his programmes of instruction. If some of the practicable ideals are ever kept in view, teaching methods will secure greater transfer.

Configuration Theory: This theory put forth by Gestalt Psychologists is a hypothesis of the Gestalt Psychology. It is a negation of the Theory of Identical Elements. According to this, it is the 'insight' gained in one situation that transfers. So, unless a task is carried out with insight, training cannot be transferred. It emphasizes that the more meaningful an experience, the richer its conceptualization and deeper its understanding are, the greater will be transfer possibilities.

Configuration theory is also known as Transposition Theory. Transposition means that it is not the specific skills or facts or principles which are the basis of transfer but the understanding of the relationships between facts, processes and principles. Gestalt psychology emphasizes the total pattern of behaviour, wholeness or unity of response. Parts do not function in isolation and transfer is dependent upon the whole part relations, between the old and the new situation as well as upon the learner's perception of these relations.

In an experiment chicks were trained to peck at corn from a six inch circle and not from a four-inch circle where corn was glued. Later on, they were presented with four-inch and three-inch circles and they chose the previously ignored four-inch circle, showing preference for the bigger circle. They had responded to the relation rather than to parts. A song learned in a certain key, may be recognized even in a different key, even though the components of the song are different. Some studies have demonstrated that transposition does not occur with very young child and occurs increasingly with older children.

Educational Consequences

Education is essentially a social process. It begins with the psychological nature of the child, but ends with the needs of the society. The new education is progressive and aims at preparing the individual for the community life. It aims at enabling the individual to take his place as a worthy citizen in his complex social order, particularly in a democratic community. For this aim in view, the new education seeks to develop desirable social attitudes, moral sentiments and good habits in the children. In order to achieve this, the content of education, method of teaching, school environment and the whole of situation in which the child is educated should be such as the greatest amount of transfer of desirable attitudes, habits, emotional patterns and ideals may take place. Education should be so planned as the way of life cultivated in the school may continue in the community life outside the school. Thus, transfer-problem becomes fundamental to all education. The teachers can bank upon the following suggestions :

> Transfer depends upon the content of education, methods of teaching, subjective conditions of the pupils, mental ability of the pupils and the environment in which learning takes place.

Transfer value of the subjects of the curriculum is very great. This is essential for the intellectual development of the pupils. Transfer occurs from Sanskrit to Hindi and Persian to Urdu. In each of the field the languages, the social sciences and the natural sciences, there are interrelationships that should be emphasised by the teachers. Facts in various fields, should be brought together. The thrilling relationship of knowledge makes it educationally unwise to try to approach a problem in too commercialized a way. Related facts should be brought into connections regardless of the fields from which they are taken. Much better education will be produced by bringing to bear on a subject the pertinent facts from many fields. Teaching should be planned for this purpose. History should not be taught as a mere narration of dates, facts, wars, battles and events. It should be taught as a story of the past describing and explaining the forces and factors that cause people to behave as they do. True History of this type will help to understand people, interpret their behaviour and predict what they will do under certain circumstances. Thus, history should be made the foundation of the present.

The problem of new education centres largely around the actual social life. Education is life and not a preparation for life. So, for maximum transfer, the teacher should instead of relying upon the subject of the curriculum and formal teaching should choose those occupational activities which are most typical of life, which offer the greatest opportunities for enrichment of experience and the practice of the social virtues. The habits, thus formed, may transfer to life to be actually lived in the larger community. In this way, education may contribute to the reconstruction of the social life..

Two movements have got spurred in education. The one is that education should have some utility for the child. Transfer of training may be made a good basis for social-utility-movement. Many valuable social dispositions transfer to the actual situations of life, if the subject matter and activities of the classroom are similar to those encountered in the community life. Methods of knowledge and insight, technique of learning and problem solving, interest, poise, habits and ideals of caution, honesty, accuracy, thoroughness and initiative are a few things that may transfer. All these are of great social utility. But, success in this depends upon the conditions of the environment, the methods of teaching and approach by the teacher.

Second movement in education is a logical outgrowth of the Theory of Identical Elements. It assumes that methods of teaching must be suited to real life. It must be problem-solving, as people are largely engaged in solving practical problems. Initiative is required everywhere in every walk of life. So, methods of teaching must foster it in the boys. In other words, problems and activities of the school ought to be. The most life-like the problems are, the greater the transfer will be to the out-of-school life.

It signifies that education be more closely related to significant personal and social activities, and that it should be less academic, artificial and isolated. The school must teach the pupil how to participate fully and effectively in all phases of modern life. The same is the ideal that lies behind the 'Community School' and 'Project method' of Dewey. It emphasizes that education should be real. Only then maximum and useful transfer can take place.

A life-situation in the school and real problems of life alone are not enough. Subjective conditions of the pupils are also important factors in the determination of what and how much will transfer. W.C. Bagley opines that generalizations must be raised to the level of ideals to ensure transfer. A sort of emotional generaliaztion around the ideals, attitudes and dispositions is essential part of community life.

Transfer may fail if the pupils are not able to find out the common identical elements. So, the teacher should pay attention to it. He should train pupils to 'dig-into' situations as a whole and find out their more subtle features. He should himself point out the critical or essential facts of relationships which a pupil otherwise will miss. This he may achieve through thought provoking questions and arousing curiosity at right time. Insight as a whole will transfer in this way.

The amount of transfer also depends upon the mental ability of the pupils. The teacher should keep this fact in mind. Bright children profit more from a situation than average children and average children profit more than dull children. Thus, transfer value of subjects and situations vary according to the mental ability of the pupils. The teacher should adjust his planning, therefore, accordingly :

1. The teacher must decide what he wants to transfer to the child.
2. He should help the students to apply their old experiences to the new situations.
3. He must learn by experience and experiment as how he should adjust or organize his teaching to allow maximum transfer.
4. He should stress the general aspect of all that is learned.
5. He must take into consideration the subjective conditions and abilities of the pupils.
6. He should take pains to integrate different items of the curriculum so as to bring out their affinity.

7. Students should be encouraged to detect similarity between two situations.
8. The teacher must have the long-run view rather than merely for the sake of its immediate utility.
9. Students must be made conscious of as many widely useful relations as possible.
10. The teacher must avoid spoon-feeding his pupils and supplying them all sorts of information himself. He should rather provoke independent thinking in them, create in them a desire to explore and devise the solution of given situations themselves.
11. Theory of identical components must be taken into consideration while teaching similar subjects viz., History, Geography and Civics can be well correlated.
12. Insight may be promoted by Heuristic method or Project method.
13. The teacher must devise appropriate methods of teaching, create proper school environment and adopt himself a favourable attitude and desirable disposition. Thus, the teacher can best fulfill his responsibility towards society.

9

The Perception

A concept is defined as a class of stimuli having common characteristics or attributes. They are experiences coded in words or ideas or mental images. The experiences may consist of objects, events, things, persons, etc. It is a name given to these objects and happenings as experienced by a child or an adult; for example trees, men, animals, students, boys, girls, intelligentia, mentally ill person, leaders, teachers, school, church, and so on. All these concepts refer to classes or groupings or categories of stimuli. Particular stimuli such as persons or events or happenings can not be considered concepts; for example, Mohan, Dr. R.D. Singh, the school principal, Chandra Gupta (Jai Shankar Prasad's Novel), France, England, India are not concepts. This is so because a concept is not a particular stimulus, but it is a class of stimuli. Mohan is a particular person.

It does not include any other individual. So, it is not a class, and hence not a concept. Concepts are variously described in the literature as abstractions, grouped experiences, assertions, constructs, ideas, decisions, identity (single instance), inferences, meanings, mental images, terms, units of thought, symbols, and so on. Kendler (1968) defines a concept as a set of connections between some response and certain attributes or cues in stimulus pattern. A person is said to have formed a concept when he is able to classify, generalize, discriminate, and apply it on a predetermined criterion or criteria. They are constructs which mostly arise from incessant physical encounters with environment.

Concepts are formed on the basis of attributes (characteristics) of stimuli which enable a child or a person to put that into a class, group or category. An attribute is a specific, distinctive feature of a concept. Attributes are neither fixed in number, nor have fixed values. The attributes may vary in number from concept to concept. For example, cricket ball has two attributes, shape (round) and purpose for which used or made. Purpose makes it a different class from other kinds of balls. This attribute, thus, varies from one concept of balls to other concepts of balls. Similarly, the shape (round) is another attribute which differentiates it from other objects of different shapes such as squares, flat, hollow, triangular, etc. Thus, concepts are grouped or classified on' the basis of their attributes. Attributes may have different values for different concepts.

For example, large schools, small schools according to attribute size or elementary schools, secondary schools, degree schools according to attribute level and similarly black pens, red pens, green pens, and so, on according to the attribute colour. Thus, depending on variations in attribute values of colour, size, form, shape, level, purpose, etc. the concepts may differ from one another for the same object, event or stimuli. Sometimes, it is more than one attribute that determines identification of a concept; for example, shape, size, colour and texture all taken together determine identification of the concept of orange. Such attributes have a wide range of values.

The number of attributes also varies from concept to concept. For example, the orange has several attributes such as shape, colour, texture, etc. Larger the number of attributes, more complex the concept becomes. For example, good teacher may have a large number of attributes which may vary from one class of good teachers (primary level) to another class (say college good teacher).

Dominance of the attribute is another characteristic of the concept. It refers to the most obvious or prominent feature of the attribute. Dominant attributes constitute dominant concepts. More dominant concepts are learnt more easily (James Archer, 1962). Lee Sechrest and Judith Kaas (1965) and John Wallace (1964) also reached the same conclusion on the basis of their experiments.

"Associating meanings with the objects and events and the names that embody them is the beginning of concept learning" according to Klausmeier and Goodwin (1966). Concepts range in inclusiveness from two units in a class to millions of units arranged in a hierarchy of classes as held by them, although they say that there is the identity concept represented in only one of a kind; for example there is only one person that is you.

The Feature

Klausmeier and Goodwin describe following properties that make something a concept :

Psychological Meaningfulness : An individual's concept of anything is the organized inferences, i.e., meaningful associations that an individual forms of objects or events. These inferences enable the individual to categorize objects as belonging to the same class. "A concept is not a word; however some words stand for concepts" according to Klausmeier and Goodwin. The common attributes or responses alone do not make a concept. Psychologically organized inferences or the meaningful association are essential ingredients of concept formation. Abstracting common elements of objects may also lead to concept learning in some cases.

Intrinsic, Functional and Formal Properties : Intrinsic properties are observable characteristics which allow certain objects to be put in one distinctive category; for example, 'birds' whose flying attribute distinguishes them from other kinds of living organisms. This is the intrinsic property of the concept of birds.

Objects can be classified and conceptualized on the basis of their use or function or purpose. For example, bread, butter, vegetables all can be put in the category food, although they have no common intrinsic properties. But, since they serve a common purpose of being used as food, they constitute a meaningful concept 'food'.

The concepts of numbers and alphabets are based on man-made formal properties. These are as usable as intrinsic properties in determining the class inclusion.

***Abstractness, Inclusiveness and Generality*:** These are also attributes or properties of concepts. The concepts may be concrete or abstract, less abstract and highly abstract. Trip to a hilly station is a concrete concept having observable intrinsic properties, but the "pleasant trip" is a highly abstract concept. No one knows what makes a trip pleasant. Moreover, it may be pleasant to one person, but not to another person.

Concepts range in inclusiveness from one member to an unspecified large number of members or exemplars. The identity concept includes one exemplar only. Continents (few), nations (many), stars (infinite numbers) are concepts which have varying degrees of inclusiveness.

Concepts vary in generality also. Low generality concepts refer to only the members of the same lowest-order class, while the high generality concepts refer to unspecified number of members of the highest super-ordinate class; for example, men, animals, living beings. Men and animals have lower generality level while living beings have higher generality level.

***Structure*:** Concepts have an attribute of structure or organization also. From structure point of view concepts are classified as (a) conjunctive, (b) disjunctive, and (c) relational.

***Conjunctive Concepts*:** They are also called joining or connective concepts. In these concepts the appropriate values of several attributes are jointly present. For example, the concept of "sentence" is a conjunctive concept because a sentence has a subject and a predicate. If either of these is missing, the group of words is not a sentence. Similarly, the attributes of mammal are warm-blooded having mammary glands and bearing live offsprings. If any of these is not present in an animal, it is not an animal. Conjunctive concepts are easier to learn. Most of the concepts are of this type.

***Disjunctive Concepts*:** Disjunctive means not joined or separated. These are concepts in which the attributes are not present in all the exemplars. Hence, disjunctive concepts can be defined in a number of different ways. For example, "two boys and two girls" is a disjunctive concept in which the attribute number remains the same while the attribute sex differs from one another. Another example is that of 'strike' in the game of baseball which occurs in a number of different ways. Yet, each is called a strike. "Teaching" is a disjunctive concept as it includes different kinds of teaching, different levels of teaching, teaching by different teachers, teaching for different purposes, and so on. At a more abstract level Hindus, Muslims and Christians are included in the concept of religious people, although they differ in many ways from one another.

Relational Concepts : These concepts are determined not by attributes only, but by the relationship between the attributes. For example, "distance" and "direction" are relational concepts as they are determined by the relationship, i.e., difference between two points in space and time respectively. They involve dependencies as is implicit in the words such as bigger, smaller, higher, equal, order, younger, wider, between, smaller, higher, equal, order, younger, wider, between, up, down, and so on. They also include 'if-then' statements. Geographic concepts such as south, north, east, west, warm, etc., are examples of relational concepts as we can not give their attributes without considering their opposites or parallels.

The Working

Concept learning is extremely important because the concepts perform following functions as described by DeCecco and Crawford (1977).

They Reduce the Complexity of the Environment : Life would have been very miserable, if the individuals were to attend to, respond to and treat each object, event or experience of the environment afresh and a new every time. Grouping or classifying objects makes it possible to deal with thousands of objects by using one word or concept, for example books which may be millions of them. We need not enumerate all individual animals for the concept of "animal" does the job quite satisfactorily.

They Help Us to Identify the Object : In the absence of concepts we can not distinguish cats from dogs or any other object. Different objects in the world around us are known to us only through concept formation.

They Reduce the Need for Constant Learning: Once a concept it formed it becomes a part of our knowledge. For example, if the concept of a dog is formed and next time when the person comes across a dog he can immediately identify that. It is not to be learnt afresh. They save us from repeated learning.

They Provide Direction for Instrumental Activity: By using concepts one can know in advance what action he has to take in a situation. If one suffers from a disease and if he has a concept of doctor, he can plan to consult the doctor. They are very helpful in problem-solving, reasoning, planning, performing daily routine activities.

They Make Instruction Possible: Verbal instructions and communication involves the use of a large number of concepts. Teaching-learning is impossible in the absence of many previously formed concepts.

Besides these, concepts are indispensable for transmitting man's previous experiences, interpreting present situations, and projecting plans into the future. Interaction among people is possible only because of concepts developed by them.

Formation Process

The initial stage of concept formation is experience, which in other words means child's encounter with the environment, his interaction with objects, incidents and people around. The first stage of contact with any new material at whatever age of maturity is, inevitably, of the trial and error sort. While playing with material or interacting with other age-mates and elderly persons including parents and family members the child learns many words which stand for objects, activities and processes distinct from one another on the basis of their specific characteristics. These meaningful words constitute his acquired concepts which help him in learning more concepts in future.

"Concept-formation involves essentially a way of putting unorganized information into some kind of mental-filing system by grouping together an array of dissimilar objects or events on the basis of some common property that they possess," (Hilda Taba). According to Hilda Taba concept formation is a cognitive task which involves grouping items according to some basis of similarity and the development of categories and labels for the groups. The process, according to her involves three phases : (i) enumeration, (ii) grouping, and (iii) developing categories. Enumeration calls for collecting data, which is analyzed in terms of identification of similarities and differences which, in turn, leads to making and labeling groups. Bruner, Goodnow and Austin (1956) describe concept attainment as a process by which learners discriminate the attributes of things, people, events and place them into categories. According to them concept attainment occurs by making decisions about what attributes belong in what category. It is, in other words, a process of determining criteria by which certain attributes are placed into certain category. She developed a complete model or strategy for developing concepts which is known as Inductive Strategic Model derived from analysis of mental process. Under these strategies the learner performs three overt activities:

(1) enumeration and listing, (2) grouping, (3) labelling and categorizing. Each of these overt activities involves covert mental operations such as (i) differentiation, (ii) identifying common properties i.e., abstracting, (iii) and determining the hierarchical order of items; super and subordination respectively. Concepts are hierarchical in nature in the sense of representing different degrees of complexity, abstractness and generality, combining lower-order concepts into higher-order ones progressively and forming a developmental sequence:

Ausubel's Subsumption Theory of learning meaningful verbal material (1963) prescribes a process of concept learning in which a concept of more generalized nature and more inclusive (called advance organizer) is presented first followed by less general and less specific concepts (i.e. organizers). The continuum going from concrete to the specific is reversed prescribing going from more inclusive and general to less specific and less abstract. Thus, in this process one concept is included within another more general one and the organizational principle is that of progressive differentiation from regions of greater generality to lesser generality.

Kendler (1961) defined concept learning as "any situation that involves the acquisition or utilization or both of a common response to dissimilar stimuli". Hunt (1962) rewords this definition by adding "identifying" before response and holds that such acts as learning to call particular animals "dogs" will be classified as concept learning. Learning of the use of names is, to him, an example of concept learning. Concept-learning is certainly an example of pattern recognition which follows categorization of sensory input in which the use of a name learned is included under the rubric "concept-learning". In short, concept-learning is learning the use of names. Bruner, Goodnow and Austin (1956) consider concept-learning only as the process of concept-acquisition which they say is different from concept formation, in which case the concept former discovers a new way of ordering objects into sets so that a meaningful classification rule can be found as it happens in case of the process of creativity. For Piaget (1957) a concept is just an explanatory rule or law by which a relation between two or more events may be described.

The behaviourists explain the process of concept formation in terms of S-R connections. When a picture or object or the real being as of "dog" is presented along with the sound "dog" and the process is repeated several times the child learns the meaning of the word which becomes a concept acquired by the child. Welch (1947) presented a concept-learning model based on the idea of direct conditioning of a response to a stimulus trace assuming that any stimulus object was represented inside the object, by a neural condition which was isomorphic with the stimulus.

Many concepts are such whose denotations are specified by symbols rather than by objects; for example "sin". Such concepts are learned via symbols at progressively more and more abstract levels. This is explained by the term "mediating response", an explanation which begins with the assumption that responses produce stimuli which may serve as cues for further responses. When a stimulus is presented its image in the organism is presumed to evoke certain previously learned responses. These provide stimuli which evoke another response, and so on. This chain of S-R may consist of overt and covert responses. In concept learning the chain is ended with the occurrence of an overt naming response.

Human beings are not found anywhere in nature. There are only individuals. The individual differs from the human being because he is concrete event. He is the one who acts, loves, suffers, fights and dies. On the contrary, the human being is a platonic idea living in our minds and in our books. Thus, the individual is a particular being and the human being is a universal, a general being. It is, therefore, important to define and discover exactly the part of the human being and that of the individual. Educational Psychology is concerned with the individual. Indeed, individuality is fundamental in man. It permeates our entire being. It gives uniqueness to the self.

Personal Distinctions

Individuals can be easily distinguished from one another by their gestures, their ways of talking, acting and their appearance. And, these changes cause every man to be himself and any body else. Identical twins coming from the same single cell are two quite different persons. In the same way there are no individuals of identical mentality. The richer the personality the greater the individual differences.

Thus, it is an established fact that the individuals differ in mental abilities as well as in physical abilities and personality traits. The individuals not only differ from one another, but also each individual differs from one ability to another within his own self. Thus, there are variations not only amongst individuals, but there are variations within the same individual among his own abilities. The problem of individual differences, therefore, can be viewed from two sides :

(a) Differences in abilities from individual to individual.

(b) Differences in abilities within the same individual.

There is no definite measure of the extent of the Individual differences. It has been found that there is a continuous gradation from one extreme to the other. Freeman of Cornell University holds that the nature and extent of individual differences on a particular trait or complex of traits is represented by the unimodal curve which portrays the range of human potentialities for development in that trait under conditions as they now are. We can not, therefore, say that all persons fall naturally into two distinct types such as athletic or non-athletic, intelligent or unintelligent etc. The only thing that we can definitely discover is the average (mean) deviation. This can reveal to us the extent of differences.

Reasons of Differences

Thorndike discusses the causes of individual differences under five main heads. These are :

1. Sex, 2. Race or remote ancestry, 3. Maturity, 4. Heredity, 5. Environment

Sex : As regards sex, it has been discovered that girls are superior to boys on tests of memory. Superiority of females over males has been found in linguistic ability. Small differences have been found in favour of males in reasoning, computation, arithmetical ability and number concepts. Males are found to be superior in manual performance and mechanical ability.

However, there are also found great overlappings between the sexes. According to these differences there have been found marked differences in interests, habits, preferences, educational and vocational preferences.

Race or Remote Ancestry : We generally enter into our common talk and make observations like-Do individuals differ because they belong to different racial, national or cultural groups? "Russians are tall and stout," "Ceylonese are short and slim," "Germans have no sense of humour," "Yellow races are cruel and revengeful," "Americans are hearty and frank," "Indians are timid and peace-loving," as the myths of racial, national or cultural differences. Many studies have been conducted in the field of psychology, sociology and anthropology to see whether there are some significant inborn differences in mental abilities among the several racial or national groups. But, the investigations have not given any clear indication. There is no evidence of any national superiority in mental abilities. Similar studies have been made with white and non-white children. The fact should be subject to the general principle that the degree and form of mental development is the result of interaction between inherited abilities and the environmental influences. In fact, racial or national groups are compared by group averages and these cannot be more significant psychologically and educationally than are differences among individuals.

Maturity : As regards maturation, individual differences of mental growth are found in infancy. The rate of growth is not the same at all the stages. It differs from stage to stage. Not only the rate but the character of growth, differs from one age level to another as maturation marches on. Yet, the children tend to maintain their relative positions of mediocrity, superiority or inferiority.

Late in life, persons suffer from a decline in mental abilities. The decline proceeds gradually at first, then increases with age especially after sixty. But the relative position is maintained even now.

Heredity : The importance of heredity is now fairly accepted. An individual's height, size of his bones, the colour and texture of his hair, the colour of his eyes the shape of his face, nose, mouth, hands and feet, the nature of his entire physical structure, and in fact all that he is physically and mentally is determined largely by his inheritance. The general principle of heredity is that children resemble their parents and that "like tends to beget like." Children resemble both their parents but even within the same family children differ because they do not develop out of the same combination of genes. That is why even in large families complete correspondence of abilities is absent.

Further, children of bright parents tend to be less bright and the children of very inferior parents are often less inferior. Heredity is said to move towards the average. This is called regression as traits when passing from parents to children tend to move towards the average. The genius son of a genius father is a very rare thing. Again, there is a tendency among the off-spring to be higher in the traits in which their parents are low and lower in which their parents are high. They move towards the average, that is they regress.

The heredity of a child is not solely determined by his immediate parents. He inherits from all his forefathers and ancestors also or from the same stock their parents have inherited. It is said that one-half of inheritance is from the parents, one fourth from grand parents, one-eighth from great grandparents and one sixteenth and so on from gradually further removed ancestors.

Thus, heredity unquestionably has a considerable influence on individual differences.

Environment : The nature of the human being is shaped through the interaction which takes place between the human organism and the environment. Our environment is our habitation in the fullest sense. Not only our physical surroundings but also the people around us, social customs and traditions, culture, education and training, all constitute our environment. What we call our social heritage, ideas and ideals, is a part of our environment. A number of studies have been conducted to see the influence of the environment on the individuals. These are :

A study was conducted to compare the intellectual status of children coming "from different occupational and social groups. The occupational status of the father was treated as a general index of the mental abilities of the child. It was revealed by the study that (a) the I.Q.s, of the fathers correspond to their occupational status and that (b) the intelligence of the children would correspond to the occupations of the fathers.

In another study conducted on canal-born children and gypsy children it was found that their environment was very poor, they were isolated from the world, cut off from school and society, and lived and worked under the most humdrum conditions. The most striking fact revealed by this study was that with increase in age their I.Q. was depressed.

A detailed study was conducted to see the effect of environment on foster and adopted children. Their I.Q.'s., and progress in school behaviour were assessed. As the foster parents are not the true parents and the hereditary, relation does not exist, the influence of superior borne environment can be better evaluated. It was revealed that intelligence as well as development of the children was remarkably better in richer and more stimulating home environment.

A similar study was conducted on identical twins placed in different and similar environments. The study revealed that in later case there was high correlation between their physical traits, mental capacities, educational abilities, while in the former case in the same twins there was less difference; but other different environments did make a difference in educational achievement and I.Q.

On the basis of above studies, one can easily hold that environment unquestionably has a considerable influence on individual differences.

Types of Distinctions

Inter and Intra Individual Differences : Inter-individual differences are differences between two individuals. It may be possible that two persons differ in their intelligence, attitudes, and interests. No two individuals in this world are identical. Each one of them differs from one another.

On the other hand, intra-individual differences deal with the differences within an individual. These differences exist within the individual. A person may have variability in intelligence, interest, attitude, etc. It may be possible that he has high intelligence but other traits are lower than that.

Physical and Physiological Differences : Some individuals according to the structure of the body may be found differing in regard to height, weight, physique and colour, etc. But physiological differences indicate differences which refer to biological functioning like blood etc.

Differences in Ability : This has become an established fact that individuals differ widely as regards their I.Q.s. The distribution of intelligence quotients obtained by examining first grade children with the Standford Revision of the Binet Test has a range from 60 to 160 with 100 as its mean. Other tests of intelligence are used with groups at all levels and ages. The results so obtained go to assert that individuals vary greatly on the scale of mental ability.

Heredity and environment are two great factors that cause individual differences in mental ability.

Differences in Aptitudes : When we speak of a person's aptitudes, we refer to his potentialities. They may be high or low, different in different fields. They vary from individual to individual. Aptitude of a person is one's ability to carry on a task to maximum success. It refers to one's special abilities. Scholastic aptitude pertains to potential learning ability. It is determined by one's intelligence. It is also called general aptitude.

But, as individuals differ from one another in the degree of intelligence, there are bound to appear differences in their general aptitudes. It is a common experience that all people cannot perform a particular activity with the same amount of ease and perfection.

Special aptitudes refer to the relative fitness of the individual for special types of work. But this "fitness" calls forth the requisite amount of various special abilities involved in the activity. But, as individuals differ from one another in the amount and degree of these abilities possessed by them, differences in their special aptitude too, appear.

Differences in Personality : Personality is not one single entity. It is a blend of a number of traits and abilities. But, these traits and abilities and their integration and the process of their blending differ greatly from one individual to another, Therefore, we find differences in individuals personalities. The individuals differ greatly as regards the physiological and biological conditions of their organs, their psychological development and mental functioning. All these individual differences find a clear manifestation in the total differences in the individual personalities. When there are differences in the component parts of patterns, there will be differences in the whole patterns too. Individual differences in intelligence, morality, sociability, temperament, etc., result into differences in individual personalities.

Thus, individuals differ from one another and they differ within themselves from ability to ability.

Emotional Difference : Some individuals are very sensitive while some others have normal level of emotionality. In the same way the ego of some persons is highly developed. As regards temperament of the individuals differences are found there also.

Real Meaning

Individual Differences in the children is a reality which is faced daily by the school teachers in their classrooms. It is never possible to lose sight of this reality and importance of individuality. Not surprisingly, they are less concerned about causes—than they are about the effects of individual differences on pupils learning ability and their adaptability to educational goals and procedures. Regardless of the cause of variability teachers of even the nursery age children must deal with these differences.

By the time children enter the first grade, differences in abilities are already marked and absolute variations become more pronounced as they progress. Whatever the reasons for these diversities, the fact is that the school should deal with them by means of differentiated curricula and individualized instruction as far as it is feasible.

A thorough knowledge of the individual differences is essential because they serve as the foundation upon which effective pupil guidance and good teaching can be built. They are often the source of one's most pronounced achievements, fullest self-realisation and greatest usefulness. They are evidences that distinguish individuals from one another.

Educationally, individual differences mean that a pupil's chronological age is an unreliable criterion upon which to base his educational programme. As the individuals differ from one another so their education too must essentially differ. Secondly, as the individual is not the same at all the stages of development and that he differs greatly with respect to his abilities at different stages and age-levels, so education should also differ accordingly at various age-levels. In other words, human variability should be given due regard in the content and methods of education. "Every person is a well-defined type and that in each type certain fixed trait-relationships exist," Education, therefore, must be adjusted to each type according to these trait-relationships. This has resulted into following specific trends in education.

Individualization : "Individualization" in the words of Courtis, "as a method of teaching or as a philosophy of education refers primarily to the attempt to adjust education to the nature of the individual." Individualization emphasizes the marked individual differences of human nature.

Homogeneous Grouping : Individual differences compel to think in terms of homogeneous grouping of classes according to the level of ability and not age. This is also known as "ability-grouping."

Adjustment to Special Interests : Individuals differ from one another as regards their interests. A great principle of learning is that education should take notice of the interests of the boys at all stages of development. This fact may be utilized in the adjustment of teaching to the special interests of the boys of various stages of development.

Assignment : The teacher should modify the assignment in amount, quality, difficulty and sequence according to individual differences. The individual differences in personality traits, previous education, capacity and other factors must be taken into consideration to fit the work to the requirements of differing individuals.

The first Acharya Narendra Deo Committee of U.P. proposed a system of secondary education based on the varied needs of pupils and said that the schools should provide diversified curricula to suit the needs and aptitudes of our students. The recommendations are based upon the recognition of the "Importance of individuals differences in ability, intelligence and personality make-up of school pupils." The Acharya Narendra Deo Committee Report of 1953 says, "Aptitudes, intelligence testing and educational guidance are of prime importance in a widespread system of higher secondary education for a free and democratic country." The recognition of the fact of individual differences resulted into four types of courses-literary, scientific, constructive and aesthetic, "Course-analysis," like job-analysis has been stressed by the committee. "Ability tests" and "scholastic aptitude tests" too have been recommended by it. All these are sound recommendations based upon the established fact of the individual differences. The same has been asserted by Mudaliar Commission Report of 1954 on Secondary Education.

Individual differences are of great significance for personal and vocational guidance purpose. On the one hand individuals differ from one another as regards their physical characteristics, general intelligence, aptitudes, personality traits, interests and likings, on the other hand there are differences in requirements of occupations. It is, therefore, essential that proper adjustment should take place between these differences so that the fittest man may go to a particular occupation and there may not be the wastage of national energy and genius.

Individual differences are of great importance for clinical and personal hygiene purpose. Students differ in personality traits and other abilities. Hence, there are differences in the adjustment that they make towards their environments. Deficiency of some traits in some of them may cause maladjustment which is to be avoided. The individual can be helped rightly only if we are able to know and measure the trait or ability that is responsible for this. Individual adjustments are to a very great extent determined by one's own abilities and traits. It is the duty of the schools, the home and the society to provide the individuals with an environment which suits their respective abilities and traits in order to avoid mental disorders. The psychology of individual differences gives an insight into adjustment problems of the individuals.

To sum up, Charles Skinner holds that, "A knowledge of the nature of individual differences is essential if the teacher is to improve the education that all children receive regardless of their ability."

If the teacher recognizes and accepts the fact of individual differences his approach to pupils will be more positive. All that the teacher can do is to provide opportunities for learning and practice. By understanding individual differences the teacher will be able to devise such remedial programmes of instruction as will help slow learners to achieve better results. In attempting to meet the varying needs, interest and abilities of pupils and to enable each pupil to grow and develop at his own rate, several teaching procedures and types of pupil classification and promotion are being extensively used in progressive schools. Some of the earlier plans and procedures were directed primarily at helping the duller pupil and almost all of them neglected the brighter pupil. Some of the recent attempts however provide for all degrees of intelligence, both inferior and superior. They are :

Individual Instruction : Individualized instruction is considered as a ready solution of the problem of individual differences. The advantages of individualized instruction are obvious. It helps to concentrate attention on the work of individuals rather than on the average work of the class, and the teacher can acquire intimate knowledge of each pupil's interests and vocational tendencies. The slow pupil is allowed to work at his own rate and shows more satisfactory results. The bright, gifted pupil instead of marking time with the mediocre, average pupil has opportunities to go ahead and work on more advanced assignments according to his choice. The teacher gets an opportunity to develop diagnostic skills in discovering how different pupils respond to a task or a problem. Thus, individual instruction seeks to meet individual differences through a degree of variable instruction.

Group Instruction : Individual Instruction misses the social value of group work and therefore group instruction is advocated. It saves the teacher from duplicate preparation and explanation and simplifies the problem of class management. Providing for group work, cooperation, and competition young people are fired with a desire to win the good opinion of others and the class work acquires strong motivation. Group work provides for the social values of education. The slow pupil is stimulated to do better by the example of brighter pupils.

Winnetka Plan : The Winnetka plan was introduced by C.W. Washburne in the school of Winnetka. Its accent is on selection of subject matter, its organization for presentation and workable devices for checking the outcomes, keeping in mind the individual interests and abilities. The first part is known as the common essentials consisting of knowledge and skills which are needed by all pupils. This corresponds to the core curricula. The second part is known as group activities. The pupil's work on the common essentials is fully individualized. It is divided into units and accompanying each unit are prepared assignment sheets, work sheets and test sheets. Each pupil works at his own rate on each unit. When he has finished his work on one unit, he compares his results with the answer sheet. If he finds that he has passed, he proceeds to the next unit, otherwise he goes over his work to correct the defects.

When he has completed a group of units he offers to be finally tested by the teacher before taking up the next-group of units. If he fails he does further work and is retested. The pupil has to secure cent percent score. Group activities like dramatics, excursions, entertainments etc., occupy nearly half the time and every day opportunities are given for creative work. The socializing influence of these activities are quite obvious.

Dalton Plan : Dalton plan was introduced by Miss Helen Parkhurst at Dalton. The main principles underlying the plan are freedom, cooperation and allocation of time. The pupils are free to continue without interruption in the work in which they are absorbed, unhindered by timetables. The work is designated as a "job" and each pupil is given a written statement of the work to be done. He is free to do it in his own way and at his own rate. The year's work is divided into monthly assignments and each assignment is further divided into daily units of work. Each classroom becomes a "Laboratory" for a special subject and it is presided over by a specialist teacher.

Each pupil may elect to work on any one subject throughout the month but he is not allowed to begin on the second month's assignment till he has completed that of the first. He is encouraged to spend more time on the subject in which he is weak. Group work is encouraged if a number of pupils are working at the same stage. General difficulties are explained in group lessons called "conferences". A pupil advances steadily job by job, through the curriculum. If in a school year of nine or ten months he only finishes eight jobs on account of balance or illness he begins the ninth job in the following year. The bright child may, on the contrary, accomplish in one year the work planned for eighteen months and the slow child working at his own rate may build a sound foundation.

Morrison Plan : Morrison plan devised by Prof. H.C. Morrison of Chicago University is based on direct guidance and stresses unit assignment. Directed guidance has five steps. The first is pretest in which the background of the pupil in determined to see what approach the pupil will have for the new unit of work. The next step is presentation. Its purpose is to present the main points of the unit of work as effectively as possible to stimulate the pupil to work. It is followed by assignments growing out of presentation. The next step is organization in which each pupil presents his own outline of the matter learned, and the final step is recitation in which the assimilated material is orally presented by each pupil. The important task in this plan is to establish learning units. For Morrison a unit is "a comprehensive and significant aspect of the environment," of science, art or conduct whose learning affects personality.

Project Method: This method was devised by Kilpatrick. In this method few problems are given to students to solve on their own behalf such as cooking, tailoring, carpenting, playing drama, writing a letter, story telling, picture appreciation, to learn writing, solving problems like why population of Delhi is fast increasing? etc. A project has its own purpose and is activity -oriented. A pupil is free to select work of his own choice and capabilities. He works in his own way. From planning till execution of the project he is completely free to complete his work in accordance with his needs, interests and potentialities.

Decroley Plan : This plan was devised by Ovid Decroley, an educationist of Belgium. The underlying principle of this method is that for life a child receives his education from the life itself. The classification of the students to their classes is made such that with regard to their interests, intelligence, potentialities etc., they look alike. The child is given complete freedom at school to work. Attempts are made that the child should feel relaxed at school like his home. Students' interests are given proper importance. The teacher treats his pupils in a psychological manner with sympathy and pays proper attention to their needs and interests.

Contract Plan : Contract plan is the same as Dalton plan. In this plan too, the study subjects are prescribed to children, and like Winnetka plan the progress of child is tested through diagnostic tests. The teacher pays more attention to the subject in which the child is weak and is encouraged to spend more time on that particular subject. In other words we may say that Contract Plan is a combination of Dalton and Winnetka Plan.

Activity Programme : Activity programme lays stress on activity. The different subjects are taught with activity as centre of each subject. A child selects any activity according to his interests, aptitudes, potentialities etc. During the learning process the child does not sit quiet and passive but is equally active and interested like the teacher. It is thus, that whole learning process becomes child-centered instead of teacher-centred. The students plan, organize, evaluate and draw results of project independently with great success and effectiveness.

Programmed Instruction : Programmed instruction is a method in which a pupil learns according to his speed and capacity. A topic is divided into many sub-topics. There are various forms of programmed instruction, but that of Skinner's (programmed instruction) is most common in use. It is used for the purpose of self-study. Individual differences are paid proper attention in this programme. Keeping himself engaged in the learning process the child learns best according to his speed, need, interest and capacity. Simultaneously, his progress is also assessed through tests. Thus, in programmed instruction a pupil follows the entire instructions of the programme with keen zest and enthusiasm.

Grouping according to Ability : The general practice of grouping pupils for purposes of instruction is based on pupil ability. Attempts have been made to improve the system of classification by grouping pupils with greater homogeneity. The basis of classification may be age differences, mental age, I.Q., achievement, teachers rating, physical or social maturity etc. But, such grouping has been strongly criticized as harmful socially and psychologically. If bright pupils are placed in separate groups they acquire superiority complexes and if all pupils are separately grouped they may develop inferiority complexes; and all this is injurious to their social development.

In practice the same class is divided into three sections of bright, average and slow pupils. These three sections cover the same course of study but at different rates of speed. Or, these groups may be kept in the same class and given different tasks. The slow group covers less work and is given more drill. The work assigned to him is more concrete and practical. The bright group covers much more ground and the stress is on difficult problems and original work. Pupils with special abilities and handicaps have to be given special attention.

Diagnostic and Remedial Teaching : There are some children whose progress is rather, irregular owing to genetic or physical factors, habits, interests, purpose or environmental background. Ideally, then, it is the school's responsibility to find out not only each child's general intellectual level but also to discover his special abilities or weaknesses, if he has any. This may be achieved through careful observation by teachers and educational tests such as (Diagnostic, Achievement, Prognostic) or, through special clinical examinations.

In brief, diagnostic tests point out individual's difficulties or weaknesses in a particular subject, while remedial teaching suggests remedy or educational provisions to overcome these difficulties. Hence, remedial teaching is a must after diagnostic tests point out individual's difficulties or weaknesses in a particular subject. Remedial teaching suggests remedy or educational provisions to overcome these difficulties. Hence, remedial teaching is unavoidable after diagnosis.

Acceleration : In India the system of promotions suffers from many defects. The system can be improved by making promotions more frequent and flexible. Here, brighter pupils are allowed to skip classes and double promotions are permitted to pupils who have done exceptionally well. Some schools have a system of trial promotions in which bright pupils are promoted to the next higher class on the condition that they make good, failing which they are sent back to their original class.

Many schools hold classes for failed students during the summer vacation which follows the annual promotions and give them another chance to pass. This method of acceleration suits the junior classes but is not desirable for higher classes, as it may create some emotional problems for them.

Enrichment of Curriculum : Provision for individual differences does not end with differentiated curriculum. For, within the same course of study and within the same subjects, there may be appreciable differences in aptitudes. This is particularly true in the so called universals or constants that are prescribed practically for all pupils. Some of the pupils may be found creative in different fields.

They may be requiring more of stimulation, high level assignments, wider reading and probably, experimentation with ideas. Guidance given to them may do wonders to some of them if not to all. Hence, fostering creativity in children and provision of co-curricular activities may do a great deal in this regard.

10

Various Theories

Hitherto we discussed philosophy generally organised around specific problems which arise in the "study and practice of education" without maintaining any continuity with reference to any particular school of educational philosophy or system of thought. It would now be appropriate to assemble the "like segments of these various educational philosophies into their respective system of thought".

These systems of thought or, schools of philosophy, maintain their distinctness caused by their respective outlook and faith in a world order that commensurates with their cosmological and ontological viewpoint, in turn determining their total approach toward education and various components and problems of the educative process, and are central in nature to the very existence, coherence and continuity of a system.

This approach provides a student-teacher with ready made systems of thought based on their approach to life and reality, arranged around the educational problems and admitting philosophical intervention. Schools of philosophy centre around thinkers sharing their common views on educational components and process in a concerted manner, and come under an umbrella.

as denoted by a respective school of thought. Commonality of thought and purpose is the essence of a school/system of thought and should be viewed as such.

Realism Philosophy

The stability and firmness that the essentialist philosophy roots itself in is enshrined in a reality that is idealistic: ideas rather than the external objects constitute ultimate reality. However, some of the essentialists envisage a more solid foundation for their educational philosophy if the reality could be independent of the mental phenomenon, right out in the external world, all by itself, hence more reliable and durable, beyond alteration and interference. Realism, therefore, "is the doctrine [that upholds] that objective reality or the material universe exists independently of the conscious mind, its nature and properties are being affected by being known". (C.V. Good). Things are, as they are, and we perceive them as realities. Hence, perception is the only source of knowledge; whatever enters perception, is real.

Major Exponents : Following are the major exponents of Realism:-

Erasmus, Rebellias, John Milton, Lord Montaigne, John Locke, Mulcaster, Francis Bacon, Ratke, Commenius, Whitehead, and Bertrand Russell.

Definition

1. "The doctrine of realism asserts that there is a real world of things behind and corresponding to the objects of our perception". (U.S. Ross)
2. "Realism is the reinforcement of our common acceptance of this world as it appears to us". (Butler)
3. "Realism is the instinctive belief of man". (D.M. Dutta).

Fundamental Principles of Realism

1. The phenomenal world is true and real, and is the only world that can be known, as only this world enters experience.
2. Senses are the doorways to knowledge; are the oracles.

3. The universe is a vibrating organism in the process of evolution change is the fundamental feature essence of reality is process mind is the function of organism.
4. Reality is rooted in the external world: the world is here and now.
5. Man is as much material as rest of the world.
6. Knowledge is empirical, experiential and is subject to scientific observation and experimentation.
7. Consistent with the facts of common life and the development of physical science.

Forms of Realism

Humanistic Realism **:** So as to promote human welfare and success, education should be realistic. Humanistic Realism, therefore, recommended study of Greek and Roman literature as they were considered to be containing all the essentials for successful and happy life. It considered study of Greek and Roman literature necessary for personal, social and psychological development. These two languages contained the best of the two ancient civilizations, and were believed to provide necessary depth, grace and fillip. Its chief exponents have been:-

Eramus (1466-1536) **:** Condemning unrelated and irrelevant education, he advocated broad and liberal education. "Knowledge seems to be of two kinds, that of things and that of words. That of words comes first, but that of things is more important". Real knowledge is knowledge of the things existing in the external world, on their own, and would be known when they enter our experience. Realism maintains the duality of what is known, and the one who knows i.e. between the knower and the known, because will there be any knowledge of things in the external world, without someone who perceives and organises them into human experience?

Erasmus was deeply affected by the movement called Renaissance. The Renaissance "was not a period of great achievement in philosophy, but it did certain things which were essential preliminaries to the greatness of the seventeenth century" (Bertrand Russell). Firstly, it broke down the rigid scholastic system;

secondly, it revived the study of Plato thereby demanding independent thought to choose between him and Aristotle, and thirdly, shaking up of dubious orthodoxy, and setting genuine and firsthand knowledge free and by regarding knowledge as an intellectual activity as a delightful social adventure with no predetermined bars attached to it. It is an attitude of breaking away from the dull, dubious supremacy of the church, and setting man free to explore around. It was the beginning of humanism, though initially, "most of the humanists retained such superstitious beliefs as had found support in antiquity" (Bertrand Russell). Nevertheless, the era of human emancipation had been heralded in Italy, France, England and Germany, though the last two differ from the Italian renaissance, mainly because of their emphasis and relevance to public virtue. It was more concerned with spreading learning as widely as possible.

Erasmus was influenced by the Northern Renaissance which followed the Italian Renaissance, and steered itself clear of the Reformation that beset the path of its Italian cousin. Renaissance is marked by the spirit of immense curiosity which later got transferred from the books to the world—the world of things and objects, and gradually became scientific. Erasmus, on his part, generally remained attached to the literary aspect of the Renaissance and, therefore, recommended reading of Latin and Greek as the doorways to the vast epitome of knowledge.

Rebellay (1483-53) : Rebellay or Rebelias, a French scholar, advocated the cause of liberal education in place of old wordy idealist education prevalent before the advent of the renaissance. Laying stress upon the religious, social and moral education, he was in favour of giving knowledge of things to the students by drawing them out into the external world of things and objects. His view on education had no place for grammar, literature and logic, and were concerned more with down to earth world of things that exist outside and independent of us. According to him, knowledge of practical environment was more necessary. He favoured all-round development of education, and evaluated education on the basis of its usefulness to life.

John Milton (1608-74) : Milton in his book Tracts of Education, opposed emotion charged education, and laid great stress on liberal and complete education, when he said "I call therefore a complete and generous education that which fits a man to perform justly, skilfully and magnanimously all the offices, both private and public, of war and peace." A man of religious disposition, faith and belief, he wished education to foster love for Him in all children. Imagine his state of deprivation on his having been born blind yet he had no grudge and bitterness, and expresses complete acceptance of God's Will when he said "They also serve who stand and wait" in the service of God. He was against mere academic education, and favoured that education should give knowledge of things, objects and facts. He also favoured physical education for the overall physical development of the child. He opposed mass and oral education. He even designed a curriculum of study for 12 to 21 years of age, which is as under:—

First Year: Knowledge of Latin, Grammar, Mathematics, and Geometry.

Next Four Years: Knowledge of farming, physics, crafts, geography, economics and physiology.

Remaining Years: Bible, Hebrew, Greek, Roman, Saxon, Economics, Political Science, History, Poetry and Law.

Undoubtedly, a down to earth realistic curriculum for the youth to enable him fit into the assigned role in society on his coming of age.

Comments : Erasmus, Rebellary and Milton were the three chief exponents of Humanistic Realism of their time, laying more emphasis on the practical aspect of education, and restricting knowledge to what enters human experience. The external world of things and objects exists on its own but acquires meaning and significance only through possible human experience and intervention. How does human experience yield a sound system of knowledge about things in the external world, and with how much of fidelity, kept the realists busy ever since.

Rational Approach

Referred to as Philosophia perennis, rational humanism finds its sturdiest support from Artistotle and St. Thomas Aquinas, and is so sound that it has generally remained unchanged since the middle ages, having its appeal to generation after generation. Aristotle based his philosophy on human reason alone hence rational humanism. Whereas St. Thomas made such modifications in Aristotle's position as the advent of Christianity seemed to demand, and his philosophy is entitled as scholastic realism or Neo-Thomasism. (Robert H. Beck).

Basic Tenets : "The major premise of rational humanism is an assertion that the essence of human nature is its rational character." (Brubacher) Rationality, therefore, is the distinguishing feature between man and other living creature with whom he shares the common feature of sensuality. It is when he rises above that animal level by exercising his capacity to judge and discriminate that man acquires that distinct characteristic. Reason is what separates man from other living forms. Whereas man shares the characteristic of mortality with other sentient beings, it is the element of rationality that sets a distinguishing stamp, it is the differentium of the genus, and rational humanism capitalises on it. Rationality is also a common mark amongst humans whose nature, because of this feature, would be the same all over, for all times to come.

Bearing on Education

1. Since rationality is the essence of human nature, the principal aim of his education would necessarily be intellectual. Further, as human nature is universal, the aim of education must be the same for all men in all times and places.
2. In spite of this universal element in human equipment, humanistic rationalism makes room for individual differences within the common framework. These differences are, however, accidental and not essential.

Curriculum : Rational humanist, while selecting the learning experiences, would be interested in choosing the essentials i.e. what is uniform and recurrent in human experience. As the school is woefully inadequate, it cannot include everything that meets this criterion. However, since the man is essentially rational, the larger the rational content of the subject matter, greater its claim to preference in the curriculum, so as to meet the overall cultivation of intelligence. Rational humanism, therefore, recommends liberal arts and humanities.

Student : The curriculum thus envisaged does not give any choice to the student, and is, sort of, prescribed but since it is congruent to his rational nature, it commensurates and gives freedom.

Method : While planning his teaching lesson the teacher must arrange the subject matter in a manner the subject demands. This order, arrangement, or management of the subject matter is called logical arrangement, i.e. the arrangement as dictated or required by the subject matter. One has to discover this order as it facilitates teaching and learning.

Secondly, another order of learning would conform to the nature of the learner, his disposition, ability, interest, aspirations, etc. This is called psychological order of teaching and learning.

Finally, teaching starts with child experience. Instead of ordering/arranging the lesson according to the abstract and universal, the teacher commences with the concrete and the particular at the level already attained by the child. As such, there is more emphasis to the direct, first hand experiences, contraventions and visualisation. Teaching-learning, therefore, is child-centred wherein one does not cut the child to the curriculum, but cuts the curriculum to the child's nature, interest and ability.

Comments : Rational humanism emphasises that "man's humanity lies in rationality with which he was invested from the beginning of time and tends to think of the character and quality of rationality as fixed and is concerned with an educational role for mind as knowing the world as it is constituted" (Brubacher). In matter of pedagogy, it considers child to be the centre of all educational activities and programmes, and advocates primacy of direct first-hand experiences.

Approach based on Scholasticism

In the Western philosophy, scholastic realism generally refers to the Roman Catholics, and to the system of rational humanism as modified by St. Thomas in view of the demands of Christianity, and is also called as Neo-Thomasism. Whereas rational humanism goes as far as reason and metaphysics permit, it stops short of the "further vistas which revelation and theology open up". It is here that scholastic realism takes over and leads one to the glorious realm of the supernatural: a jump from natural to the supernatural, but in and through the natural. It, therefore, seeks deeper meaning for its educational philosophy.

Basic Tenets : According to Brubacher "the educational philosophy of scholastic realism is fundamentally dualistic." It is dualistic because it recognises an order of nature as well as that of the supernatural, in this regard, it goes farther that Rational Humanism which considers rationality of man as the basic category or the universal premise to base all its educational deductions. Both are essentialists. Scholastic realism soars into the realm of the supernatural and, perhaps, superhuman, wherein God is central to its metaphysical theology, and nature is His manifestation; all knowledge is revelation, and individuality and novelty are only accidental, and are there only if viewed from the standpoint of an immutable eternity, which is not only changeless but also above change, is the only exception to the law of change, and cause and effect, in fact, is sui generis, and is the source of whatever is perennial.

Educational Assumptions

1. What is fixed and unalterable through all time is essential.
2. Justifies unwavering educational objectives.
3. Sufficient warrant for a prescribed curriculum.
4. Educational process helps man lift himself to his eternal status.
5. Educational values of immutable character help one form a universal programme.
6. All progress takes within nature and is primarily a matter of improving the means of gaining the final objective.
7. Knowledge is approximation of truth.
8. Learning is neither incidental nor accidental, it needs to be learned, and antedates any project work.
9. Learning can be appropriated directly.

10. Knowledge is objectively conceived.
11. Ultimate function of mind is cognition and to seek the true.
12. Curriculum should help mind to penetrate what is profoundly true.
13. Education must cater for natural as well as the supernatural.
14. Truth and good are separate categories, but what is good must be judged as good.
15. Objectivity of values.
16. Employment of interest in learning: interest is an assertion by the learner of a recognition of value in the object of his studies. Nevertheless, curriculum takes precedence over interest.
17. Permanent is to be preferred to the transient.
18. Permits indoctrination.
19. Individuals are of supreme worth.
20. Dependence on authority, hence flourishes in aristocratic or democratic conditions.

Bearing on Education : According to scholastic realism the ultimate aim of education is the approximation of the individual to the infinite, changeless supernatural order where God is the author of all, and helps him to lift himself up to the eternal. Education should help man understand the natural and the supernatural order, and help advance toward this progress. Aims, therefore, are fixed, changeless, universal and eternal Curriculum

As rationality is the essential nature of man, education should consist of subjects that help in direct apprehension of reality, and improve the means of gaining the final objectives. Here it is in agreement with rational humanists in studying liberal arts, humanities and, physical sciences to understand the natural order, but adds study of theology for its approximation to the supernatural and toward salvation.

Students : An individual is an instance of already complete reality, and hence, has a universal rational character. Scholastic realism admits of the individual differences within the general frame of universal character of man, and allows adequate freedom of action. He should be able to master the essentials of culture by training. Though scholastic realism allows freedom of action, academic freedom is not absolute, and is proportioned to expertise.

The individual differences in students are only accidental, and have no bearing on their ultimate nature, as there is no difference in the quality of immortality. Individuals, hence, are of supreme worth.

Method : As scholastic realism maintains its fundamental dualism between the natural and the supernatural, the temporal and spiritual, its methodology is rather authoritative and does not tolerate individual aberrations. It does not permit pupils to arrive at their own conclusions independently as there is danger of extravagant waste of time. Academic freedom, is proportionate to expertise. The natural order is known through cognition, but the supernatural is known through revelation. It may even take recourse to indoctrination as there is no uncertainty of the final values, and therefore, is intolerant of error.

Comments : As the natural and supernatural order are objective in character, knowledge is also objectively conceived, and is the approximation of the true and the good. Revelation transcends the duality of the subject-object order of nature, and reveals what is beyond it, the supernatural. Cognition and belief become the sources of all knowledge, and education should help man toward this approximation.

Approach based on Sociality

Social realism capitalises on the contact of man with the thing, which exists in the external world on its own merit and is independent of subjective intervention, except the social contact between the two. Learning, therefore, is experiencing of things in their natural setting, and one may have to go about in an extensive manner. Books, therefore, are of very limited value, as real knowledge comes on one's pulse, in an extensive interaction.

Attainment of real knowledge in social environment is essential because it acquaints one with the useful to life in nature. Hence, education should promote the working efficiency of man for a happy and successful life in a socially compatible environment.

Bearing on Education : Emphasis on attainment of real knowledge which comes from the social contact of man with thing in a socially conducive environment, so as to promote working efficiency, happiness and success.

Curriculum : According to social realists, education should consist of subjects like Geography, History, Arithmetic, physical exercise etc. so as to promote social qualities.

Method : Education should not be 'bookish'. It should take the child to the world outside, help him explore it, and know it. Hence, not much of classroom lecturing. Instead, they prescribe travelling, touring, observation and, experiences as tools of really effective, useful and meaningful education. "The social realists, looking in askance at bookish studies, stressed the value of direct studies of man and things ... which would give real experience of the varied aspects of life" (Ross). There is a slant toward oral education of the select in their mother tongue.

Student : A student is an actively participating agent in the process of education. He must experience the world with an open mind, and grasp the maximum of the socially useful knowledge and information, to develop in him "virtue, wisdom, breeding and learning" (John Locke) as well as develop his physical, mental and moral faculties.

Varied Thinkers

Montaigue (1533) : Montaigue did not accept anything without understanding it because he did not believe in education for the sake of education. Education, for him, should be instrumental in making practical and rational so as to make them successful in life. The purpose of education should be to develop intelligence and self-discrimination in children to facilitate smooth and successful living. He was also against the bookish knowledge, and laid exclusive emphasis on experience as a source of knowledge.

Bearing on Education : Education should develop intelligence and self-discrimination for happy and successful life. It should also make one practical and rational.

Curriculum : All subjects which acquaint pupils with nature are essential for their rational and practical development. Art and craft, humanities and languages, geography and history, natural science, should be included in the curriculum.

Method : He favoured sending children on tours to explore the land and nature. Travel is a great source of knowledge and mental, social and emotional maturity, as said by Francis Bacon. Nothing should be accepted without understanding it. He condemned cramming and recommended learning by experience. Practical and experiential approach is the crux of his method. For him, learning should be firstly through the mother-tongue, later by the language of the neighbours, and finally through the classical languages like Latin and Greek.

The reader may note the progressive development and expansion of social contact. According to him "a boy should not so much memorize his lesson as practise it. Let him repeat it in his actions".

Discipline : Montaigue was against repressive discipline, and allowed greater freedom of movement and action by sending children on tours and travels.

John Locke (1632-1704) : An empiricist to the core, Locke assume the independent existence of things in the external world. Experience for him, was a bundle of sensations leaving an imprint on the blank state of the mind called tabula rasa. According to him, we only get to known things through the sensations caused by them, but never the cause itself. Education, hence, should be through the senses as there is no other way of getting in touch with them, or, knowing them. Experience, therefore, is the source of knowledge.

Training of senses becomes central to the Lockean thesis. He, however, admits of reflection also as a source of knowledge, but reflection adds another dimension to the sense experience and included believing, doubting, willing, accepting and rejecting.

Bearing on Education

(a) Locke rejects the concept of the innate, as for him sense experience is the only legitimate source of knowledge which is extraneous to man. Locke is a dualist as the external reality, whatever it may be, exists independently. As sense experience is the only source of knowledge, training of senses becomes the first aim of education.

(b) Locke, being a social realist, emphasises on cultivation of virtue which is the basis of successful social interaction which should be devoid of evil deeds.

(c) Cultivation of wisdom because it would help appropriate foresight to choose wisely, among alternatives. Sense experience is essential but the individual has freedom of choice to accept or reject.

(d) Breeding, social graces and good manners, such as dancing, riding, fencing and wrestling, etc. These were, perhaps, the presumptions or prerequisites of a successful life in the English society, and helped one go about with elan and confidence. This also implies the physical and agility development of the individual. The English society is no different even today where good manners and etiquettes are considered as virtues and, social graces.

(e) Education should provide knowledge and information, but Locke relegates this aim lower than those mentioned above. Knowledge should also help acquire suitable attitudes.

Curriculum : Education, for Locke, should include such subjects as would help physical, mental and moral development of the individual, as well as to cultivate good manners and social graces in him. History, geography, literature, languages, physical and natural sciences, dancing, music, riding, fencing and, wrestling etc., form the core of Lockean curriculum of education.

Method : Social interaction is the source of knowledge, hence maximum use should be made of it in teaching. Being an individualist, he did not recommend education for the masses. Education, for him was an elitist affair wherein a child was to be taught by a private tutor who was to be well versed in the customs and beliefs of society. Education, for Locke, was grooming of a child as a gentleman. He recommended "pleasant and lively" method of teaching through the mother-tongue and was against physical punishment.

Approach based on Sensuality

Sense Realism plays a dominant role in education, and is the forerunner of the modern day concept of maximisation of senses in teaching-learning. As Munro wrote "the term itself is derived from the fundamental beliefs that knowledge comes primarily through senses. Inspired by the scientific discoveries and inventions of the seventeenth century, the sense realists considered only such knowledge as came from the senses as valid knowledge. Bookish education brings artificiality and dogmas. Observation and contact are the only legitimate sources of knowledge of the objects/things existing independently in the external world. Nature study is central to such perceptions and gives knowledge of natural objects, natural phenomena and, natural laws. Francis Bacon even went to the extent of calling the senses as "our oracles and compasses" of knowledge.

Educational Assumptions

1. Sense organs are the doorway to knowledge.
2. Truth is known by observation and contact.
3. Inductive method of teaching and reasoning.
4. More emphasis on nature-study and sciences.
5. Education for the masses, unlike the social realists who considered education to be elitist.
6. Education to be imparted in the language of the common people.

Mulcaster (1530-1611) : According to Mulcaster "the end of education and training is to help nature to her perfection". He emphasised the physical and mental development of the child and to achieve the fullest development of his nature. Education, therefore, should be child centred, and should develop his intelligence, memory and judgement. He advocated use of psychological methods of teaching, and recommended that a teacher be trained in the methodology and techniques of teaching. Use of mother-tongue was his favourite medium of instruction.

Bearing on Education

Develop physical and mental faculties of a child in consonance with his nature, interest and needs to the fullest.

Curriculum : Curriculum should include such subjects that may develop knowledge, logic and memory of the child. Curriculum should include mother-tongue, reading, writing, painting and music, and other such subjects, at the primary level, and should include scientific subjects at the secondary level.

Method : Use of psychological methods in teaching-learning.

Teaching should be child-centred and consider individual differences of intelligence, interest and aspirations.

Teaching through mother-tongue.

Teaching should be pleasant and interesting.

Teachers should be trained for successful classroom performance.

No coercion in teaching.

Francis Bacon (1562-1623) : According to Bacon "the object of all knowledge is to give man power over nature" and should make a child useful to society. Knowledge should be acquired piecemeal i.e. inductively, wherein experiences add up to an edifice. Use of senses and limbs is essential for a child to observe and feel nature. As such, natural laws should be discovered and followed by a child so as to control nature.

Bearing on Education : Education should give man power over nature.

Education should help training of senses, and an acute sense of observation and inductive synthesis.

Education should make a child useful to society.

Curriculum : Francis Bacon was inspired by the advancement in the field of scientific research and knowledge. He, therefore, gave sciences the place of honour in his curriculum. The curriculum should be so designed that it gives a child an ingress into nature, develop in him a critical and unbiased sense of observation and of drawing inductive conclusions and results. Other subjects included in his curriculum are languages, literature, religion and philosophy.

Method : Education should be child-centred and should take into account child's nature, interest and intelligence level. Teaching was to be conducted inductively wherein general laws could be discovered through piecemeal sense experiences, giving child full freedom for observation and experiment. Bacon recommended fullest use of the senses and limbs and is the forerunner of activity-culture in classroom teaching-learning. Teaching, therefore, should proceed from particular to general, simple to complex, concrete to abstract, ending up in the most general axioms.

Ratke (1571-1625) : According to Ratke, education is a process of development of a child according to his nature. For him, senses are the gateways of knowledge. He was the founder of a new system of education later developed by Commenius. Ratke developed the following axioms of education:

(a) *Obey the Natural Laws:* To follow nature and to understand the natural phenomena, one should know and obey the natural laws which are essential even for one's survival. Education must help discover such natural laws.

(b) Necessity of recapitulation for making knowledge permanent or, its consolidation.

(c) *One Subject at a Time:* To avoid confusion and to promote understanding of the subject, only one subject should be taught at a time. The modern concept of school timetable bears it out.

(d) *Mother-tongue as Medium of Instruction:* It will facilitate learning and grasp the teaching content as it comes to a child naturally.

(e) *No Coercion:* A child should not be forced to learn which should be an outcome of natural maturation and readiness. No repression.

(f) *No Cramming:* Make a child understand and develop correlation between aspects of learning; no rote and no stress on memorising the content.

(g) *Principle of Similarity:* A thread of similarity should run in the entire process of education.

(h) *First things, then Words:* First show, then tell.

(i) *Knowledge through Senses:* Sense experience is the only legitimate source of knowledge hence, senses should be trained for accurate observation.

(j) *Knowledge through Experience:* Experience is the outcome of interaction between things and observer, both are independent of each other.

Bearing on Education : Education should develop a child according to his nature.

Curriculum : The curriculum should include subjects that help a child to understand nature, its laws, and to know the things existing in the external world. Study of physical and natural sciences, history, geography, languages and graphics would help sharpen the senses and observation of a child.

Method : The forerunner of modern visualisation of processes and product of learning, Ratke was the first to emphasise the graphic representation of things in learning. First show, then tell, is his greatest gift to the child. He does not recommend verbosity in teaching, and considers recapitulation essential for consolidation of learning. The medium of instruction should be the mother-tongue. Open the world to the child through his senses and capitalise on it. No pressure or coercion on a child for learning. Efforts must be made so that the child understands the material rather than crams it.

Commenius (1592-1671) : Foremost amongst the advocates of sense realism, Commenius considered that "ultimate end of man is eternal happiness". Education should, therefore, make a child learned, moral and God-fearing. Commenius advocated general education for all; even the poorest of the poor should get the benefit of education as it helps his social and spiritual unfolding. Considering the inductive method as inadequate, he recommended natural method of teaching. For him, the source of knowledge transcends mere senses and lends credence to intelligence and, divine inspiration.

According to Commenius, nature has its timetable and schedule, and makes a child bloom accordingly. Dr. Jaiswal summed up that "the object of Commenius was to make human beings successful in life, and to develop the moral and religious feelings through education". A child should be taught his mother-tongue first and then other subjects. For him, all learning should be linked and interrelated. He was opposed to all forms of repression, and recommended a universal pattern of education.

Bearing on Education : Education should make man achieve eternal happiness, as such, it should make a child learned, moral and, God-fearing. Education should be general and, for all, without any discrimination and bias.

Curriculum : As knowledge does not come from sense experience alone, the curriculum must help develop intellectual and moral faculties of the child. Mother-tongue should take precedence. "My curriculum will include all those subjects which make a man wise, virtuous and pious." His curriculum further responded to various stages of learning.

Method : It is in the area of teaching methodology that Commenius breaks fresh ground and has been the forerunner of modern concept of teaching-learning. His influence was so profound that a chain of successive philosopher-educationists such as Rousseau, Pestalozzi and Herbert accepted and developed his views and, took pride in it while doing so. No wonder, Commenius is called the father of modern education.

His views on methodology are as under and, may be called Commenius principles of education:-

1. Teaching method should be simple, straightforward and relevant to the situational environment and subject.
2. Correlation between life and education i.e. education

should be life-related, and must have utility value. Therefore, the purpose of the learning material must be explained. The child must be rationally involved in the classroom proceedings.

3. Knowledge should be useful.
4. Teaching should be done in an effective manner by use of visualisation and contravention where first hand direct experiences are not available/possible.
5. Explain general rules.
6. Teaching should be progressive in that the material/lesson should be divided in logically and psychologically related steps.
7. Follow chronology to avoid mixing up details.
8. Various parts of the subject-matter should be discussed thoroughly to establish correlation, and to develop understanding and comprehension.
9. Continue teaching till learning takes place. For this use comprehension and recapitulation exercise to gauge the extent of learning.
10. Do not rush: Nature has its own timetable and schedule.
11. First teach the mother-tongue and then other subjects.
12. No repression and physical punishment.

Comments : Commenius advocated synthesis of educational psychology, educational organisation, and educational methodology, to ensure that teaching-learning is a mutually satisfying experience, is meaningful, successful and durable. His views on education are so profound that they have the respect of both the essentialists and the progressives. The UNESCO honoured Commenius by adopting his ideas for its blueprint on education.

Concept of New Realism

According to Rusk "the positive contribution of neo-realism is its acceptance of the methods and results of modern development in physics." For them, all rules and procedures, including that of science, are changeable, and are valid only in certain conditions and circumstances. Neo-realism recommends study of humanities as well as the sciences to give a child balance world view. Its chief exponents are Whitehead and Russel.

According to Bertrand Russell "whatever can be known, can be known by means of science; but things which are legitimately matters of feeling lie outside its province." He further says that "in the welter of conflicting fanaticism, one of the few unifying forces is scientific truthfulness, by which I mean the habit of basing our beliefs upon observations and inferences as impersonal and ... divested of local and temperamental bias."

He and Whitehead belong to modern analytic empiricism which differs from that of Locke, Berkeley and Hume by "its incorporation of mathematics and its development of a powerful logical technique." Knowledge is through perception, and anything to be called perception "must be in some degree an effect of the object perceived, and it must more or less, resemble the object if it is to be a source of knowledge of the object." Corresponding representation gives knowledge of the objects that exist in the external world.

So far, Russell and Whitehead are realists, but they add a new dimension to the existing dualistic realism, when they reduce the distinction between mind and matter and "making possible the doctrine of neutral monism". This coming closer of mind and matter is the basic tenet of neo-realism

Bearing on Education

Whitehead : Whitehead considered living and unliving, conscious and unconscious, movable and immovable, as organism. Therefore, education should give the child full knowledge of organism. He further advocates understanding of scientific and empirical values so as to enable a child have a fuller world-view.

Curriculum : Whitehead recommends study of scientific subjects but gives due weightage to arts and humanities, languages and literature, to understand and grasp the feeling component in knowledge. Giving it the importance that it deserves he says that "when you understand all about sun, all about the atmosphere, all about the rotation of earth" which takes place at cognitive level, but one may "still miss the radiance of the sunset", which is a feeling component and takes place at affective level.

Method : Observation and verification is central to any sense experience. Senses must be trained to report truthfully and independently of any bias or prejudice. A child must have freedom of action and expression.

Bertrand Russell : According to Russell philosophy generally consisted of two parts inharmoniously blended: "on the one hand a theory as to the nature of the world, on the other an ethical system or political doctrines as to the best way of living". Russell, however, rejects this dichotomy, and suggests "neutral monism" wherein the dualistic world of mind and matter moves closer, tending to become one, and where moral contradictions get resolved.

Bearing on Education : As all knowing is through senses, education should emphasise the sensory development of child resulting in right perceptions and understanding. Education should also be liberal to develop finer aspects of a child's personality.

Curriculum : Russell lays singular emphasis to mathematics and physics. He also advocates study of arts and humanities for all-around development of a child. He recommends liberal education but keeps religion out of it. He, however, opposed emotional exuberances in children as there is "as little emotional strain as possible in connection with the acquisition of knowledge". The two are distinct and different as they operate on different domain, cognitive and affective, respectively.

Method : Knowledge is through senses, hence maximum use of senses should be made. Experiential knowledge is piecemeal and needs to be synthesised by analysis and classification. He recommends scientific method of observation and verification, but added that "whatever can be known, can be known by means of science; but things which are legitimately matters of feeling, lie outside its province".

Effects on Education

Though Realism affected education in a big way with regard

to source, extent and nature of knowledge, its special contribution to education is, firstly, that it tried to remove the gulf between life and education. Education is not only life-related, it is in direct communion with the world of objects existing in the external world, independent of our perception. Secondly, it recommended the principle of scientific experimentation and observation. Realism lays exclusive emphasis on the sense-origin of knowledge and, that sense organs are the doorways to knowledge. It also advocated inductive method in education wherein learning is piecemeal in its origin. Realism also caused a drift from the bookish knowledge, and brings about a union between nature and man based on one's own experiences.

Chief Characteristics of Realistic Education : The following are, in brief, the salient features of a realistic educational system:

Scientific Attitude : Realism lays exclusive emphasis on science subjects and the scientific attitude of observation and verification wherein education is not only natural but also direct. Understanding of the laws of nature and their acceptance is the essential of this attitude.

Status of Child : Realism deals with life here and now, and as such, avoids plunge into the world of ideas and ideals. It concerns with the immediate and real problems that may confront a child, so as to promote his welfare and good. The status of the child, therefore, is central to all its educational programmes and activities.

Experiment and Application : Knowledge for Realism is through observation and verification. It confirms the view that knowledge howsoever subtle and sublime would have no significance if it does not have any value for life: knowledge, therefore, should be life-related and find its consummation in human application and experience. As such, it encourages creativity, urge for practical work and, learning by doing. Knowledge, therefore, is an active ingress into the external world of objects and experiences.

Opposition to Bookish Knowledge : As knowledge is application to life, Realism opposes bookish knowledge which inversely encourages rote and cramming tendencies among children. Education should enable a child to understand the natural phenomenon and, natural and social environment. Their slogan is: Do not tell, show and help a child develop his intelligence and judgement.

Freedom to Child : As child is the focal point of all realistic programmes and activities, it allows reasonable freedom to the child to exercise his natural tendencies, interests, aspirations and abilities. There is thus, a limited external control in realistic education, and a child would on his own impose upon himself the constraints of discipline required by nature and society.

Training of Senses : As sense organs are the source, the doorways, the oracles of all knowledge of the external world, the senses should be trained to provide information with utmost accuracy and variety. Maximum use of these sense organs should be made to develop them by use and experience.

Individuality and Sociability : The aim of realistic education is to develop both, the individual and the society of which he is an integral part, as the two are inseparably related, each acquiring meaning and significance from other. Hence, realism lays equal emphasis to individual and society.

Merits of Realism

1. Education to be practical and utilitarian.
2. Educational aims are directly related to life.
3. Introduction of science subjects in the curriculum.
4. Use of inductive method of teaching leading to emergence of heuristic, experimental and, correlation devices in teaching.
5. Emancipatory Discipline; no repression, no physical punishment.
6. Emphasis on objectivity in teaching-learning.
7. Changed the pattern of school life wherein schools are not only temples of learning, but also places of meaningful activities and interaction resulting in the all-around development of a child.

Limitations

1. Lopsided emphasis only on the physical world without going into its metaphysical existence, extent and nature, thereby ignoring the non-sensual.
2. Does not account for illusion, such as, of seeing the snake in the rope. If knowledge is linear and direct, how come this illusion?
3. Ignores emotions which it considers as a strain and a drain.
4. If everything is real in life, how to explain suffering and disease?
5. Exclusive emphasis on science subjects upsets the curriculum.
6. No place for ideals and values bringing pessimism and retardation.

Aristotle : "Aristotle, as a philosopher, is in many ways very different from his predecessors, first to write like a professor his treatises are systematic, discussions divided into heads, he is a professional teacher, not an inspired prophet" (Bertrand Russell). He is described as "Plato diluted by common sense", a difficult situation as Plato and common sense would not be an easy mix. For him, the world is continually evolving toward a "greater degree of form" and thus becoming progressively more like God. The process is ceaseless and continuous as perfection of matter and form is difficult to achieve continuously backoned by the ultimate perfection that is God. Aristotle, hence was biological in his approach to religion and creation. He was a perfectionist who believed in the essential nature of man and the world. Hence, an essentialist who believed in the existence of matter in its own right and purpose.

Effects on Morale

Aristotle is known for his theory of universals. He described it as "which is of a nature as to be predicated of many subjects, by 'individual' that which is not thus predicated". Universals, therefore, entail 'substance' or things to which it can be predicated.

It is not 'substance'. Whereas substance relates to proper name, such as, this or that, a universal signifies an adjective or class-name, such as, 'human', 'man', etc. Substance describes 'things', whereas universal indicates sort of things, not actual particular thing. As such, a "universal cannot exist by itself, but only in particular things. The duality of universal and substance lead to the dichotomy of matter and form. Matter exists in form, much the same way as universal exists in substance. Matter, therefore, is the substance of the things.

It, however, does not mean that form confers substantiality; it gives "Unity to a portion of matter", like 'chair' and 'wood'. Matter without form is a mere potentiality, only a possibility. This distinction between matter and form and their existence independent of mind, turns Aristotle a realist who believes in the duality of matter and form, as well as of 'mind' that performs functions of perceiving potentiality of turning matter into form. This form is generally compared to Plato's ideas. God is pure form as he is no matter, hence eternal and unchangeable, yet Aristotle speaks of "rational soul in man and also God." He is a rationalist and considers God only as the First Cause, the Prime Mover who is eternal and good.

Aristotle demonstrated throughout his writings, the typical Greek "love of static perfection and preference for contemplation rather than action." The life of the rational soul consists in contemplation, which is the complete happiness of man though not fully attainable. For him soul is the form of the body as it makes body an organic whole. He differentiates mind from soul as it is bound more with body. In fact, it is soul that confers substantiality upon things. It is the final cause of the body, and as it is bound up with the body, it perishes with the body, hence no transmigration. Aristotle distinguishes between rational and irrational soul: the former is divine and impersonal, the latter is connected with the body: the former, as universal mind, is immortal, the latter as irrational, hence perishable.

Mind or reason is immortal as impersonal and divine, but this immortality is not of individuals or separate men. He shares with Plato and later with Christianity that "so far men are rational, they partake of the divine, which is immortal." Man has the capacity to increase the element of divinity in his nature, and to do so is the highest virtue.

Educational Implications

1. Education should aim at providing opportunities to enable man attain his rational self and raise his level by increasing the divinity in him by forsaking the matter that forbids his upward movement. Let him achieve the rational soul that he shares with God, and let him be one with him by transcending his personal and irrational soul that perishes with the body. Refinement of reason and mind should find priority in our education programmes. Aristotle, however, does not forsake body or the physical because it is as much essential till it lasts as a symbol of the universal form.
2. As contemplation may bring complete happiness to man, necessary opportunities should be afforded to him toward this end. Complete happiness by increased divine potential is the highest virtue, and education must help achieve this through suitable educational programmes. Happiness, therefore, is the highest goal and is the activity of the soul.
3. Virtues are of two kinds, intellectual and moral. Intellectual virtues result from teaching, moral virtues from habit. Men become good by forming good habits. Let education, therefore, provide for such environment that helps one acquire good habits which in due course of time may provide "pleasure in performing good actions."
4. Education should define the good whereas virtue is defined as action "tending to produce the good." Virtues are means to an end, namely happiness, hence virtues are concerned with means which have to be equally pure and rational. Virtue, as such, may include ends of action. Aristotle described "Human good is activity of soul in accordance with virtue in a complete life." Educational programmes should, therefore, provide for such situations that may help one become good.

5. Virtues are not to be judged by their consequences as generally believed by Christian moralists, but should be valued on their own account. As such virtues are pathways to reach 'good' which is a value. Virtues and values are, therefore, inversely related, and education must help arrive at this equation.
6. Distinguishing 'pleasure' from 'happiness', Aristotle states that "Happiness lies in virtuous activity and perfect happiness lies in the best activity, which is contemplation." Education should, therefore, develop virtuous living which is contemplative in nature.
7. In political backdrop, Aristotle is for democratic practices. His concept of "equality according to proportion and for every man to enjoy his own", is rather difficult to measure, but nevertheless worthy of pursuit. Educative process, therefore, should aim at developing democratic virtues.
8. Aristotle lays special stress on teaching of physics, mathematics, biology and logic to sharpen the intellect, and enlarge the expanse of knowledge. Education should, therefore, provide for intellectual and moral development, to goad one toward action. Action is the goal, knowledge merely a means to it. Education should, therefore, be based on realistic precepts, and should not get wasted in the world of ideas.

Educational Establishments

According to Aristotle, the child should be taught on the basis of experiences. Thus, Aristotle indicated the principle which was accepted by other scholars centuries later. It is necessary to prepare the mind of the child for higher subjects. Aristotle was of the firm conviction that the mind inclines to move from known to unknown. Therefore, it is necessary that the children should be given knowledge of different subjects through direct experiences. He was of the view that the knowledge of the principle regarding any subject can be acquired through experience.

Importance of Aristotle : The educational principle of Aristotle could make very little influence on the people of his time. The same can be said about Plato. However, the influence of the ideas of Aristotle is clearly visible in the schools of today and in the curriculum of Universities. The attainment of liberal education has never been as great as in the present age.

It would not be an exaggeration to say that the influence of Aristotle is clearly visible in the modern period. Aristotle has the credit of organising many subjects and giving them a scientific form. According to Paul Munroe: "Universally recognised as the greatest of the ancients, Aristotle was supreme down to the time of 15th century renaissance."

11

Naturalistic Theory

Ward described Naturalism as "a doctrine which separates Nature from God, subordinates spirit to matter and, sets up laws as supreme". By robbing God of nature, it does away with the supernatural, and restricts itself only to what is natural; by marginalising mind, it consolidates what is material, and is often called as materialism; and by setting up unchangeable laws of nature and matter, it builds up a world-view rooted in scientific attitude, approach and method. Nature reigns supreme, and is the only reality, the rest is all governed by its laws. Hence, submission to nature and by following the track formed by it, one can discover what all there is, seen or unseen, as the essence of a thing does not lie in perception alone and may have to be discovered through the "mutual aid of science and common sense".

The Approach

(1) According to Joyce "Naturalism is a system whose salient characteristic is the exclusion of whatever is spiritual or indeed whatever is transcendental of experience from our philosophy of Nature and Man". It considers reality at the empirical level alone, and nothing that transcends experience could be the subject

of knowledge. As spirituality has trans-experiential origin, it has no place in this system which is outrightly materialistic in outlook and precepts.

(2) "Naturalism is not science but an assertion about science. More specifically, it is the assertion that scientific knowledge is final, leaving no room for extra-scientific or philosophical knowledge". (R.B. Perry)

(3) "Naturalism is a doctrine which separates Nature from God, subordinates spirit to matter, and sets up laws as supreme". (Ward)

(4) It may be summed up that "Naturalism is a term loosely applied in educational theory to systems of training that are not dependent on schools and books but on manipulation of the actual life of the educated" It considers Nature as the source and inspiration of all knowledge.

Various Thinkers

Aristotle, Rousseau, Comte, Hobbes, Bacon, Darwin, Lamarck, Huxley, Herbert Spencer, G. Bernard Shaw, Butler are its chief exponents spread over centuries, yet maintaining its intrinsic affinity. While touching others in a passing reference, emphasis would be laid on Rousseau, and Herbert Spencer as representative models of the system.

The Growth

Going as far back to the nature-worship of the early Greek and resulting in the worship of natural elements of civilisations, Naturalism got a spurt in the biological theories of evolution propounded by Darwin and Lamarck, who traced the evolution of man in a naturalistic order through the twin principles of the struggle for existence and survival of the fittest in a purely physical and biological backdrop. Adaptation and adjustment to natural laws spell success in meeting natural situations and interventions.

However, the revolutionary change in thought and practice in physical sciences during the eighteenth century ushered in far reaching changes in social and political order of the state. Whereas despotism and absolutism, even aristocracy, went for the authoritarian and totalitarian regimens ignoring the essential nature of man as well as the spirit of natural laws and phenomena, a new thought pattern started emerging wherein freedom and the essential nature of good was considered to be naturalistic hence, common to all in equal measure. Reformation and renaissance movements lent credence to the natural and free society and helped in developing new and revolutionary concept of state craft, growth and development, society, religion and education.

Voltaire and Rousseau spearheaded the movement of freedom and equality in everything that concerns human society. Education was no exception. There was no inequality in nature, then why in society? The ideals, concepts and practices of the French Revolution in 1789 had its reverberations throughout Europe and other like-minded countries. Naturalism in statecraft and education had travelled a long way together, and became a force to be reckoned with. There was no looking back.

Forms of Naturalism : There are three forms of Naturalism:

1. Physical Naturalism.
2. Mechanical Naturalism.
3. Biological Naturalism.

The Evolution

Also called naturalism of physical sciences, physical naturalism studies the external world, as that is the only world, through its processes and phenomena, and explains human nature in terms of the material objects existing outside on their own, and the laws of nature that allow nature to move the way it does. Nature is not blind though it is restricted only to the external material world. Mind is a by product of matter. Nature, therefore, has total control on man and his activities, and does not let him have any respite, hence no freedom but to tow the line in accordance with the laws of nature.

Physical naturalism, because of its exclusive stress on the external world and the physical science, does not give any useful contribution to the field of education which is a dynamic and developing process.

Approach based on Materialism

Mechanical Naturalism considers the external world as a huge machine getting its form through matter and motion. Man is no exception and is also a cog in the machine. All movements of heaven and earth are, in the final analysis, attributable to the mechanical nature of the phenomenon which is destined to move, if move at all toward a blind end, if there is an end at all. Matter and motion are the only two categories, how they work, how they come together, why they come together, why matter needs motion and, why motion works on matter, are some of the lay questions that beset a mechanical naturalist who, perhaps, is more of a machinist than mechanical. It was with much of reluctance and contradiction that mechanical naturalism admits of someone who manages the machine, the machinist and, called deu ex machina. Yes, there is a machinist but he is outside the machine, above the laws of matter and motion.

This knave philosophical explanation of cosmology does not give anything to education. Why education if one is a helpless, blind, dead clog in a machine which is beyond repair and rectification? If life has no purpose, no teleology, why education? That life is dynamic, purposeful and progressive phenomenon is the key of any educational programme and activity: the programmes that may have desired effect on man as he is pliable, amenable, biological, rational and spiritual entity having some purpose in existence, and consciously grows toward it. Behaviourist psychology may be considered the only contribution of mechanical naturalism, and that too, only if mechanical naturalism admits of some kind or level of consciousness, mind.

Approach based on Biology

That "man is the product of evolution" is the basic tenet of Biological Naturalism. But again the question arise: was this evolution blind or purposeful or, was it also a mechanical process ending in man as a by-product? Or, was it a gradual progression toward perfection? Attributed to Darwin's theory of evolution, biological naturalism believes that man has evolved from the lower animals, and therefore, is the best of the species: ashraf-i-mukhlooq, as the Quran says: the best of the creation. The process of evolution underwent a timeless growth, and admits of some purpose in evolution. It considers man as a natural product (and not a by-product) inheriting the best of the racial past, impulses, instincts and, primitive emotions. It, however, does not take in to account the spiritual in man, if at all there is any. That is why Biological naturalism restricts itself to the biological growth and development, and is rightly called so. Its aspects of growth and development makes it relevant to any educational thought and approach, theory and practice. Biological naturalism subscribes to the following principles of evolution:-

(a) Adjustment and Adaptation to environment for base survival otherwise life would have become extinct.

(b) Struggle for Existence i.e., life is a struggle in which adjustment helps it.

(c) Survival of the Fittest i.e., adjustment and struggle help one survive, but in this struggle only the fittest survive and the other species decay and perish. Remember, these principles are at the animal level and, do not consider of the higher rational faculties of love and sacrifice. If at all there is sacrifice in Nature, it is blind, instinctive and unvoluntary, hence has no significance except biological. The world is governed by the laws of nature.

Educational Impact

Capitalising on its precepts of adjustment and harmony, the educationists consider Biological Naturalism relevant to life, and consequently, to education. According to Rosa "education is seen as the process of adjustment to environment, it aims at enabling the individual to be in harmony with, and well adapted to his surrounding". This school gives us the "doctrine of natural man [as against the theory of divine creation] and prefers instinctive judgement and primitive emotions as the basis for action, reflection or, experience that comes from association with society". These are, therefore, the spring of action. Instinct is the outcome of evolutionary process which helps freedom of the organism, and conversely strengthens instinct. These instincts are the springs of action as later advocated by McDougall and mankind has grown and developed through these processes. Let "education of the child be in accord with, both in mode and arrangement, with the education of mankind, considered historically". In education, nature acquires two meanings, firstly, like that of Rousseau's call for "Back to Nature" wherein only natural processes should be allowed to nurture a child; secondly, that a child should be developed in accordance with his inherent nature, abilities, interests and other endowments. Education should not interfere with this growth and development, but should help further it, so as to arrive early, by putting the child at the centre of all educational processes, programmes and activities, naturally.

Diverse Facets

Back to Nature : Rousseau's clarion call was a desperate scream of a philosopher-educationist against formal, verbal and artificial education prevalent during his time, and exhorted one and all to consider education as a means to bring about natural and normal development of a child in a healthy, natural environment. His first sentence in his famous book Emile and Education, sums up his attitude: "All things are good as they came from the hands of the author of Mature, everywhere they degenerate in the hands of man". Naturalism, therefore, considers Nature as the sole source of inspiration. Further the teacher should remember that a child's nature is not static, it is dynamic, it is developing. A teaching programme or activity should, therefore, be in accordance with the changing nature of the child providing variety and interest.

Child Centred : We have already discussed somewhere in the body of the book that the education process has three components: Teacher-Content-Child/Pupil. There has been varying emphasis on any one of the poles during the long history of education: sometimes it is the teacher who is the hub of all teaching-learning activity; sometimes the weightage is given to the content irrespective of the other two components, but in Naturalism the entire focus and attention is the child, the most affected component of any educative process. As a matter of fact, all three components are essential for a successful educative process. Teacher teaches John Latin. However, Naturalism considers child as the focal point, therefore, education should be child-centred, in accordance with his potentialities, interests and aptitude, and the other two components should be incorporated in a suitable manner wherein the content should be according to his needs and aspirations and, the teacher should be well versed and well practised in child education. The teaching procedures and learning materials should be cut according to the child, and not vice versa. Treat a child as a child, and not a mini adult: "Nature would have them children before they are men". Munroe sums it up when he says that "education finds its purpose, its process and its means wholly within the child-life and child-experience". Let education be not only child-centred, but also child-oriented.

Progressive : We have mentioned a little while ago that the content should be child-centred. Education should be progressive and, not sudden and abrupt; it should go along with the child, and also take the child along. That 'Child is the father of man' is a figure of speech and should not be taken literally, and that 'education is preparation for life', should not rob a child of his pleasures, needs, experiences and values. Hence, the educative process should progressively grow with the child. If we rush the child we "may produce forward fruits without ripeness and flavour". (Rousseau)

No Bookish Knowledge : Let a child learn from his experiences and interaction with Nature. Let his senses be the oracles and pathways to truth. Let him not suffer excessive verbalism, and let him see the world as he does. You be a remote control to oversee that he does not hurt himself. The only book that Rousseau prescribed for early childhood education was Robinson Crusoe for the exploits, bravery and, presence of mind of its hero in alien situations guided only by his natural tendencies. All education, therefore, should be self-learning.

Freedom of Child : School should not condition or affect his natural tendencies and provide free environment wherein a child could move around and gather his experiences. Unnecessary external intervention may stunt his natural growth and development. Do not spoil a child's dream-world by introducing checks and restraints. Let him enjoy that sublime feeling of being free, and suspend discipline for later life. Whatever little discipline a child may have should be a part of his routine and not extraneous. Do not rob his today for some uncertain tomorrow.

Training of Senses : As all knowledge of the external world comes through senses, enough care should be taken to train the senses for correct and timely reporting of events, experiences. Senses should be able to detect illusions and hallucinations, or from presenting a distorted or a berated view of nature. Senses should be so well trained that there is no confusion in perception and reporting. According to Rousseau "education should prepare the way for reason by the proper exercise of senses".

Negative Education : According to Ross "a negative education does not mean a time of idleness, far from it. It does not give virtue, but protects from vice; does not give truth yet protects from error. It disposes the child to take a path that will lead him to truth when he has reached to understand it, and goodness, when he has acquired the faculty of recognizing and loving it". In a way, it is a kind of familiarisation of situations wherein truth and goodness may be experienced at an appropriate time.

Psychologically Sound : Naturalism is grounded in sound psychology wherein it incorporates researches in that field for the betterment of an educative process.

Comments : The clarion call 'Back to Nature' was first given by Francis Bacon and Commenius but Roussaeu gave it a startling shape and meaning, and Herbert Spencer, Pestalozzi, and Froebel further formalised it. No wonder, the slogan is the backbone of any naturalistic educative process or activity.

Bearing on Education : Because of disparity of views among various branches of Naturalism where is no unanimity of aims as such and we would, therefore, describe the educational bearing of each form of Naturalism and later attempt, if it so warrants, a synthesis of their varying viewpoint to give it a characteristic look.

Mechanical Naturalism : Aim of education should be to establish "the conditioned reflexes that are habits of action and thought appropriate to modern life". Curriculum should be such that it helps one understand the laws of nature, operates, more or less, at the animal level.

Biological Naturalism : Education, for this school, should aim at establishing happiness in mankind. Now, happiness does not mean only sensual pleasures but points to something more enduring behind its experience. By using the word happiness instead of pleasure, the naturalists transcend the charge of being hedonistic, which is more base and animal in nature. 'Maximum pleasure of the maximum people' is another variation of it.

However, at the animal level the basic principle is: Seek Pleasure, Shun Pain. No wonder, McDougall supported heuristic attitude and applied it to the study of natural phenomena. He prescribed Direct Method in teaching of languages. Heuristic and laboratory methods should be applied in learning sciences and mathematics; Observational method may be adopted for study of Geography, etc. Nature study was given priority.

Darwin Theory

Also called biological evolutionism, this school recommends study of such subjects that may help one to survive nature which is hostile. Survival should, therefore, be the aim of all education with emphasis on physical and natural sciences, physiology and health regimen.

Education should aim at developing such ability that helps one adjust with environment so that the individual must be in harmony and well adapted to his surroundings.

Discipline Study

Aims

(a) "Education should make the human machine as good a machine as possible by attending to its constitution, by elaborating it and making it capable of more and more complicated tasks". (Ross)

(b) Attainment of Present and Future Happiness in that education must emphasise emancipation, moulding and guiding of the basic impulses of a child so as to attain natural progress and development. (McDougall)

(c) *Preparation for Struggle:* Evolution is through the struggle for existence and survival of the fittest. As such Darwin and others consider education to aim at developing human capacities to enable survival.

(d) *Adaptation to Environment:* Lamarck unlike Darwin asserts that human being is unlike the other animals, has a tremendous power to adapt to nature to his advantage by coping up with all kinds of hostile and benign circumstances. It gave man an edge over nature. Education, therefore, should strengthen this innate capacity of man to stand up and be counted.

(e) *Improvement of Racial Gains:* Naturalism considers education as a mode of transferring cultural and civil achievements of a people, as the same cannot be transferred by the natural process of inheritance, yet are an important endowment, and cannot be allowed to dwindle. Education, therefore, develops, conserves, enhances and transmits such cultural achievements of a race acquired over years of dexterous efforts.

(f) *Natural Development:* Rousseau laid exclusive emphasis on the physical development of a child so as to make him strong. Besides, education, while preparing a programme and activity, should take a serious view of his nature, individual differences, inborn tendencies, interests, aptitudes and abilities, and help them to develop in a free and conducive environment. Nature, in this sense, is a wider term including the physical nature as well as the child's nature both are inclusive and complementary.

(g) *Autonomous Development:* According to Nunn, a child's development should be free and autonomous, acquired by the child with his own effort: no spoon feeding.

The Curriculum

Since self-preservation is the basic tenet of Naturalism, the curriculum should contain only those subjects which help toward this end. As such study of religion, culture and music does not find a place in Herbert Spencer's views. For him, the study of physical and natural sciences, sports and games, are the legitimate subjects compatible with his views. He further includes History and Geography, and Mathematics as essential for a child's total natural development. For him, History is the study of the past experiences of the race, and helps in explaining the present and its origin, and determines its futuristic outlook. However, later Naturalists like Huxley, include the study of literature, languages, Art, Music and other cultural subjects, as subsidiary subjects, but necessary for a child's physical, intellectual, moral and social development.

The Concept

According to Rousseau, "Give your child no verbal lessons: He should be taught by experience alone. Teach by doing whenever you can: and only fall back on words when doing is out of question :... Book knowledge should be as little as possible". It may sound too much, but remember, it was a reaction to verbalism, and the generally exaggerated. Huxley, later relaxed the extreme views held by Rousseau, and cautioned about the risk factor in experience. Nevertheless, Naturalism was a tirade against verbalism, parent-domination and repression.

Following are the essentials of Naturalistic methodology:

1. Learning by Doing.
2. Learning by Experience.
3. Learning by Play.

These principles ushered in new methodology by way of progressive approaches toward child-education, such as, Observation, Playway, Project, Heuristics, Dalton Plan, Kindergarten and Montessori methods of early childhood education, and lay singular emphasis on self-learning as it "fosters the spirit of joyful, spontaneous, creative activity, its applications are endless". Froebel, Pestalozzi, Montessori, McMillan sisters,

Gesell, Gandhi, Tagore, Tarabai Modak, Gijubhai Bhadek, Annie Besant, Sarla Devi Sarabhai, and a host of other Indian and foreign educationists, are happy travellers on the naturalist bandwagon.

Role of Teacher

Naturalism generally believes in non-intervention with a child's natural development. A teacher should, therefore, guide and nurture children in the spirit of a gardener who tends each plant with equal care and dexterity. No artificiality; no inhibitions. Let there be an unchecked flow of child's playful activities in a joyful manner. A child is inherently pure and good, and he must develop according to his nature, interests, abilities, desires and aspirations. A teacher must help him achieve this by being sympathetic and kind, resourceful and imaginative, and by setting the stage for the children to freely act in accordance with their interest and ability, and by being a remote observer and guide. He must guard against the risks by controlling the environment without altering them so that no harm comes to a child. A teacher should have a genuine sense of humour and fun; children love fun, a teacher should capitalise on this. He should not impose his views on the child and should help have his own experiences, observations and conclusions. Let all learning be self-learning and let every teacher be a pivot, a source of unending inspiration and guidance: a friend, philosopher and guide in the real sense of the phrase.

The Naturalism

Naturalism believes in discipline by natural consequences wherein pleasure and pain are the guiding factors. No repression, no corporeal punishment. Herbert Spencer's exclusive emphasis on natural consequences may cause untold damage to a child's psyche, growth and development. J.S. Mill, therefore, recommends caution and warning to the child to beware of a lurking danger in not all that innocent nature. John Dewey also is of the similar view when he recommends some kind of direct disapproval to avoid "some courses of action which are far too discomforting and obnoxious to pursue". A child, therefore, should have freedom within the carefully controlled environment, of which he may be unaware thus giving him the impression of absolute freedom. A child will later on, in his own course of action, develop a sense of self-discipline. School, therefore, should provide ample opportunities for self-learning and self-discipline.

The Evaluation

As a rule, evaluation consists of the pros and cons of an issue and, as such, refers to its overall assessment, merits and limitations.

The Limitations

1. Narrow, limited, one-sided and unsatisfying aim of education, as Naturalism concentrates only on natural environment and natural development which may result in a lopsided development of a child ignoring his social aspect which necessitates a child's growth and development in a social environment as well.
2. Emphasis on present needs and solution of a child's present problem becomes the summum bonum of all educational activities, marginalising spiritual values and development of intellectual and aesthetic aspects of a child's personality, with no reference to preparation for future life.
3. Avoiding any reference to books and any other form of recorded information will create a void as all knowledge does not come from experience howsoever extensive and intensive they may be. As such, books and other means of contraventions, should as much be the part of a child's educational programmes and activities, as the natural activities are.
4. Rousseau recommends twelve years of natural education to a child. This lays emphasis only on physical development of a child and ignores his social, moral and spiritual development. No wonder, Pestalozzi rejects it when he says "specialised development of one side of human nature is unnatural and false to consider any one capacity exclusively is to destroy man's natural equilibrium".
5. Consequently, a naturalistic curriculum is also one sided with emphasis only on science subjects. Spencer did

relent to consider humanities, art, literature, language etc. as subsidiaries. It is needless to say that curriculum should be as comprehensive and varied as human life is so as to ensure its overall, all-around development.

6. Unlimited freedom to a child is dangerous as it may cause him physical harm and social and moral aberrations. As freedom is in social context, it also implies freedom of others which a child must learn to respect as early in life as possible without being detrimental to his own growth and development. Freedom should, therefore, be curtailed not only by natural consequences but also by social dictate.
7. Discipline by natural consequences, as advocated by Spencer, in its extreme form, is dangerous, impractical and unwise. Self-learning should not mean self-injury wherein a child should learn from others' experiences without putting himself to unpalatable consequences. Discipline, therefore, should be self-discipline in a personal and social context, under the watchful eyes of the teacher howsoever remote he may be in any given learning situation.
8. Naturalism considers teacher as a detached observer whereas, in fact, teacher is a guide who would restructure experiences for a child's observation and understanding; he is sympathetic, kind and considerate, nurturing the child as his own, through thick and thin of the life-experiences; he may have to take recourse to deliberate interventions so as to make an experience intelligible and meaningful. An actively engaged and inspired teacher is a must for a child's all round development: physical, intellectual, emotional, social, moral and spiritual.
9. Too much emphasis on individuality might develop socially undesirable attitudes in a child as he would be totally unaware of social interaction, cooperation and social graces. An extreme naturalism is a double-edged weapon which may cut either way hurting the individual and society in the process.

The Merits

1. Child-oriented approach and child-centred activity programmes distinguish Naturalism from other schools of educational philosophy. Child is the focal point; the centre of all progressive approaches to child growth, development, needs, abilities, aptitudes, desires and aspirations. As such, much more detailed attention was paid to the child in order to understand his peculiar nature leading to the emergence of an exclusive study of child, called child psychology. The theory of early childhood education and the practices of educational psychology were never so close as of now.
2. Study of society in all its socio-cultural ramifications, demographic and sociological tendencies, and its evolution to the present form and content, received a sudden and powerful spurt because of naturalistic trends in education, and gave it an ingress into its purpose and direction, and inversely helping it to understand the processes of development. Sociology became integrated with Education.
3. Activity-based Curriculum, learning programmes and experiences were central to the Naturalistic doctrine, as it lays sole emphasis on self-learning, learning by self-experience, learning by doing and, learning by participation. The child-centred learning experiences and materials were designated as learning programmes, covering a vast and varied area of child-experiences and capitalising on his playful nature. Child education became totally child-centred and most of the early childhood experiences were activity based, and accepted by all progressive educationists from Rousseau downward passing through the great galaxy of Commenius, Pestalozzi, Froebel, Montessori, Dewey, Kilpatrick and a host of other Indian and foreign educationists. That 'child is the father of man' was never as true as of now and is an exclusive contribution of Naturalism.
4. If the learning experiences are child-oriented, could their

transmission be otherwise? Child-orientation not only affected construction of learning programmes and experiences, but also helped devise such modes and means of transmission of information in as much painless manner as possible, and by sparing the child the agony of growing up. Naturalism in education, therefore, brought in its wake such teaching techniques and methods as Activity-method, Playway method, Observation method, Kindergarten, Nursery and Montessori methods, Dalton Plan, Heuristic method, Project method, and a host of other combinations that revolutionised childhood teaching-learning.

5. And finally, naturalism advocated sparing the child of the rod, and was against all kinds of repressive and oppressive measures in the bringing up of a child. Later naturalists dropped the concept of natural consequences as a source of discipline, and advocated self-discipline in a free, congenial and conducive environment, where a child has a reasonable degree of freedom to act and explore.

The Comments **:** Romantic Naturalism of Rousseau and Froebel, and later of Bernard, is essentially based on a theory of human nature which considers child as spontaneously self-active and inherently pure. It implores the educationists to determine the laws that govern and help understand child's nature so as to ensure his all-around development in a creative manner. The basic premise of the Naturalistic philosophy is that "what is, is right", and whatever a child is trying to do may be an expression of some basic built-in urge and self-assertion. Romantic naturalism (a term coined by Brubacher so as to distinguish it from Pragmatic Naturalism of John Dewey) is, therefore, a child-oriented approach centred around child-centred learning programmes and activities. Its abrupt reference to natural circumstances and interventions may be exaggerated, so as to appear distinct from the current formal practices of the day, but are true, fair and practical in the overall growth and development of a child in a free, friendly and supportive environment and atmosphere, and is, therefore, the forerunner of all subsequent, progressive theories and practices of childhood education.

12

Humanistic Theory

The order of the day in the philosophy of Indian education is Neo-realism and Humanism. Idealism can't work and Naturalism is out dated. All that is left is Neo-realism and Humanism. The knowledge of Humanism is very necessary-more so how we can use it in education. And to humanise education is a baffling problem. (Neo-realism is omitted for the present).

The Approach

Humanism implies both a human and a humane approach to educational problems; human in the sense that human nature (including likes, dislikes, interests, aptitudes etc.) should not be suppressed by religion in favour of an ascetic ideal and a narrow dogmatic interpretation of the world; humane in the sense that the nature of the child and its growing mind should not be suppressed by cruel discipline, teachers and rigid methods of teaching. Taken in this way, Humanism was a revolt against the medieval dualism of mind and body. It was a revolt against the monopoly of theology and church dogma in the theory and practice of medieval life. It may be mentioned that Humanism was not directed against Christianity. On the contrary. Humanism accepted its close connection with Christian tradition and Christian morality.

In other words, it can be defined as that which is not supernatural but natural, that which belongs to the nature of man and not to the external nature and raises him up high and provides him satisfaction is Humanism.

Still in more simpler words we can say that when human world and human being become the concern of philosophy—the result is Humanism.

Humanism is taken from 'Humaniora'-which means study of human body and surrounding nature. The word 'Humanities' is also taken from it.

After having known about the definition, we now proceed further to analyse the definitions in order to find out the meaning of the term Humanism. Humanism, let it be known at the outset, means many things. In its original setting, Humanism meant the liberation of the reason from the shackles and chains of dogma, it very much involves a critical study of nature and humanity through the observation of actual facts.

Secondly, to early humanists, it meant reasonable balance of life.

The third interpretation may be the study of humanities or soft subjects or of polite letters.

Fourthly it may be called a philosophy, the centre of whose study is man. Man is the measure of all things and man again is the architect of fortune. Humanists believe that way and as such they want to study man. Important philosophers who were humanists were Descrates and Locke.

Potent Role in Education

What then is the task of humanism in education? It is as follows:

Aims

(i) The first principal function of humanistic education is that the tender spirit may drink in the seas of piety.

(ii) The next is that he may love and learn through liberal studies and that he may be informed concerning duties of life.

(iii) From the earliest childhood, the individual may be habituated in the courteous manners.

All that is mentioned above was and is possible through the revival of graceo-roman literature and in part ideals of Christianity and in part in the continuation of knighthood and chivalry. These only could help the people to realise the aims of education.

Milton, one of the humanistic educationists had laid the aims of education as such-the end then of all learning is to repair the ruins of our first parents but regaining to know God almighty. He brings in the knowledge of Chemistry, God, Religion etc. His oft quoted words are, I call therefore a complete and generous education that which fits a man to perform justly, skillfully and magnanimously all the offices-both private and public, of peace and war."

Thus the aims of humanists as a whole laid for their education are:

(i) To produce a broadly educated man possessing a well rounded personality who could assume leadership in church and state.

(ii) To produce individuals who are at home in the field of classical learning and yet they may be men of action. In this sense classical knowledge should not make men soft and passive.

(iii) To produce men who should have a wide range of accomplishments. They be able to express themselves in poetry, song, dance, etc. All men must be physically and mentally healthy.

Jacks says that according to humanists, human perfection must be its final objective.

Regarding Aims of Education for Girls. An ideal woman will be a versatile and charming companion of the ideal courtier. Education should make woman able for the ideal companions.

To conclude, the aims of humanistic education were anticlerical, broad, generous. Their defect, however, was that those outstripped the ability to devise suitable curriculum and methods for their realisation. How could these scientific aims be achieved through humanities and languages alone?

The Curriculum

The main tenet of humanism i.e. education for all and the child is the centre of all education and the broad aims of education reflect on the type of curriculum. Hans says that the humanistic curriculum had in it the 'real' studies so that those could light the minds of children since it was the pupil who came first or got priority-method and theory later.

(i) Accordingly, curriculum included the study of old classics of Greeks and Romans since early humanists considered these to be possessing profundity of content, literary style etc. and they believed that all the values such as wide learning, all round development, life of action, qualities of artistic enjoyment could be achieved by teaching Greek and Roman literature. In comparison with literature and classics, they gave slight attention to mathematics, natural history, music etc. and much less attention was given by them to the vernaculars in their curriculum. They believed that if history and ethics is to be studied-we should study those as a part of the work of the old classical writers. This meant that learning of history and ethics is incidental. We are not to study these separately.

(ii) Physical Education was also included in their curriculum and there was due place for it. It aimed at producing a new brave class of people.

(iii) Training for Good Manners such as modesty was also stressed.

Criticism

(i) Learning of history and ethics was incidental.

(ii) Curriculum can further be criticised for its verbalism and narrow literary professions. It is all verbal.

(iii) Since the curriculum was verbal and it appeared to be quite easy, many people went in for it without knowing that they were not capable for this. And there could be no check on this as humanism meant education for all.

(iv) This type of curriculum was single track or one sided. There was emphasis on humanities alone. Later on there were attempts to reform the curriculum.

Academician J. B. Florin and his Humanistic Curriculum. In the 18th century Florin asserted, "Philosophy and the sciences ought to be made the principal study of young persons." He classified all subjects of instruction into three groups: (i) Relation of man to nature, (ii) Relation of man to himself, (iii) Relation of man to other men.

He advised a ten years course for the ages seven to seventeen presuming that the boys would enter his academy with a fair knowledge of writing and reading. The subjects included all branches of mathematics, history, applied sciences for the first group, Latin, French, Italian, Grammar, Rhetoric, Poetry, Drawing, Music and exercise for the second group. History, politics, economics and biography for the third group.

Methods of Teaching

(i) We can know about the methods when we go back and scan through the works of Erasmus. It was he who had left in writing about the method. He had tried the old methods in teaching literature and he told us. "Do not give the personal account of the author-rather appreciate the work of the author." We should talk about his style, about his vocabulary etc. rather than become personal with him.

(ii) Talking about difficulties in the way of learning, humanists say that the teacher should give few simple directions to overcome difficulties. Do not hurry because learning comes easily when the proper stage is reached. Avoid difficulty which can be easily ignored. Postpone things.

(iii) Later on, the above stand of postponing things was amended since it was not wise to postpone things. It lead to undue tension. The difficulty must be handled.

How? Whenever a difficulty is handled, the approach of the teacher should be gradual and as interesting as the teacher can make.

(iv) Next item in the method of humanistic education was to set exercises for the matter taught. It should not be literal reproduction. The subject should be reproduced. He did not favour taking notes. He would encourage memorisation, understanding and reproduction. The substance be memorised. Let the child understand critically and then reproduce. The maxim was: - Understand-Arrange-Repeat.

(v) For mature students, early humanists recommended lectures and debates. Independence and individuality were introduced in learning of lessons. It was a protest against verbalism and cram work.

Diverse Facets

Discipline. Humanists believed in discipline in the schools. It was a discipline of kindness than of vindictiveness. There was an appeal to pride and ambition in the child rather than to rigors of punishment.

Role of Teacher. It is the teacher who is the chief agent in this enterprise of sensible integration and success or failure depends upon his outlook and methods. It he lives a unified life himself, he will help his pupils to find a unity in the multiplicity of their experience, but if he is to do this he will need a different training from that which he has received in the past.

It requires intuition and imagination, insight and sympathy, faith and charity and wisdom that is bred of experience and these are the qualities over and above academic qualifications which we are seeking and finding in the humanistic teacher of today.

Developments Ahead

Humanism today is altogether different from what it was in the early days of its inception. The reason being that many factors in the passing years had influenced it and as such it had to change.

We shall briefly examine those factors and their influence on humanism.

Democracy and Humanism. The first factor that influenced it was the coming of democracy. In a democracy, we believe in the education of all and education for more and more people. When we have to educate all it is understood that curriculum has to be simplified. Old classics like Latin Greek lost their hold and importance. Common knowledge that was followed by all and understood by all was advocated. This aristocratic touch in the form of Latin and Greek stood abolished.

Language and Humanism. The second factor was that of acquiring a common language for mass education. Common language helps to promote religion even. Things of mind and philosophy were conveyed in very simple terms to people. Even Gandhiji was charmed by the language of the people.

Rationalism and Humanism. The third factor that influenced it was that it was an era of Nationalism and people had begun to take pride in what was their own. Accordingly came the literature in modern languages and this literature replaced the classics. The gap stood filled up.

New Subjects and Humanism. The coming of new subjects like Sociology, History etc. and the beginning of the era of science influenced humanism extremely. Scientists saw that Latin and Greek were obstacles in learning.

Philosophies and Humanism. Philosophies like naturalism and sense realism drew people to the teaching of knowledge through sense objects. Abstractions were ruled out.

In the light of the above changes, let us see what contributions did humanism make in education Today even Indian education has felt its impact. It is fair to say that our outlook in education is strongly tempered by humanism and the great majority of the teachers are ready to agree and cooperate about human ends in education.

After having studied the pros and cons of three schools of philosophy and their hearings on education, we may ask "which is the best philosophy which we must accept and adopt in our system of education?" The answer is that we must adopt all that is good in the three. We must follow what is called Eclectic approach in our education. Eclecticism means adopting good from all streams of thought.

It is indeed true that there must he some sort of meeting ground and various philosophies do meet at certain points. We will first see the areas of agreement in different philosophies and how educational thinking stands influenced by this agreement. Various philosophies agree at the following points.

Values. Values are of two types utilitarian and instrumental. Every philosophy holds the importance of studies in curriculum and equipment in class room in a way that they are of use to the children. This value of use is always accepted by all philosophies.

Again all philosophies agree that same values are aesthetic and they are to be enjoyed on their own or for their own sake.

Spiritual Aim. Whatever he the philosophy, it does accept one spiritual aim—aim of knowledge. All the philosophies strive to get knowledge. There is an indefinite quest for knowledge.

Consideration for Pupil. Consideration given to the pupil is the next thing where the philosophies agree. All philosophies recognise the dignity of the individual. This ensures some sort of freedom. So all philosophies profess their faith in theory of freedom because they have pupil's value.

All Philosophies Agree that All People must Get Education. That is why we are attending to backward areas.

Conserving the Past. All philosophies have another aim in common-conserving the past. Pragmatists, Idealists and Naturalists—all believe in conserving past.

All Philosophies have Some Norm (Criteria) in Selection of Social Heritage. Only nice things are cut out and preserved.

How This Agreement Influences Education?

Aims. All philosophies agree on proximate aims of education, although ultimate aims are different. Every philosophy enjoins upon educators to command over fundamental processes i.e. 3 R's, speaking, health, family life, civic and vocational relations.

Here all philosophies, agree. They differ only in how they will help in realising ultimate goals of education.

Curriculum. All philosophies agree that experience be taught to all i.e. history, grammar, logic, sizeable portion of race and physical sciences—all must learn.

Methods. All philosophies agree that there are several methods of teaching and their selection and depends upon circumstances or local conditions or equipment.

All philosophies believe in the utility of drill, in problem solving approach as life is full of problems so let children think and solve their problems.

Freedom in teaching methods is also accepted.

All philosophies believe in motivation of pupil and instructional principles. Individual differences are also accepted by every philosophy. Lastly all philosophies accept science of education. They recognise contribution of psychology.

All philosophies encourage child's association in running of school.

And all philosophies believe in providing good material, buildings, protection of pupil and his health care.

The Distinctions

Views About Order of Nature. To the concept of world and the notions of reality, the answer is different. If the philosophies profess their faith in temporal order, then they accept change as inevitable. Certainly then aims and curriculum of education must also change.

If philosophy has a belief in changeless, then it must also affect aim and curriculum.

Theory of Knowledge. Theory of knowledge pertains to how do we know the world? According to Naturalists, it is the experience of senses and their experiences are product of interaction between the individual and the environment. And they do not accept any final truth. Others believe in insight. Still others believe that knowledge is got from initiative.

Differences in Educational Outlook. These differences are there because of economical and racial outlook e.g., in U.S.A. despite all liberalism. Negroes are neglected. On the other hand, we have communists who educate all yet do not believe in liberalism.

Should education be subjected to the differences that do not promote harmony? Should we allow these differences? The answer is that these differences are not created by the philosophies—all are born alike. These differences are the outcome of social environments and social prejudices. We can eliminate and minimise these groups and differences. Science can help us in synthesising the philosophies.

Up-to-date Version

The Meaning. Humanism is a very old cult of philosophy. It has been interpreted in various ways, such as- a reasonable balance in life, vivid interest in all sides of life, freedom from religiosity, responsiveness to all human passions, a philosophy which holds that man is the centre and measure of all activities. It is in the last sense in which Humanism is generally understood since the sixteenth century, and it is with this that we are principally concerned in this chapter.

Humanism as a philosophy has its definite concept of man, human problems and universe. The term Humanism was used first for the first time by the sixteenth century writers and scholars of the European Renaissance. Today this term is used to convey a philosophical belief which believes in rendering service for the greater good of all humanity according to the demands of reason and democracy.

The Postulates

1. Humanism does not believe in supernaturalism. It regards nature as a system of constantly changing events. Hence the universe exists independently of mind.

2. Humanism believes in science and thinks that man being a product of nature is a part of it. Man's body and personality are inseparable. Hence he does not survive after death.

3. Humanism considers that human thinking is a result of the interaction between the complex living organism and the environment.
4. Humanism thinks that man is competent to solve all his problems on the basis of his own reason and scientific method.
5. Humanism believes that man is the maker and master of his own destiny.
6. Humanism thinks that man's happiness lies in this world. For the achievement of this happiness he should be made free in this world to progress culturally, economically and ethically.
7. Humanism wants to make man free to have the highest aesthetic experience of art and beauty.
8. Humanism stands for national and international democracy in order to establish an everlasting peace in the world.

The above eight points may sum up what Humanism stands for today. By the term Humanism it is understood today that man has a right to be happy. His happiness needs no justification. It does not require any support from any supernatural source. According to Humanism man is endowed with the requisite power to make this earth a place of peace and beauty. Humanism is against any tendency which is likely to encourage some kind of fatalism in man. It infuses hope and courage in man and reminds him that his only home is in this mundane world, so he must find his destiny here on this earth.

The ethics of Humanism is to serve one's fellowmen. Humanism may be regarded as human-being-ism. It believes in the interests of human beings. It does not tolerate any kind of discrimination against any race, community or nature. Modern Humanism stands for cosmopolitanism, international friendship and essential brotherhood of man.

Self-growth

According to Humanism this mighty and abundant nature

is our home. All marvels of life are produced by nature. We are sustained by nature. This earth has to be accepted as good. It is here that we can experience all worthwhile and happy existence of humanity. Men on this earth may possess all glories of art, culture and science. This life, earth and nature have to be accepted as total.

Different Approaches

Humanism holds that man is not an alien in this world. Today man is displaying an increasing control over the brute forces of nature. He can even foresee some of the cataclysms that usually took him by surprise in the past.

To Humanism mind is a function. Human thinking is as natural as walking or breathing, and it is indivisibly conjoined with the functioning of the brain.

Concept of Right to Liberty

The reality of human freedom has to be assumed. It is necessarily grounded in natural processes. It can prefer one thing to another and can adapt itself to all things. In fact, freedom comes out as a result of these qualities of preference and adaptability.

Logical Approach

Humanism stands for the method and spirit of science to all human problems. It believes that the acquisition of this method and spirit is far more important than acquiring information about facts. So, in the study of even the social sciences and in the world of public affairs we have to apply the scientific method and spirit. Humanism holds that in the absence of scientific methods man will face disastrous consequences in many of his endeavours and projects.

Moral Aspects

1. Humanism wants man to accept freely and happily the various great gifts of life. It further impresses the point that human life in its own right may be as splendid and beautiful as any concept of immortality. Humanism

emphatically accepts joys and beauties, the braveries and idealism of existence of this earth. It believes in the beauty of love and the love of beauty. The Humanist's emphasis is always affirmative and positive. He stands for the greater and more frequent and discrete enjoyment of earthly goods by all human beings everywhere and unendingly. Thus his ethics stands for buoyant this-worldliness and rejects ascetic other-worldliness. It is in favour of high standards in relation between the sexes, but it does not think that sexual emotions are evil in themselves. It does not want any supernatural explanation or sanctions at any ethical point. In solving any ethical problem, the Humanist relies upon reason based on the method of science. He does not depend upon any religious revelation or any kind of authority or intuition. He thinks that no human act is good or bad by itself. Its goodness or badness is to be judged in terms of its results for the individual and society. Thus he draws his guiding principles from human experience and wants to test them in human experience. The Humanist thinks that from the standpoint of human happiness today is just as important as tomorrow.

2. Humanism stands for modification and socialisation of human motives. Hence, human nature has to be reconditioned and reshaped, or regenerated. This is possible because human nature is essentially flexible and educable. The reconditioning and reshaping of human nature should take continuously throughout the whole, i.e., from birth till old age. Thus Humanism does not believe in the dictum that "You cannot change human nature." The reconditioning, reshaping and transformation of human nature has to be directed toward the good of the individual and society. Humanism defines man as what he does and likes to do. The Humanist concept of human personality rejects the false antithesis of the individual and society. So Humanism wants to carry out a systematic and skilful programme of training human motives and emotions in

order that the social and sympathetic propensities and impulses of human beings may be encouraged. It does not want to encourage the egoistic tendencies of man.

3. Humanism stands for an abundant life for the individual. It thinks that no human happiness is possible without good economic conditions. Hence the tremendous potentialities of modern technology must be utilised for ensuring abundance for man. It is on the basis of this utilisation that the good of the individual and of the society can be assured.

4. Humanism is apprehensive of the current danger of a third world war in which atom bombs, rockets, hydrogen bombs and bacteriological devices besides other weapons of mass destruction are likely to create alarming situations. But even in the face of this impending danger Humanism stands firm in its vision of the good of the entire humanity. Its note is always optimistic and positive as regards human welfare. Therefore, it advocates social cooperation for expanding the possibilities of individual fulfilment. So, its attitude is one of activism and not a passivity. For the fulfilment of the goal of human welfare, the Humanist wants that the individual must renounce some of his desires and observe some control and restraint over himself in the interest of ensuring human happiness on this earth.

Democratic Standpoint

1. From the ethics of Humanism we may safely infer that this philosophy stands for the widest possible application of democracy to all relevant aspects of human life. We have to keep in mind that the democratic spirit is not dogmatic. It recognises the value of constant challenges to basic assumptions. So no limit to the growth must always be conceived in a social context and this context implies the good of the entire mankind. Toward this end, Humanism wants people to rule themselves according to the principles of democratic governance. The people should be able to outline their own pattern

of freedom, happiness and progress. It is immaterial if they make mistakes in this process, because by doing so they will learn from their own experience and grow wiser.

2. Humanism thinks that democracy is of permanent validity for mankind. Democracy has not to be thought of in terms of political democracy alone, In fact, it must include within its purview, the social, economic, religious, philosophical, educational and various other aspects of human life. Complete and true Humanism implies a real full-fledged Humanism.
3. Humanistic religious education is based on secular point of view but it transcends secular education when it builds religious education on the base of secular education for its plus-value. This quest for "plus" values beyond secularism centres around some conception of God. Gandhi, Tagore, Vivekanand, Tilak, Dayanand Saraswati, Aurobindo, are some of the eminent Indian thinkers and educationists who subscribe to some sort of humanism in religious education. It makes religious education more tangible and relevant. Even the convent schools which swear by "moral" education, centre these religious teaching around Lord Jesus, without giving an obvious religious touch to the proceedings.

"Humanistic religious education is inclined to make his approach to God through the agency of human experience" (Brubacher). For him, all education has religious overtones and implications. Religious education therefore, is simply education, in the most complete sense of the term.

The Results

1. According to the ethics of Humanism schools, colleges, universities and research institutions will benefit greatly from the enlarged financial resources of the State, because these units of the society will be regarded as centres from which will flow all that is good and needed for the good of mankind. Due facilities will be made available for the advancement of all individuals irrespective of

caste, colour, creed and sex, rich and poor, high and low, dull and brilliant. In all the educational endeavours the accent will be social rather than only individualistic. This implies more emphasis on the study of social studies, such as, sociology, politics and economics. Ethics will be included in the curriculum in order to help the youth to imbibe broad Humanist attitudes which will imply loyalty to the social group and to mankind. The teaching of science and scientific method will be greatly emphasised. The students will be taught to learn how to think rather than to memorise individual facts. There will be no opposition between science and the humanities. Both will receive due attention without excluding either.

2. In the Humanist educational programme an attempt will be made to spread in the people a fundamental awareness of literature and art so that they may be able to appreciate and imbibe the good and beautiful in life. This will not mean lowering the standard of literature and art, but of raising the cultural standard of the people to unprecedented levels. Thus there will be a vast extension of institutional facilities from the primary education stage to the adult level. The administration of all types of schools, colleges and other educational institutions will be governed according to democratic principles. There will be academic freedom to all. Teachers and students will be free to establish and join organisations of their choice. There will be freedom of thought in all educational institutions. In the literary, artistic and intellectual fields, no undue pressure and deterrents, fears and conventions will be imposed because they are likely to cripple or kill freedom of thought, opinion and creativity.

Role of Tagore

Education has been defined as "a consciously controlled process whereby changes in behaviour are produced in a person, and through him, in a group". It is a gradual adjustment of the individual to the spiritual possessions of the race. Hence, education is considered to be normative in that it explores various aspects of human personality so as to prescribe a generally suitable and acceptable programme of learning which should be conducive for the attainment of its objectives and goals. However, there has been a continuous change in the nature, extent and import of these objectives which are inversely related to the meaning and reality ascribed to human nature and to the environment in which education takes place. Hence, education is in dire need of some sort of a philosophy which may provide it with direction and roots, stability and purpose.

Life is dynamic, it is a continuous change. Since education invariably occurs in a social matrix, it also acquires the same characteristic. The ideals of life are eternally at variance, due to contemporary socio-economic conditions and political ideology, and their conflict for whatever reason, reflects itself in educational theories. Hence, as long as life is what it is, there can not be a universal aim of education. In all ages the singular aim of education had been to educate man to achieve his complete self in accordance with the concepts prevalent from time to time. Education therefore, is a means to achieve philosophical aim.

An interesting corollary of the normative functions of philosophy in the field of education has been that their exponents are possessed by their respective philosophies as the final means of shaping the young minds toward attainment of prescribed goals. Education, in this sense, is an offshoot of philosophy and it translates those desirable objectives through its inherent processes and spells out means for doing so. Ross speaks of this "inevitable tendency of the philosophers to turn into educationist" as the great philosophers of all ages and of all countries, have also been great educators. This is but logical because if one does not preach his own philosophy who else would and the best means of preaching one's philosophy is to ensure it as an instrument of human regeneration. Rabindranath Tagore based his philosophy of education on human regeneration. The main tenet of his philosophy is the ultimate affinity between Man, Nature and God. His educational philosophy is an attempt at self-realisation by means of communion with nature and God. He lays special emphasis on education as a means of self-realisation which consists in the realisation of the universal soul in one's self. According to him "the fundamental purpose of education is not merely to enrich ourselves through the fullness of knowledge but also to establish the bond of love and friendship between man and man".

The spark of divinity that Tagore saw in man lends a special significance and import to his philosophy of education as it singles him out as a visionary who had his feet planted on firm ground. His philosophy is as much relevant today as it was during his time: it is a philosophy of love and compassion responsive to human hopes and despair. It is a philosophy of man in search of himself in this myriad of wonderland called universe. Man is not only the centre of this edifice but is the "measure and the sanction of all things".

Tagore believes that the chief end of human life is to work for happiness of man upon this earth within the confines of nature which is his home. His philosophy of education is an elaboration of this central theme and provides ample opportunities to reconcile and resolve apparent anomalies in our day to day life. Tagore is a champion of humanity, of human values and ideals. His philosophy of education aims at producing enfranchised citizens who may hold their heads high without any fear in their hearts.

1. Rabindranath Tagore was one of those contemporary philosophers of education who may be called humanist in the most strict sense of the term. His humanism is not naturalistic but is integral to the tradition of Indian humanism. His philosophy was cosmopolitan humanism of which his theory of education was a direct corollary.

2. The aim of education, according to Rabindranath was self-realisation. He was a great poet and a saint who, through his imagination and insight, realised the universal soul within himself and in Nature. This realisation by every one, according to him, was the goal of education, Self-realisation means the realisation of the universal soul in one's self. Man's aim in life is to achieve this status, a process which cannot be realised without education. Education, therefore, is integral to

life. In the absence of education the individual will be deprived of self-realisation. Rabindranath did not find any incompatibility between thought and life, philosophy and education: both are inversely related and are inclusive of each other.

3. Rabindranath believed that every one is potentially divine and every one can realise this potentially. Man has a spark of divinity in him which inspires him for self-attainment, self-realisation, the realisation of his true nature. Education should, therefore, provide opportunities to harness these innate potentialities. His philosophy was influenced by the great Indian traditions contained in the Gita and the Upanishads, though Rabindranath had the added advantage of familiarity with the educational ideas prevalent in the west. Therefore, like other Indian humanists, he synthesised the ancient Vedic traditions with the modern western scientific attitudes in formulating the goals of education.

Cosmic Man's Concept

1. Tagore's philosophy of education can not be understood without understanding his metaphysical theory which revolves around the concept of Cosmic Man: a vision, a poet's dream which Tagore cherished and lived by. Referring to Cosmic Man as the ultimate reality Tagore said: Truth is the infinite pursued by metaphysics, Fact is the infinite pursued by science, while Reality is the definition of the infinite which relates truth to the person. Reality is human: it is what we are conscious of, by which we are affected, that which we express". The Cosmic Man is known by individual not by his reason or logic but through direct realisation, a sort of communion. In the words of Tagore "Reality, in all its manifestations, reveals itself in the emotional and imaginative background of our mind, we know it, not because we think of it, but because we directly feel it. It is not banished from our conscious mind". This further affirms Tagore's emphasis on the feeling aspect of human

experience. He considered man more central to the scheme of things. Man is more than reason, a soul, a spirit, a finite-infinite being, an angel who seems to have lost his wings, and is now in the process of becoming.

2. The idea of Cosmic Man is in conformity with the message in the Gita: the message of Vishvaroopi Darshan. The Cosmic Man is at the back of all movement, all change, all order and system in the universe: he is the measure of everything and is central to all movement. The relation between him and Nature is pantheistic which finds meaning in the concept of God. Cosmic Man includes both Nature and God. Rabindranath admitted "I have never looked at God, Man and Nature as problems which can be considered in isolation from each other. I could never conceive of their occupying watertight compartment". Cosmic Man lives even in the humblest person, therefore, even the lowliest of the low should not suffer from personal and social neglect. The worship of the poor is the direct corollary of Tagore's vision of the Cosmic Man. He said "He is where the tiller is tilling the hard ground, where the path-maker is breaking the stones. He is with them in sun and shower, and His garment is covered with dust (and sweat). Put off your holy mantle and like Him come down on the dusty soil". That work is worship, was an essential tenet of Tagore's Cosmic Man, and he lived by it.

3. Concerning the metaphysical problem arising from assigning personality to the ultimate reality, it should be remembered that for Rabindranath personality is not something limited and mundane but unlimited and supra-mundane. While in the man it is found in the first form, in Cosmic Man it may be seen in the second meaning. Elucidating this meaning of Cosmic Man he writes "This personality which is the conscious principle of oneness, the centre of relationships, is the reality ... therefore the ultimate object of attainment ... this world

exists only in its relation to a central personality. When that centre is taken away, it falls to pieces, become a heap of abstractions, matter and force, logical symbols, and even those, the thinnest semblance of reality, would vanish ... if the logical person in the centre to whom they are related in some harmony of reason were no where. He is more for the 'saguna' form of reality rather than 'nirguna' form of reality which blinds human mind and soul by its sheer brilliance.

4. God is the perfect person, Man is a person in an imperfect sense: he is always in the process of becoming, moving towards the attainment of his true self. He is an individual whereas God is a person. He is a Cosmic Man. He is the super person who is seen in different forms which are virtually all-inclusive. He is anthropomorphic and is endowed with human attributes which make Him intelligible to man. It is in Him that human beings share their experiences. "The relational world is for the both individual and universal. My world is mine but it is also yours... it is not in my own individual personality that Reality is contained, but in an infinite personality."

5. Tagore avoids the sophistic and mentalistic tendencies inherent in the philosophy of Berkeley, as well as the pitfalls of the philosophy of Nietzsche whose super man is the negation of both man and Reality. Tagore's idea of Cosmic Man is human, is in and through the work and toil that spells human life, is responsive to human hopes and despair.

Nature of Humanbeings

1. Reality according to Tagore is one in which God, Nature and Man reside in a spirit of intimate relationship. The three are infact three dimensions of the same reality. Man is intimately related to God and Nature. Man and Nature are but two expressions of the same Divine. Divinity is pantheistic, it runs in and through the fabric of all creation; it permeates the cosmos. In his philosophy

of education, Rabindranath considers the intimate relationship of man and nature as the basis of self-realisation. His system accepts both in a spirit of mutual dependence and harmony. Nature is propitious, is conducive toward man's attainment of his spiritual and material excellence. Nature and Man are mutually amenable. Tagore says "In the west the prevalent feeling is that Nature consists exclusively of inanimate things and beasts, that there is sudden unaccountable break where human-nature begins. According to it, everything that is low in the scale of beings is merely Nature, and whatever has the stamp of perfection in it, intellectual and moral, is human nature ... the Indian mind never has any hesitation in acknowledging its kinship with Nature, its unbroken relation with all".

2. The intimate relationship between man and nature is the hallmark of Indian thought. This relation is conceived as companionship, a permanent source of inspiration, a state of communion. A life divorced from nature can not be a complete life. According to Tagore, even in the liberated state, our relationship with Nature continues. "The soul's birth in the spiritual world does not coincide with severance of relationship with what we call Nature, but freedom of relationship".

3. It was this firm conviction of the intimate relationship between man and Nature that made Tagore emphasise so much on the natural environment in schools. He wanted that "young mind should be saturated with the idea that it has been born in a human world which is in harmony with the world around it". Even the superiority of man lies in his ability to be in union with Nature, an ability which is not quite possessed by other living beings.

Derived from Latin 'Homo' meaning human being, Humanism is the philosophy in which man is the measure of everything. In historical retrospect whatever had been found to be useful for human welfare has been attached with the concept of humanism. Such as the idea of social welfare, scientific attitude, progress of democratic institutions and other such concepts emerging out of the process of democratisation of man and society are concentrated in Humanism. As a philosophy, humanism has a definite notion regarding man, his problems and universe. Greatest good of the greatest number according to democratic means is the mainstay of this social and philosophical concept. Its major contributions have been:-

(a) Belief in life in harmony with the noblest ideas and the highest values.

(b) Affirms the dignity of man.

(c) Faith in the necessity of establishing a social order based on peace.

(d) Commitment to peace as a meaningful concept must have far reaching influences on the social and educational aspects of a society.

The educational impact, in brief, is as under-

(a) Education is considered an important part of man and society.

(b) Education has a creative role in establishing an ideal society.

(c) Education is an agency of freedom and responsibility.

(d) Employment-oriented education.

To sum up, man is not only the centre, he is the measure and the sanction of all things. Humanism believes that the chief end of human life is to work for happiness of man upon this earth within the confines of nature which is his home.

Pointing out the human element in Tagore's philosophy, Humayun Kabir wrote "Rabindranath Tagore was one of the greatest humanists that the world has known. The keynote of his life was resistance to tyranny in all forms. He struggled against economic exploitation, political subjugation, social inertia, injustice, religious intolerance and insensitiveness". These words, however, do not convey the most important aspect of Tagore as a humanist. Undoubtedly he fought for human virtues but the more important point is that he presented a humanistic philosophy and a religion of man which again were the foundation stone of a gigantic system of humanistic education.

Tagore was essentially a poet therefore his Humanism is generally expressed in his literature. Pointing out this facet, K.Sen writes "Humanity is the very epitome of the wide and varied universe. To know it properly is to realise the highest manifestation of Brahma since in all its worldwide aspect humanity is permeated with the spirit of God. The universal greatness of humanity has truly found its triumphant poetic expression in our age in the literature of Rabindranath".

Besides literature Tagore's Humanism is expressed by his idea of religion of man. His works bear testimony to his unstinted emphasis upon the uniqueness of the human individual, his greatness in the world of the living, and his intimate relationship with Nature and God. It was due to his Humanism that while he opposed the British, he was not against the British people. It was again his humanism which made him work relentlessly for the establishment of a cosmopolitan educational institution in the form of Shantiniketan. His educational system is as much the embodiment of his Humanism as his literature is its expression.

13

Pragmatic Theory

"Pragmatism is essentially a humanistic philosophy maintaining that man creates his own values in course of activity; that reality is still in the making, and awaits its part of completion from the future" (Ross). Pragmatism, as such, is an attitude of mind which views that reality is in a flux, in a continuous process of action, making and dissolution, and is in a state of becoming, responding vigorously to the needs and demands of human experiences, and fluctuating with the insight and progress that man may acquire during his journey on earth. Man is central to all creation and his experiences determine the nature and extent of reality of truth. He is measure of every thing. Life, therefore, is experiential, is growing and, is progressive: moving forward, creating in the process new and emergent values useful in this progression and development.

Utility and results are the touchstones of the values that emerge from this evolution. Nothing is absolute except, perhaps, change which is the heart and soul of pragmatism: change, therefore, is real though "things change neither at the same time nor at the same rate" (Brubacher), thus giving an impression of continuity and progress finding its vindication in experience.

The Concept

Derived from Greek pragma meaning activity, and pragmatics meaning practicability or utility, Pragmatism is described by Reid as "activity, engagement, commitment and encounter". Activity and utility are considered as central to this doctrine which neither believes in idealism nor in naturalism, though Brubacher refers to it as pragmatic naturalism as against Rousseau's romantic naturalism.

He further suggests that it could even be called instrumental or experimental naturalism as the three terms, pragmatism, instrumentalism and, experimentalism are interchangeable, and assume the basic character of man and nature. As such, pragmatism believes in experiment as the only criterion of Truth and, experience as the only instrument of knowledge, the two being together in an integrated manner, changing from place to place and from time to time. Change, therefore, is the essence of Pragmatism.

Role Players

Peirce, William James, John Dewey, Kilpatrik all Americans, and Schiller are the Chief exponents of Pragmatism in its modern form.

Definition

1. "Pragmatism offers us a theory of meaning, a theory of truth of knowledge, and a theory of reality". (J.B. Prett)
2. "Pragmatism is essentially a humanistic philosophy, maintaining that man creates his own values in the course of activity, that reality is still in the making and awaits its part of completion from the future, that to an unascertainable extent our truths are man-made products" (Ross).
3. "Pragmatism is merely a state in the development of a new idealism that will do justice to reality, reconcile the practical and spiritual values, and result in culture which is the flower of efficiency and not the negation of it" (Ross).

Significant Facets

Action rather than Thought : Though thought creates means for action yet it is subservient to action. Proper and suitable thought would create proper and suitable means for action. Ideas are the tools.

Experiment as a Source of Verification : Knowledge is through observation which is vindicated by verification. Thoughtful action by its very nature is a kind of testing of provisional conclusions and hypotheses. Experiment makes a thought pure and is its justification.

Practical Experience : In contrast to Idealism which considers education as the dynamic side of philosophy, Pragmatism considers philosophy to be the outcome of educational practices. Practical consequences or results are basic to this doctrine and help evaluate experiences.

Utility : Only those experiences are accepted as true which on evaluation yield utility, purpose or, result.

Man is the Measure : Only those activities which are likely to be useful to man should be taken recourse to, as there is no need to pile up knowledge which has no relevance and significance to life. As such whatever measures upto man's requirements should be central to knowledge.

Mirrors American Society : Though having its origin in Sophist philosophy of the Greeks and passing through a grand galaxy of philosophers like Socrates, Hume, Bacon, Locke and Berkeley, Pragmatism in modern times found its application in the American philosopher, C.S. Peirce in 1878 when he asserted "our beliefs are really the rules for action". William James, another American, carried on the torch later picked up by John Dewey and Kilpatrick, both Americans. It is, therefore, strongly believed that Pragmatism mirrors the American way of life and is in accordance with the American genius which was confronted with changed circumstances, thus initiating a new approach to problem solving through practicability, utility and usefulness. Relevance became the key word which considered life compulsions and circumstances as the sole criteria of growth and development of reality and truth. It is a forward-looking, dynamic way of life looking for new environment, pastures, circumstances and opportunities. It is a response to challenges of life, as and when they show up.

No Fixed Principles : As reality is in a state of flux, Pragmatism does not believe in fixed principles: reality is in the making and principles emerge in interaction with experiences, their verification and utility.

No Verbosity : Verbalism was considered the greatest bane of traditional educational practices causing referent confusion, boredom and monotony, and making teaching-learning a dull and drab affair. There is no scope for verbalism in Pragmatism as it goes for direct experiences felt on one's own pulse. Show rather than Tell.

No Closed System : Pragmatism does not believe in absolutes. Life is an open book, the script of which is written by the individual himself in accordance with his experiences. As such, Pragmatism prefers concreteness to abstruseness. Let life be as clear and distinct as first-hand direct experiences in their totality and fullness.

No Fixed Values : Values are in the making and exist in the world outside. As such, they are empirical and subject to a possible change, hence transitional and not fixed, standard or, absolute.

Emphasis on Social Interaction : Social interaction helps polish one's personality as it is in this context that man acquires and develops such tangible graces like humility, love, sympathy, cooperation and, fellow feelings, that help him adjust and be a useful member of his group. Personality develops through interaction.

Spirit of Enquiry : As reality is in the making, the only way to understand it is by enquiry which is the basic source of knowledge in Pragmatism. Enquiry implies open-minded forthright, honest, inquisitive, practical and experimental bent of mind, which is a fair reflection of the American attitude toward reality, nature and truth. Dewey defines Inquiry as the "controlled or directed transformation of an indeterminate situation into one that is so determinate in its constituent distinctions and relations as to convert the elements of the original situation into a unified whole" and that "inquiry is concerned with objective transformations of objective subject-matter". It is a general process of attempting to make the world more organic as an inquiry yields unified wholes. Truth is the outcome of inquiry and Dewey quotes Peirce that "Truth is the opinion which is fated to be ultimately agreed to by all who investigate".

Forms of Pragmatism

1. *Humanistic Pragmatism:* It considers only those things or principles as true which satisfy the needs, requirements, aspirations and goals of human beings thus furthering the cause of mankind. Truth is the index of human satisfaction. "Whatever fulfils my purpose, satisfies my desires, develops my life, is true." Hence, Truth is relative, and contingent subject to satisfying human needs.
2. *Experimental Pragmatism:* According to Experimental Pragmatism only those things and principles are true which can be verified by experiment: Whatever can be experimentally verified is true, or what works is true. "Truth is the opinion which is fated to be ultimately agreed by all who investigate", it is, therefore, the outcome of experimental verification.
3. *Biological Pragmatism:* Brubacher calls it pragmatic naturalism. According to it whatever helps one adjust and adapt with environment or, help change the environment, is valuable and important. Truth, therefore, is biologically useful. Dewey says "the test is found in the function of thought, in adapting the human organism to its environment". It may also be called Instrumentalism as it considers thought as a means, an instrument, for solving problem-situations to achieve adjustment and harmony. It is also called as Chicago School of Thought, as Dewey propounded it while working at Chicago University.

Cardinal Rules

Changing Nature of Truth : As reality is in a state of flux, as such, truth may change from time to time, place to place, and has no element of finality in it.

Truth Lies in Successful Application and Results : It is not fixed or absolute, and is a relative term with relation to situations and circumstances that it may help a person to cope up with, hence is formed by its results.

Problems Act as Motivators for Truth : It is discovered in problem-solving or, as Dewey says, help in developing unified wholes.

Faith in Social Interaction : It is the sole source of human development, and help acquire desirable social and moral attitudes.

Principle of Utility : As seen earlier, utility is the touchstone. Only those things or principles are true which serve some purpose and, are useful, "It is true because it is useful" (William James).

No Fixed Values and Ideals : Truth by nature is transient, hence no hankering after permanence. Values and ideals are in the making, hence temporal. Values and ideals would change with circumstances. Nothing fixed.

Human Initiative : Pragmatism has total faith in man's prowess, capacities and initiative, as man is competent to mould his circumstances to his advantage as well as to that of society. Man is the creator of his environment, and has unbridled initiative in this regard.

Activity as Central : Action precedes thought and is its forerunner. Thought is the outcome of action, hence action/activity is central to human life wherein man is an active being. Learning by Doing is a necessary corollary of this principle.

Forward Looking : Pragmatism does not brood about the past, which is gone and dead. Life concerns the present and the immediate future, not very long distant. It again smacks of the practical attitude of the pragmatists; control your present, make it as flourishing and fruitful as possible, because you have a hold only on the present which one may manipulate to the best of one's advantage and ability.

Pluralistic : Pragmatism considers reality as pluralistic, neither monistic nor dualistic, hence truth is also pluralistic determined by man's experience. It sees "no necessity for seeking one fundamental principle or explanation is content to admit several principles and, accordingly is pluralistic" (Rusk).

Flexibility : Life is flexible and so is reality; nothing is fixed; everything is in a flux, is changing. This gives one a lever to deal with circumstances in search of unified whole which is the building material of knowledge and truth. Flexibility gives maneuverability, freedom and openness. Apply all your faculties and experiences to the circumstances that confront you at the moment, with no hang up, and forge ahead on the way to progress and development. Flexibility gives freedom of application.

Reality in Making : As nothing is fixed and absolute, permanent and transcendental, truth is in the process of becoming what it may depending on the intervention and manipulation of man and circumstances. As such, man is the creator of truth which is subject to change according to his experiences.

Diverse Role in Education

Progressive education spurred the present extensive interest in educational philosophy of which Pragmatism may be considered as the root. The keyword is progressive and needs attention. Progress, if one may recall, is naturalistic and implies change which in turn yields novelty. Novelty and Change are the crux of the world which confront the pupil.

As the two characteristics of human experience create situations and circumstances that need to be resolved, one turns to problem-solving attitude of mind which helps develop initiative and self-reliance notwithstanding individual differences. The progressive education has a specific criterion as it does not accept any general formula or, fixed values. Progressive educational philosophy centres around pupil-interest, capabilities, aptitudes, needs and aspirations, which in turn determine its educational aims, learning programmes/materials, and the means of putting these across for pupil-comprehension, learning. Progressive education is modern education which is primarily child-oriented. Pragmatism is one such version.

The Features

We may conclude from the above discussion what could possibly be the characteristics of pragmatic education:-

Education is Life-related : Experiences are the sole source of knowledge; experiences are life, hence experiences are life-related, and education, in as much as it concerns experience, is life-related, and provides a child with concrete and specific opportunities to enable a child create his value-world for a better, happier and, fruitful life.

Education is Growth : Life is change, so is society. Education should create such circumstances that it helps the growth and development of the individual as well as society. Growth occurs through change and is continuous. Education, therefore, is a continuous, unending process of growth and development.

Reconstruction of Experiences : There would hardly be any state in which man is not experiencing. These experiences are, however, in a state of flux, and need orientation or reorganisation into unified wholes which constitute reality, transforming child behaviour into a characteristic pattern of adjustment and personality structure. Dewey described education as a "process of reconstruction or reinstitution of experiences".

Social Process : Education is an interactive process that takes place in a social matrix, helping a child not only to acquire knowledge and information through experience, but also help him to acquire socially desirable attitudes, habits and qualities, which would eventually help him for social adjustment, well-being and happiness. Education should make a child better adjusted toward himself and society.

State Responsibility : Ministry of Human Resource Development is responsible to provide facilities, direction and guidance to society for the development of all in accordance with their ability, interest and aptitude. State should not control education, and should only spell out general line of direction in discharge of its constitutional obligations.

Educational Impact

Aims : The progressives or pragmatists do not consider any aims or values fixed in advance. Aims and values emerge during reconstruction of experiences, and as such no way to education is true way. Aims of education, therefore, are emergent and subject to change from time to time. As seen earlier, pragmatism is a "humanistic philosophy" and that "man creates his own values in course of activity." To quote Ross "the most general educational aim of the pragmatists is just the creation of new values". Secondly, education should enable the human being to be fairly adjusted to his immediate environment. "The social objective of education may be conceived as a better organised environment". Thirdly, education should create dynamic adaptability and problem-solving capacity of an individual in a social matrix. When Dewey said "Education, as such, has no aim", what he meant was that it has no prefixed or absolute aim as such, and that aims of education are emergent, are responsive to the experiences of man. In nutshell, education must foster competence in children, and that will be an all-inclusive aim.

The Curriculum

If curriculum is constructed in accordance with the aims of education, it shall give place only to those subjects of study which fulfil these aims according to this philosophy. Pragmatistic philosophy gives several criteria for the construction of curriculum.

Principle of Utility : The curriculum should provide only that information which is beneficial to the pupils. Subject should impart practical knowledge and useful skills to the students. These skills should also prepare them for future life. Thus, the curriculum should include physical training, hygiene, language, history, geography, mathematics and sciences. For girls domestic Sciences or Home Sciences and for boys agricultural sciences are prescribed. This criterion supports the view of vocational training after a satisfactory and requisite general education. Different studies are preferred, but the nature of these studies must be problem-solving.

Child's Natural Interests : Stages of development are followed by the stages of interests. The curriculum should be constructed in due regard of these stages of development and interests of the children.

"The child in the elementary school is interested in conversation or communication, inquiry, construction and artistic expression; hence the elementary school curriculum will include such tools of knowledge as reading, writing, counting and nature study, hand work and drawing."

Child's Occupation and Activities :This principle in regard to curriculum construction stresses the necessity of child's own experiences in the field of education, "Book-learning" as with the Naturalists is not preferred by the Pragmatic School of Philosophy. In the curriculum the activities must be purposeful. As observed by an eminent educationist, "If these activities take the character of the activities of the Community of which the School is an organ, they will develop moral virtues, result in attitudes of initiative and independence and will give training in citizenship and promote self-discipline."

The Principle of Integration : The principle of integration is very important in curriculum construction. According to this, Pragmatists believe in the unity of knowledge and skill, Subject wise independent teaching will not suffice of the purpose of bringing about integration. Pragmatist warns us against teaching subjects as "watertight compartments." In the words of Descartes "All the true learning must be integral and the educators ought to abstain from dividing and parcelling out what nature has made one and indivisible."

Methods of Teaching

Traditional and customary teaching is not preferred by Pragmatists. They want to create new procedure by adopting a new method. In the view of Pragmatists the method which is based on the child's interest and is able to solve the problem of the child, is most preferable. Child is the centre of the educational system.

The teacher must be experimental in his dealings and should not be the follower of established principles and fixed methods. Pragmatists say that we may accept a principle only after testing and examining. "Principles and methods of teaching should be forged afresh in the light of real-life situations."

Relation with Life : The first principle should be to establish a relation with the life of the child. The method should not be apart from child's real life situations. His interest, desires and inclinations should also be considered while adopting a method of teaching. "The most effective learning comes from whole hearted purposeful activities."

Principle of Action or "Learning by Doing" : Pragmatism believes in actual working. Merely theoretical knowledge or facts are not at all accepted by this philosophy. A pragmatist believes in the fact that learning process should be rooted in experience. In other word this philosophy accepts the principle of 'learning by doing.' According to Ryburn "experience is the first and best master" whose lessons we never forget. The child has a natural aptitude for doing and making things. This principle stresses the fact that a child should be put into real situations, and through education he should be able to study those situations intelligently and to solve them absolutely.

Principle of Integration : The whole learning process should be based on the 'Principle of integration'. A human mind has no watertight compartments, therefore knowledge and skill should also be integrally imparted. The integration or correlation should lie in the different subjects and also in the different aspects within a subject. Various aspects of learning should be integrated as a whole. Gestalt Psychology also believes in the 'whole'. According to this psychology learning process should run from 'whole to part'.

Concept of Project Method

After considering these principles, the 'project method' is introduced. This method implies all the principles and fulfils the conditions of a good learning process. This method is enunciated by Kilpatrick. While defining a project he says that it is "A whole hearted purposeful activity, proceeding in a social environment."

The boys should be clearly told about the task they are going to perform, and they should also know why and how do they do that.

Experimental Method : Another significant contribution of pragmatism is "Experimental Method" which holds that knowledge is gained after experimentation. Like Socrates, pragmatist wants "his pupils to think and act for themselves, to do rather than to know, to organise rather than repeat." Only those techniques of teaching are valid that would cultivate a dynamic and adaptable mind. This method is nothing more than helping the students to use intelligence, and solve problems that are meaningful to the child.

Role of Teacher

A teacher's work is to guide and put a child in the real situation of his life, so that he might be able to understand his life's problems and thereby solve them. Pupils should be inspired to follow the principle of "learning by doing or learning through experience."

"Doing is more important than knowing, like Socrates the pragmatist teacher wants his pupils to think and act for themselves to do rather than to know, to originate rather than to repeat." A teacher must also be a practical man. His teaching should not be based on lecturing and repeating only. He should create a problem solving attitude in his pupils.

Significant Role in Discipline

Pragmatism believes in social discipline. Personal discipline is disapproved by this philosophy. Dewey says that discipline is a 'mental attitude' and in order to maintain this attitude, socialised activities are essential. Project method deals with all such essentials. Socialised activities' can be easily performed in 'social project'. Cooperative feelings and socialistic attitude can be developed through various project techniques. Pragmatists believe that 'play' and 'work' should be combined and this combination will perform a mental attitude—discipline, inner discipline cannot be maintained through force and domination. Children should be left free in order to develop freely and harmoniously. Let the children feel that disciplined mind and actions are the part and parcel of human development.

According to pragmatists, rewards and punishments are of no significance in the process of learning. All the activities are done in a social sphere. In society, according to pragmatism, every member should be treated equally. No fixed moral standards or values should be accepted. These standards are established through their own experiences by every new generation.

In this way, this philosophy believes in discipline, but the discipline should not be the outcome of external force, it should be backed with freedom and joy.

The Evaluation

Pragmatism, in spite of its progressiveness, is antitraditional; against everything that has any claim for permanence and absolute, and reduces the world and reality to a state of flux and reconstruction. It has the following limitations:-

The Limitations

Opposition to Eternal Truths : Pragmatism believes in plurality of truths, each one designed and contrived by individual experiences, and changing with time and place. Results may not always justify truth; there may be something that transcends experience and points toward a non-experiential permanence; primordial and basic. It has no place for truth for truth's sake as it makes truth contingent.

No Fixed Values : As reality is in a state of flux, there would not be any fixed, predetermined values and ideals which are created by circumstances: values are experiential, circumstantial, emergent. It is a necessary corollary of negation of eternal truths, how could predetermined values and ideals exist in a world where there is no eternal truth; contingency of truth reduces values to superficiality.

Aims of Education : As Dewey says "there are no aims of education". He says so because the end results of education, if any, may be incidental, a matter of chance. It is stretching change rather too far: change is not chance and education cannot be a rudderless ship on the high seas without a compass and bearing. A directionless education is a purposeless activity leading not even to chance. Pragmatic education may suit the American people, but round the world, there are countless people who look to education for permanence, inspiration and direction. It would be unkind to say that "no way to education is true". (Brubacher)

No Spiritual Values : By not supporting spiritual and cultural values, pragmatism is proving its logical consistency as anything beyond experience is contradictory to the basic tenets of pragmatism. That reality is empirical and not temporal may run counter to the faith and belief of as many people, if not more, who support it for its empirical satisfaction and utility. Is life only a utility-service? Has past no place in the history and achievement of a people? The fact is that the Americans do not have a history, they only have a comfortable geography which tucks them away at a safe distance, meddling at will. See in contrast Churchill's History of the English Speaking World wherein every word stands for permanence, authority, grace and benevolence because a world of English speaking world exists outside the geography of the Island-state, and integrates people with divergent background into a formidable whole: pity, Americans do not even speak English.

Limited Use of Intelligence : Pragmatic theory of truth "implies very distinctive role for intelligence" (Brubacher). It is more an instrument of verification and helps adaptation with precariously shifting environment". This is also in line with the pragmatist line of thought which places exclusive emphasis on experimentation. But, is it the be all? Is intelligence only adaptation? Is intelligence subservient to innate tendencies or, is intelligence itself an innate and basis ability which controls, directs and moulds man's innate tendencies? As a matter of fact, Pragmatism treats man at his animal level, anything more or less, is merely incidental and contingent. It is an extremely skewed view of intelligence, hence unpsychological.

Denial of Past : We have made passing references to the fact that Pragmatism is essentially an American creed developed in consonance with the American ethos and psyche. As such, it does not consider past of any consequential relevance, and is dead. Even the distant future has no place in this doctrine, only the present and the immediate future have any empirical relevance. All because, the Americans have no past, have no history except of slavery and deprivation. Their attitude, therefore, is to break away from it, in search of new pastures and glory.

Delimitation of Formal Curriculum : If experience is the only source of knowledge, it would be rather difficult to select projects from the natural circumstances, situations and environment. Hence, it may tend to be repetitive, which of course is a fact if one goes around and inspects the so called project work at various levels commencing from class X of ICSE/CBSE boards, and even higher classes, thus affecting the originality of the project.

No Formal Education : Advocating direct first hand experience as the sole source of information, Dewey plays low on formal, direct, interactive classroom teaching-learning situations. Edgar Dale, another American genius and the father of modern Audiovisual education, put direct-firsthand-experiences at the base of his Cone of Experience and went up along the various bands to the most abstract, conical position. What the Cone suggests is that the first band is so placed because of intensity and directness of experience, and it in no way decries the importance of other learning materials placed in order of increasing abstractness, thus making formal learning as much relevant, though recommending that the learning should not shift so much away from the first band that one lands in totally unfamiliar, abstract and abstruse situations, and that learning should be as near to the first band as possible and desirable.

Pluralistic Concept of Truth : As truth is emergent, contingent and incidental, it is neither monistic nor dualistic, but pluralistic. There would be as many truths as thrown up by circumstances, making truth as a flexible outcome of experience multiplying through activity. This lackadaisical treatment of Truth is, to say the least, unwarranted and inadequate as one does look for primordial, fixed and absolute truth which may act as a beacon in the pursuit of the real.

But it may be said that by sticking to the pluralistic concept of truths, Pragmatism avoids any contradiction with its basic tenets and maintains a logical consistency within the system.

Excellent Method : Restricted to its methodology, Pragmatism is an excellent means of acquiring knowledge and information. In fact, but for its methodology, Pragmatism does not have much to convey as it ends up generally in negation of the established theories and practices. Even William James accepts that Pragmatism is not a school of philosophy when he says "there is absolutely nothing new in the pragmatic method it is just an empirical attitude has no dogmas and no doctrines save its methods". The experimental method does help in developing an inquisitive mind, a progressive attitude and open mindedness.

The Merits : In spite of the above-mentioned limitations, Pragmatism has a great message for education in that it lays exclusive emphasis on some progressive aspects of modern teaching-learning technology. In this respect, even some of the objections mentioned earlier would also turn to its advantage as there is nothing much wrong in them except their exclusiveness and narrow application. With this we turn to the positive side of pragmatism in educational process.

Project Method : Project method is the lasting and exclusive contribution of Pragmatism in the field of educational activity. It enables a child to be creative and responsible to natural circumstances using manipulation and intelligence, resulting in his natural progress and development. A child learns to manage himself as well as his surroundings.

"Crucial in the pragmatic or experimental way of gaining truth is methodology" which defines the difficulty as precisely as possible, surveys the "resources available for its solution", and proposes a hypothesis which is later "put to the test". Activities are initiated at this stage to match the results thrown up by the corresponding circumstances with the consequences expected out of the project.

Child-centred Approach : In contrast to the traditional approaches to learning, Pragmatism lays exclusive emphasis on child, his growth and development in accordance with his interests, ability, aptitudes, needs and aspirations; child is the focal point and everything else is oriented around him. Thus all aspects of an educational activity, such as aims, curriculum, method etc. are valid only if they help a child develop his individuality.

Activity Oriented : Credit goes to Pragmatism for its activity-oriented approach to teaching-learning. Child is playful and active by nature and Pragmatism capitalises on this tendency. Learning by Doing, therefore, is a major contribution of this doctrine. This relates to the importance of activity curriculum, as the activities are "necessary both to make education lifelike and to make life yield the truth" (Brubacher). For pragmatism, knowledge is "wrought out in action" short of which it only remains information. "Information becomes knowledge when it is judged to be relevant to the solution of a particular problem". This judgement is later "tested in the crucible of experience". Throughout this process there remains an exclusive stress on activity. That explains why in pragmatism programme is activity-oriented.

Life Related : Experiences are related to a child's life. Therefore, teaching should be through life-related situations and prepare a child for life. Teaching-learning should, therefore, be pragmatic to life.

Social and Democratic Education : Freedom is the keynote of pragmatic approach to teaching-learning wherein a child is free to negotiate circumstances in his individual manner and thereby develop self-confidence, initiative, equality and entrepreneurship, democratic values, mutual well-being and social efficiency which would make him a gainfully and harmoniously adjusted person. "Society is a mode of shared experiences" and "participation in society is one of the most important ways in which education takes place" (Brubacher). The more free and "unimpeded this sharing is, the more democratic the society is said to be, and certainly the greater is the educational opportunity" (Brubacher). Education is, in fact, socialisation of the child.

It should, therefore, not come as a surprise if pragmatism is warmly attached to democratic process. "The two have much in common because both encourage the individual to specialize in cultivating his unique talents". This interaction is evident both at the level of curriculum construction and the classroom interactive process wherein a teacher avoids all kinds of artificial barriers, and shares with the children as many decisions "as to objectives, curriculum, and discipline as possible".

Face Lifting Education : Pragmatism by its forthright and fresh approach and outlook toward the educative process, not only revolutionised the theory and practice of teaching-learning but also infused new life into the decaying, hackneyed and dull educational procedures and practices hitherto in use. It is the culmination of progressive education, also called new education. Its basic concepts of teaching methodology, such as activity principle; child-centred educational programmes; learning by doing; learning through verification etc., have given a new facet to educational practices, sustaining and strengthening them by a forward looking, candid and pragmatic approach to life.

Progressive and Optimistic Outlook : Values are instrumental and take shape in the hands of the individual in conformity with his experiences. This brings optimism to life as things are possible, pliable and amenable, giving one lots of confidence and sense of entrepreneurship. Further, pragmatism is progressive in the sense that it is an open-minded approach in keeping with the demands and needs of the modern society and its mechanism.

Comments : Pragmatism is an attitude of mind and a way of life which opposes tradition in search of the greener pastures and creates a world of its own. This powerful attitude of mind needs an equally powerful approach toward experience-reconstruction which is at the root of all learning and pursuit of truth. It promises a better adjusted person fully developed in all its aspects, and consequently, a far happier and satisfied individual in full agreement with social demands and expectations, at the same time ensuring his total freedom and entrepreneurship, a spirit of adventure and creativity. Progressive education is not progressive because it is making steady advance toward some definite goal but because it is "growing in whatever direction, a novelly emerging future promises most development" (Brubacher). Progressiveness is not progression. It is an innovative, naturalistic, experimental and, problem-solving approach to life and education.

14

Realistic Theory

Realism is as old as the naturalism and materialism of ancient Greece. Throughout the centuries realism developed into many forms and it is difficult to classify them. There is irony in circumstances that the attempt to prove the existence of independent physical realities should result in such a discordant chorous of realisms. So the discussion has to be limited otherwise we have its beginning from John Locke, Johann Herbart and Herbert Spencer besides having historical idealistic realism involving Plato etc. We shall talk of realism of the common sense and application of contemporary realism to education.

The Rise

Just as naturalism came as a protest against artificiality and sophistication, similarly realism in education has arisen as a result of all emphasis on the abstract, bookish and verbal knowledge and sophistication. There came a cry-down to earth, come down to worldly things.

The Approach

Although common sense genically assigns different meanings to the same word as occasion requires, it usually considers the term realism as having to do with "What actually exists". It has to face even perversity and ugly aspects of life as described in novels and paintings as if sordid and seamy side of things were sometimes more real than their own aspects. But it is there.

Cardinal Facts

(i) *Independent Existence of the World.* Realism is fundamentally the philosophical doctrine that the material world has the independent and objective existence. Its being and properties do not depend upon a knowing mind. This philosophy does not differ greatly from the ordinary man's view point or view of this world. This way it is a form of materialism.

(ii) *Parts Different from the Whole.* These people consider parts independently than the whole and give more importance to these parts. Realists this way are opposed to the gestalt point of view of looking at the things as a whole.

(iii) *Sensory Perception: Most Important.* Realists at the outset ignore the higher mental abilities and capacities. They do not believe in high mental processes and go against Iqbal's couplet which translated means:

The wider human experience transcends sensory perception. It is the sensory perception that is most important to them.

(iv) *Universe not External.* Realists believe that universe is not external. There is a law that governs the universe and that law is supreme since it is through that law and order that cohesion prevails.

(v) *Realism Believes in Examination of Things Singly.* Realism came as a result of the scientific thought of the 16th and 17th century. Since we begin to attach meaning and significance to phenomenon and things, it became essential to know and analyse things and this was not possible till we believe in them. Man began to examine things one by one. That way is scientific way and realism also believes in studying things singly.

(vi) *Denial of Physiological Processes.* Realists forget the physiological processes in the sensory perception. They do not think that as we see things some physiological changes take place. They believe that things presented to us thrust themselves on us and there is nothing physiological. This way they go against idealism which believes in the physiological processes- perhaps the truth lies with both the points. Things are seen by brain—it is realism but the meaning is given by mind—it is idealism.

Real Facts

Any correspondence to reality is truth and not that truth is something existing earlier. Everything is sense perception. Ideas work because they are true to reality. Ideas are good if they are consistent with the world. It is the matter thus which is more important and it existed earlier to mind—mind came later as a result of evolution.

So Realism propounds a philosophy which is very appealing and is consistent with the facts of life. It is in accordance with the development of the physical world.

Weber has put the Tenets of realism in a round about manner. He says that there are five main agreements between the realism of layman and realism of philosophers:

1. There is a realm of nature which exists beyond or outside of our minds.
2. Nature existed before we knew it, exists whether or not we know it and will continue to exist after we pass away. The realist usually keeps nature in neuter gender and does not personalise or apothesize reality in the romantic manner typical of idealists.
3. The attributes of physical objects exist just as we know them except for errors of perception which are verifiable as errors. The true nature of a thing is not altered by mere circumstances of its being known.
4. Experience is the touchstone of what is real. "Seeing is believing." Whenever we cannot discover truth by direct

experiences or seeing, then and only then scientific research is done.

5. Such knowledge as man has shown that physical nature follows or manifests a network of laws. Such laws are regarded as external realities, independent of our minds and ever-independent of the physical world which 'follows' them.

Various Kinds

1. *Humanistic Realism.* It developed in the fifteenth century. It came after the period of renaissance was over in Europe. Humanistic realism believes in: (a) interpreting knowledge in simple terms (b) direct study of man and things (c) For them, man was reality and an ideal.

2. *Social Realism.* This term social realism is adopted to indicate a view of education held by educators in the previous centuries but more generally accepted during the seventeenth and eighteenth centuries. This realism is a revolt against isolated living of man. All learning is to take place in company with others. Travel was emphasised and in England, people were not considered to be educated until and unless they had considerable travel experience.

   Prominent social realist was Michael de Montaigue. The effect of social realism was that the schools stood invaded by cultural and social activities.

3. *Sense Realism.* It is also known as scientific realism. Its origins are in the seventeenth century. Many scientific discoveries had been made and all of them stressed the fact that senses are the gateways to knowledge. Thus term sense realism is derived from the fundamental belief that knowledge comes primarily through the senses and that education is consequently founded on a training in sense perception rather than on purely memory activities and directed towards a different kind of subject matter (science). Education here is based on rational grounds rather than on empirical grounds. Thus 17th century was an age of criticism and doubt. Some

people call them innovators also. Richard Mulcaste. Bacon were the representative sense realists.

4. *Scholastic Realism.* This type of realism holds that the study of eternal truth must have hold over objects of world around us. The unmistakable truths should be indoctrinated in the children. The scholastic realists think education can lead to salvation. And lastly scholastic realists believe that morality divorced from religion is hardly of permanent nature and thus worthy of emulation and respect. They consider religion as the main spring of ethics and social morality.

Other realism types are :

(i) Realism of Alfred N. Whitehead.

(ii) Realism of Bertrand Russell.

Vital Role in Education

The educational implications of only sense realism will be discussed. See humanism for educational implications of humanistic realism.

1. *Aims.* All our thinking is to be based on realities of life and philosophy of education can prove its worth by becoming more practical.

The main aim of realist education is that education should be for this world-to see that education is practical one-and has a vocational bias.

The aims of education of realists were not theoretical. These people do not believe in false values and thus their education is not directed to achieve those false values and hence it saves them from puzzles and riddles and from the mysteries of the superhuman. We know where our education is to take us.

2. *Curriculum.* (i) The main tenet of philosophy is that truth about the things is to be acquired. This reflects on the curriculum also. It means that in their curriculum the study of sciences is to be not only included but also a prominent part is to be given to it. Also to be included are practical arts.

(ii) Realists stand for the diversification of the courses but the courses should be related to life. There should be no gap between what is learnt in the school and what is actually there in life. It should not be purely theoretical information. Contemporary events should be there and a study of Civics should be included and the practical utility of all that is taught in the school should be brought out in the school itself.

(iii) The main stress of realist education is on vocational training since it is useful for utilitarian purposes and also enables a man to explore and harness sources. Harnessing the sources gives to them the maximum pleasure, the use of it will come later on.

(iv) They also emphasise mother-tongue. Mother-tongue is the most natural mode of expression and thought. Physical education is also taught as a subject since without it they cannot understand nature.

In realist curriculum, we have many subjects and activities as we want to have a rounded view of things and reality.

Methods. The realists advocate sense training. It is the senses that are the gateways of knowledge. Let the child do practical work himself and that is why there is too much stress on the teaching of science. It helps to train and equip senses.

Critical Observation, Exploration, Self-study and experimentation are the other methods of education advocated by realists.

Since they are interested in training of senses, this had led to a stress on measurement in education. It means that the stimuli are observed and regulated.

With regard to examinations, realists have placed reliance in the objective measurements.

The author has not been able to locate specifically the role of a teacher in realism.

Regarding discipline, it is teaching of morality and religion that can help.

15

Idealistic Theory

Idealism is a very old philosophical thought and it has exercised a great influence on man and his activities. It has been the most dominant philosophical theory in the ancient period. Even in the modern times, idealism has certain attractions which appeal to the human mind and exercise a good deal of influence over his thinking and activities. It represents the views of great philosophers like Plato, Kant, Hegel, Berkley, Comenius, Froebel, Lotze, Tagore and Gandhiji. It asserts that reality consists of ideas, thoughts or minds rather than of material objects and forces. Reality is found in the mind of man and not in the physical, material and external world. It is spiritual in nature, and believes in the super natural reality. The spiritual world is more important than the material world. The material world is a myth and untrue.

The Idea

Derivative Meaning. The world idealism has been derived from ideas. According to this doctrine, the ultimate supremacy belongs to the ideas. They are eternal and unchanging.

Popular Meaning. The word idealist means the person who accepts and lives by lofty moral aesthetic and religious standards and the one who is able to visualize and who advocates some plan or programme that yet does not exist. Social reformer, for example, supports something which has not yet come into existence. The idealist is a dreamer who is liable to ignore practical condition of a situation. Those who work for world peace or for the elimination of poverty may be called idealist.

Philosophical Meaning. Idealism is also commonly known as spiritualism. It seeks to offer an explanation of the man and the universe in terms of spirit or mind. The spiritual quality of man distinguishes him from other lower creatures. Rusk says, Idealism contends that the material and physical universe known to science is an incomplete expression of reality, that it exists but to subserve, and requires to complement it as a higher type of reality, a spiritual universe.

According to some others, there is no such word as idealism. Titus says that philosophical meanings have been derived from the word 'idea' than 'ideal'. W.E. Hocking, an idealist, says that the term 'idea-ism' would be more to the point.

Insisting Points

Ideas are Final. To the idealists, idea or spirit or thought or ideals is the final reality. Idea of the thing is real and the thing in itself is simply the manifestation of that idea.

Priority of Mind and the Self. Mind is prior to matter. The basic reality consists of or closed related to mind, ideas thoughts or selves. Mind is the controller and the explainer of phenomena. World is the creation of the mind and not natural phenomena. Mind and ideas are real. Matter is subordinate.

Freedom of the Human Mind. Freedom of the human mind is the highest virtue. Freedom means Freedom from ignorance, wants and passions. The consciousness of ignorance is the beginning of knowledge, which according to Socrates, is a virtue.

Universe Exists in Spirit. According to Idealism, the spirit is the fundamental constituent of the universe. True reality is spiritual. Thought, experience, value and personality are more real than the material things of the external world. Matter in its essence is also spiritual and very atom has life, mind and energy.

Belief in Universal Mind. Universal mind stands for God who is present everywhere. Human mind is a part of or fragment of Universal Mind and it is God who creates and carries forward the individual mind. His is the .infinite mind, and the finite minds are all dependent upon him God is the source of all human values. We all exist for Him. The goal of the human activities is the realisation of the infinite mind in one's own self.

Concept of Man. According to idealists, man is not only an animal who has same time to live. He is a superior creation. He possesses dignity and distinctiveness. They believe man to be a spiritual being- an eternal phenomenon. Man is not a perishable body. Behind this body is the undying spirit. According to Ross "Human" personality is supreme and constitutes the noblest work of God. "He is a little lower than the angel and is crowned with glory and honour. He has a will to perfection and an inner striving or self-realisation. He has certain powers which are manifested in his intellectual attainments, his culture, art, morality, religion and so on.

Harmony between Man and Universe. Man is at home in the universe. He is not an alien. He is not here just by chance. According to Titus, 'What is highest in spirit is also deepest in nature. Man is a part of the cosmos and a part of the world process. He it rather, in search of truth goodness and beauty. His search at its highest levels manifests itself as his constructiveness, imagination and creativity.

Values of Life. Idealism has full faith in eternal and spiritual values of life, which never change. Truth, beauty and goodness are, according to Plato, the outstanding eternal values. The idealist's goal of life is the realisation of these spiritual and absolute values. It is religion which unifies them all. These values or the truths are not man-made but their existence is automatic and permanent. Man's duty is to discover these fundamentals through proper education. Man is not an inventor but a discoverer of these values. His discovery is possible only through the awakening of spirit or knowledge.

Conceptualism or Knowledge. Idealism is conceptualism in its epistemology, because it believes that objects have no existence apart from the concept related to them. Knowledge is obtained not through perception of senses, but indirectly through the medium of concepts, ideas or the activity of the mind. It attaches great importance to the knowledge which is gathered through mental activates. Knowledge gained through the senses occupies a secondary place.

Emphasis on Normative and Social Sciences. Idealist lay greater emphasis on normative and social sciences rather than upon natural and physical science. Idealists explain the universe on the basis of normative and social sciences. These sciences are ethics, logic, aesthetics, sociology and psychology.

Diverse Sorts

There are many classifications of idealism, yet no one classification seems to be entirely satisfactory, and there is much overlapping. Here we shall briefly mention only three types of idealism:

Subjective Idealism. It is also called mentalism or phenomenalism. It holds that minds or spirits and their perceptions or ideas, are all that exist. The objects of experience are not material things, they are merely perceptions. Things such as buildings, trees exist but they have no existence apart from a mind that sees them. To say a thing exist is to say that is perceived. Berkley is the best representative of this type of idealism.

Objective Idealism. It is best represented by Plato and Hegel. This views that external world is in real sense man-made. There is an organisation and form in this world. The man discovers what there is in this order of the world. In nature, the idealists find the same principles of order, reason and purpose that men within themselves. The existence of meaning in the world however, implies something akin to mind or thought at the core of reality.

Personal Idealism. In this, the basic fact is not an abstract thought but a person or a self or a thinker. Life is more important than any verbal form of expression or fixed meanings. It emphasizes the reality and the worth of individual people, moral values and human freedom. Nature is an objective order and people transcend or rise above nature when they interpret it. Personalism is theistic furnishing both religion and ethics with metaphysical assumptions. Since personality has greater value than anything else, society must be so organised as to give each person fullness of life and opportunity.

Educational Impact

Comenius is believed to be the originator of idealism in the sphere of education. According to idealism, man is born with a spiritual self. It is through education that we can realise its spirituality. Rusk says, "Education is stated to enlarge the boundaries of the spiritual realm." Home says," Education is awakening to the life of God in the soul of man, involving praise, prayer and worship." Idealism has talked more of objectives and aims of education and less of its devices, methods and organisation.

Goals and Ends

Some of the important aims as laid down by idealism are as under:

Education for Self-realisation. This aim is also mentioned as, "exaltation of personality." Idealism aims at ideal personality to be achieved through education. It attaches importance to the dignity of man. Education has to enable the child to realize the soul, recognize his real form, and proceed towards self-knowledge. He has to be encouraged to realize Truth, Beauty and Goodness and establish identity with the Supreme Power. It also believes in divine destiny which has got to be achieved through 'Karma' and which is possible when self realization has taken place.

To Achieve Salvation. Real education is meant ultimately for Mukti- to liberate oneself from the cycle of life and death.

Individual's Physical Well-being. James Ross says "The health and fitness of the body must recede the attention, for without such health and fitness the pursuit of spiritual values is seriously handicapped. As spiritual exaltation is not possible without being physically fit, so physical aspects of education cannot be ignored.

Development of Moral Sense. So that the child is able to distinguish between right and wrong and he is able to follow the right and reject the evil. The goal of life as well as of education should be the realisation of moral values by developing the spiritual character of the child.

Values to be Passed on to Posterity. Education must ensure that the value which the present man has inherited from the past and which he has himself developed are passed on to the next generation.

Development of Complete Man. Education should aim at developing the child into a complete man with full physical, intellectual, moral, spiritual, emotional and cultural uplift.

Preservation and Enrichment of Culture. Rusk says, "Education must enable mankind through its culture to enter more and more fully into the spiritual realm and also to enlarge the boundaries of the spiritual realm." The spiritual or cultural environment is an environment of man's own making, it is the fruit of man's own creative activities, it is the product of ages and it is always in the process of growth. Every new generation has to preserve it and improve upon it.

Development of Inventive and Creative Powers. Education must foster such inventive and creative powers and the man so that he can achieve mastery over the material world. He should not remain helpless like other beings. Through these powers, he would change and modify the environment according to the purposes and needs.

Simple Living and High Thinking. It is the mind that is to be developed and controlled. Simple living and high thinking should be a maxim for the individual. Napoleon has rightly said, "The only conquests which are permanent and have no regrets are our conquests over ourselves.

Proximate and Ultimate Aims. According to Home, there are proximate and ultimate aims of education in idealism. The proximate aims are: Good health, Good skill, Social justice, Character, Art and Intelligence: The ultimate aim is the development of humanity in the image of dignity.

Universal Education. Since the idealists believe in the fatherhood of God and the brotherhood of man, they aim at making education universal. It is not meant for the favoured few. All should be given the opportunity to acquire knowledge about the self irrespective of caste, creed, colour, sex, status or religion.

Development of Syllabus

Idealists insist on the study of humanities such as literature, art, religion etc. They want the curriculum which helps in the all round development of the individual. The most significant among man's activities are the intellectual, the aesthetic and the moral. Intellectual work will involve subjects like language, history, geography, mathematics, etc. Moral impulse can he reinforced through art, poetry, religion, ethics etc. Physical activities may involve various kinds of handicrafts and manual skills.

Methods of Teaching

Teaching method is the weakest aspect in idealistic philosophy. Truly speaking, idealism does not suggest any special methods of education. It does give importance to school and to its classrooms. It is in the classroom that human mind meet any where and effort can be made for self-realization.

Only Pestalozzi and Froebel have contributed some views to methodology. Pestalozzi advocates self-activity on the part of children. He wanted all instruction to be based on psychological findings, experience, and observation and not on abstract statements and words. Froebel gave to us 'Kindergarten' method which is a playway method. Some other methods are listed below:

Question-answer Method. Socrates had adopted this method. He used to move about, engage the youth in question-answer and discussion sessions.

Conversational Method. Plato converted questioning method into conversational method.

Inductive-deductive Method. Aristotle devised inductive-deductive methods for imparting education. Hegal adopted it in the form of logical method.

Playway Method. As mentioned this method was devised by Froebel in his Kindergarten schools.

Simple to Complex. Descartes evolved the method of going from simple to complex.

Concrete to Abstract. Comenius adopted concrete to abstract as his important method.

Exercise and Practice. Pestalozzi is created with this approach. He introduced self-activity on the part of the child.

Lecture/Debate. Idealists frequently take the help of lecture and discussion as method of teaching. They have also favoured debate as one of the techniques.

Story Telling and Dramatics. The idealists suggest story telling as a method for infants and dramatics for adolescents.

Education through Correspondence. The idealists also appreciate correspondence as a method of teaching and learning.

Significant Role of Discipline

Idealism believes in the strict form of discipline. Only a disciplined mind can tend towards the highest good. One cannot expect to achieve salvation by living in a loose manner or by believing in unrestrained discipline. Idealists cannot allow total freedom or loose discipline. Discipline, however, must take the form of self-discipline, self-insight and self-analysis. It is better realized through developing such qualities as renunciation humanity, politeness, obedience, etc. There should not be any external pressure for enforcing discipline. Rather it should be created through influence and impression and not through fear, coercion repression and threats.

Role of Teacher

The teacher enjoys a very high place in idealism. The place which the teacher occupied is ancient Indian education is well known in this respect. He is the 'Guru', in the real sense. The student cannot achieve self-realization or salvation without his guidance. The teacher carries the child from darkness to light. The school is a garden, the teacher is a cautious gardener, and the child is a tender plant. Through teacher's guidance alone, the child can develop himself to some perfection.

Idealists expect the teacher to be normally high, intellectually develop and culturally advanced upto a stage of perfection in his own case. He creates the special environment whose function is to lead the child nearer to reality and to his highest possible perfection. He acts as a true friend, philosopher and guide. He is expected to lead a life of contentment, contemplation, poverty and detachment. A good teacher fired with missionary zeal and fervent desire to build men and women. He is a pious man. He leads a virtuous life. He is a man of high ideals and he is always a source of inspiration for his students. Teacher stands next to God in idealist education.

Criticism and Evaluation. Idealism as a philosophy of education suffers from many shortcomings, which are:

Impracticable. Idealism is very easy and beautiful to preach but difficult to practise. It has given us very lofty aims of education. The spiritual aim set before us too high to be achieved in this materialistic world. The ideals seem to be very attractive but reality is entirely different and sometimes beyond our control and possibilities.

Not Psychological. Idealism does not take into consideration the psychology of the child, who is more for activity and less for contemplation.

Dogmatic. Idealism is a dogmatic philosophy. It is very rigid. It introduces authoritarianism in education.

Neglects Social Aspect of Life. It is individualistic in nature and neglects socialisation of the individual.

Rigorous Discipline. It advocates rigorous discipline which is out of time with the modern concept of education.

Under-rates Sciences. It under-rates sciences and technology and gives priority to fine arts, literature and social sciences.

Over-dependence in Pupils. It overemphasis the dependency of pupils on teacher. It goes against self-effort, self-reliance and freedom for healthy growth.

Poor Contribution to Methods of Teaching. The methods of teaching advocated by idealists are not largely in tune with the present day requirements.

Overemphasis of External Values. Idealists believe the values to be external whereas this blind faith in the existing values does not fit into the thinking of a modern man

Too much emphasis is also laid on creating a spiritual atmosphere in the school, but the school can not be converted into a temple.

Conclusion. Idealism is basically a sound philosophy of life and like all other philosophical thoughts it has exercised a general rather than a specific influence on education. Its impact on education and its various aspects is significant enough and will continue to be so. Perfection is the goal before a student. The teacher has a very important role to play.

Present confusion in the educational scene can be minimised by following the dictates of idealism a bit more sincerely.

16

Secular Values

Secularism in education refers to an attitude of mind that omits religion from curriculum of 'public schools' in contrast to the religious institutions like 'madarsas' and 'maqtabs' which revolve their educative process around their religious tenets. Of late, efforts are being made to bring these institutions in the mainstream and add scientific and technological aspects to their curriculum. Nevertheless, omission of religions from the curriculum encouraged the rise of a strongly "secular temper of mind" which gets along with the educative process without any "religious observances" wherein children are well adjusted to meet the principal "scientific and social demands of the everyday world about them".

The secularist is concerned with the world here and now, and lays emphasis on continued adjustment in obedience to natural laws by means of a scientific method. He has no religion except a secular outlook which demands a non-religious approach to religion and morals "which rest on the self-sufficiency of man's own natural powers to direct his own destiny" (Brubacher). It, however, does not mean that the school dispenses with the spiritual values. Secularism in education provides equal access to spiritual values by all irrespective of caste, creed, religion, gender and cultural origin. These spiritual values are not wedded to any religion or sect, and are based on "secular views". Democracy and secularism, generally, go together, and consider "man to be captain of his social destiny". However, in the Indian context, the word secular was added in the Constitution in 1977 (42nd amendment) and has been a cause of great confusion, mistrust and apprehension, especially amongst the minorities as the political parties give it their own twist and significance.

The Approach

Derived from Latin Sacculum, the word secularism was first used by George Jacob Holydake in the nineteenth century. He accorded it a social and ethical value status. As such, secularism acquired a social and ethical connotation and referred to a system which considered all men equal in opportunity, participation and belief in spite of one's caste, creed, religion and belief. Secularism, therefore, became the hallmark of liberal and tolerant social and moral practices.

Important Facets

Secularism has the following essential features:

1. Primary emphasis on the material and cultural upliftment of individual and society.
2. Respect and reverence for truth irrespective of source for better social and moral character of society.
3. Concerns for this age or world and its improvement.
4. An independent, unbiased and positive attitude of life which does not root itself in any single divine faith and commandment.
5. Liberal, permissive, progressive and tolerant social and moral order.
6. As against the view of Bradlaugh, secularism and religion are not necessarily hostile. As a matter of fact, secularism is a state of harmonious coexistence of various religions, so much so that it becomes a religion by itself.
7. Secularism is equality of all religions in a state.
8. Secularism is absence of a state religion.

Effect of Secularism

Secularism is an essential characteristic of any democratic educational system and goes well with the accepted norms of educational theory and practice to an extent that education would, perhaps not be democratic if it was not secular. As such, the dynamics of educational change in the modern society covers the entire domain of educational objectives, content and procedures.

These may also be called the variables of education/teaching, and have the following ramifications:—

Teacher	*Content*	*Pupil*
1. Development	1. Universal	1. Interest
2. Knowledge	2. Flexible	2. Ability
3. Tasks	3. Secular	3. Aspirations
4. Instructional Interventions	4. Global	4. All-round development
5. Ideology	5. Diversified	5. Knowledge, Attitude and Skills
6. Attitude	6. Play oriented	6. Variability of individual differences.
7. Status	7. Vocational	
	8. Graded	
	9. Updated and relevant	
	10. Distance Education	

Dynamics of Educational Change : It may reasonably be assumed that the entire educative process in a democratic setup revolves around secularism and in cultivating secular attitudes and values. We shall presently discuss the role of various components of education in this regard.

Secular Perception

Aims : Aims are values in expressed form. As such, the educational aims of a democratic educative process must cherish and aspire for secularism in education. The Secondary Education Commission 1952-53 recommended the following aims of education having a direct bearing on secularism.

"Education system must make contribution to the development of habits, attitudes and qualities of character which will enable its citizens to bear worthily the responsibilities of democratic citizenship and to counteract all those fissiparous tendencies which hinder the emergence of broad national and secular outlook."

Development of Democratic Citizenship : India is a secular, socialist, democratic republic, and as such education should produce dynamic, resourceful and enterprising citizens. It should help one develop the intellectual and emotional ability and control to sift the right from the wrong in a dispassionate and scientific manner.

Training in the Art of Living Efficiency : For the wholesome development of the child, and for the benefit of society, education should develop in him a spirit of accommodation based on discipline, cooperation and tolerance. It should foster such socially desirable aims, acceptable attitudes that make the child to be a responsible and efficient member of the society.

The Kothari Commission 1966 recommended the following measures to consolidate democracy by means of social, national and moral values which inversely consolidate secular education:

Develop Social and National Unity : For national reconstruction, national unity is an essential need. In the absence of national unity, self-centred individuals try to achieve their own motives without caring for the interests of the nation. This makes the nation weak and backward. Thus, national unity is greatly essential for national reconstruction. But the feeling of national unity can be developed through education only. Hence, the aim of education should be to develop social and national unity.

Consolidate Democracy : Education is necessary for the success of democracy. Hence, to consolidate democracy is another aim of education. To achieve this aim, education should be so organised as to provide more and more effective experiences to children to inculcate in them the qualities of democratic living. Then only, national consciousness will stimulate national outlook, sense of national character and responsibility.

Comments : Whatever be the effect of the educational process regulated by the aims prescribed by society, there is a "unanimity of opinion on the point" that children at the time of leaving the school are in an incomplete state of development". This deficiency is to be filled up in later life by religion and social and moral integration, and consolidation of faculties and inclinations. Secularism is one way of doing it where integration takes place without subscribing to any religious sect and faith. Secularism, therefore, is vital for peaceful coexistence, growth and prosperity, and is, in fact, attitudinal and progressive.

Educational values help imbibe secular values, and educational aims provide appropriate direction and keep the educative process on track by exercising vigilant control and rectification, leading it to Sarvadharmambhave wherein every religious tenet and creed enjoys equal opportunity and status. National Educational Policy 1986 and India Vision 2002-2020 are the cardinal points toward total secular education as a matter of state policy irrespective of the occasional crying foul of saffronisation and appeasement.

Curriculum : The first question in curriculum construction is whether it should be shaped by the social culture and the demands of the society, or according to the needs of an individual. In spite of the profound respect for the individual in a democratic setup, preference is given to the social order in curriculum construction. Secular curriculum should be universal, flexible, global, play-oriented, graded and relevant, and should address to the society rather than an individual, community or sect. It should be culture-oriented, and as best of the culture is contained in tradition, let curriculum be tradition-oriented, permitting little permissiveness and aberrations, which will soon disappear into the body-structure.

The content of the curriculum and its presentation goes a long way in developing secularism in a society. A long history and a long line of tradition may have certain aberrations at some point, but it does not mean that these should be blown out of proportion to ignite racial and religious feelings, or to fan the fires of passion, hatred, suspicion and ill will. In contrast to it, even if there are such historical incidents of acrimony and cruelty, these should either be ignored, glossed over or toned down. As it is, one such omission would not change the course of history and tradition of a people. Tolerance is the key word. The curriculum should be so designed that it develops better understanding of each other's views with compassion and respect. Secular education should have secular curriculum presenting the learning experiences in different forms at different stages of learning and comprehension to absorb it. Inclusion of science subjects broadens one's outlook and perception, and, therefore, helps develop secular attitude. The current misconception about saffronisation of education and tinkering with the curriculum is based either on misrepresentation or misconception. Social studies, especially, History is the favourite target of this onslaught, at times rousing passions beyond reason and control.

In fact, how much of History has been distorted, if distorted at all, in the recent times by those who aim at diluting presentation of some unpleasant incidents in the course of our history. The author remembers the manner in which History was taught during the pre-Independence era raking up hatred resulting in the partition of the country. Does teaching of history aim at dividing people to the extent it did in the Indian subcontinent? We are talking about History because it is a hotbed of controversy and mistrust. The same is true of other social subjects though not related as directly and intimately with tradition.

Teacher Tasks and Behaviour : Teacher has specific tasks and behaviour in a democratic set-up: his knowledge, development and preparation; use of strategies or other instructional interventions; manipulation of environment; ideology and attitudes should be such that they help create a democratic and secular impression on the pupils. The teacher must tell what is relevant at an appropriate level, and skip the rest for the time the pupils are matured enough to understand things on their own and in their own perspective.

The teacher should be professionally honest, capable, impartial, discrete, progressive and enlightened without being unduly charged with any specific faith, creed or tenet, showing equal respect to all religions in a conscientious and fair manner. He is the promoter and upholder of creating a social climate in the society that helps generate secular values and traditions in the country. Such is the teacher who would infuse secular attitudes and knowledge amongst his students for a better, prosperous and glorious tomorrow where everyone lives in amity, harmony and peace.

Pupils and Secularism : In the ultimate analysis it is the pupil on whom all secular manipulations and interventions are working; it is the pupil who has got to be secular in his approach and outlook. The other components and variables simply help him reach there by providing necessary and amicable facilities and environment. Today's pupils are tomorrow's citizens and would be at the helm of the things in various spheres of life in their own right. Whatever they imbibe today would manifest itself in their social, moral, political, literary and religious views and actions.

Secular attitudes are those socially desirable attitudes that help one understand and tolerate others' point of view, accept it with respect and compassion in the interest of general well being, welfare, progress and prosperity. Pupils should, therefore, be provided opportunities to develop secular bent of mind, attitude and culture. This will be the signal contribution of education toward secularism in society.

The Features

Briefly speaking secular education has the following characteristics:—

1. Moral outlook.
2. Development of wider vision.
3. Pluralistic outlook.
4. Democratic values.
5. Cultural development.
6. Synthesis of spiritual and material values.
7. Humanitarianism.

Difficulties Ahead

1. Traditional bias and narrow outlook.

2. Too much emphasis on theoretical learning and absence of a solid value system.
3. Lack of knowledge of secular social and moral outlook, and a general apathy to celebration of each other's festivals to inculcate a spirit of secular understanding and living.
4. Neglect of mixed group interaction and lack of mutual faith and trust.
5. Cross purpose of various constitutional provisions which created more confusion and mistrust about the need and meaning of the word secular (1977/42nd amendment) in the Constitution which already had adequate projective devices by means of Articles 25 to 28, as well as 29 and 30, which were enough to dispel any misgivings by some sections of the society.

17

Democratic View

The Approach

It is in the political sense that democracy has been generally understood. According to Aristotle, democracy is government by many, while Abraham Lincoln gave us his well-known definition, "Democracy is the rule of the people, by the people, and for the people." The ruling power, in a democracy, according to this definition, in any country, does not rest with a particular set of people or privileged group, but belongs to every one of the members of the community, and to all citizens in the country.

This means that every adult in a democracy has a share in the governing of the country. The work of government is not allowed to fall into the hands of one person or into the hands of a small body of men, or even into the hands of one class in the community. This is political democracy—only one aspect of true democracy which includes economic as well as social democracy, as it prevails in Russia. Economic democracy means that economic power will be in the hands of the people as a whole, not in the hands of a few capitalists or of a particular class. The economic organization of the community will be cooperative rather than competitive. The economic projects will be undertaken for the benefit of the community as a whole and not for private profit. Work will be provided for every individual according to his abilities and capacities. Social democracy connotes absence of "all distinctions based on class, birth or possession of money." Everyone will have equality of opportunity—money or birth or class will not stand in the way of progress. Thus democracy, in its complete sense, means a way of living and organization of community that has political, economic and social aspects. In such a democracy, every human individual will be given the freedom to develop, to the fullest extent possible, all the potentialities—freedom to think, to express, to discuss and to work and act—freedom to create and to change, freedom to cooperate. Besides freedom, every individual in a true democracy will have an equal chance of living a full life, and of exercising his powers in social, economic and political spheres. The individual will be valued as a person, whatever his caste, creed or religion. In true democracy, faith in the common man to do the noble things in life will inspire the citizen who will serve the community realizing "that all he has and is, he owes to the community."

But democracy in education is a comparatively recent idea, and there interpretation as well as understanding of educational principles and practices from the point of view of democracy is our task here. Dewey tells us, "A society which makes provision for participation in the good of all its members on equal terms and which secures flexible readjustment of its institutions through interaction of the different forms of associated life is in so far democratic. Such a society must have a type of education which gives individuals a personal interest in social relationships and control, and habits of mind which secure social changes without introducing disorder."

The failure of many teachers and educators in understanding the significance of democracy as a way of living has made them disregard it and even oppose it as a guiding principle in the school. The traditional attitude and approach has been upheld for centuries and has resulted in the continuation of autocratic and totalitarian practices in the administration, supervision and methods of teaching prevalent in our schools. This means that the relationship between the administrator and the teacher as well as that between the teacher and the pupil, has been quite similar to the relationship between a dictator and his subjects.

The Radhakrishnan Committee Report describes democracy is "A way of life, and not a mere political arrangement." It is based on the principle of equal freedom and equal rights for all its members, regardless of race, religion, sex, occupation or economic status. In India, democratic government is based on the Preamble to the Constitution which states: "The sovereign Democratic Republic of India will secure to all its citizens, justice—social, economic and political, liberty of thought, expression, belief, faith and worship, and equality of rights and opportunity. It will further promote among them all fraternity, assuming the dignity of the individual and the unity of the nation." Democracy, therefore, is to be attained in India, through the furtherance of the principles of justice, liberty, equality and fraternity.

The National Policy on Education of 1986 Stresses the "Equalization of Educational Opportunity" for all children in the country. Proper educational facilities need to be provided for pupils in rural and backward areas. A common school system which promotes social and national integration is to be adopted. The education of girls, encouraged, and provision made for the education of the physically and mentally handicapped.

The spread of literacy and adult education among the masses is also emphasised, as one of the measures towards achieving an enlightened democracy.

Besides the educational expansion to include rural and backward areas, the minorities living in the country should have educational opportunities made easily accessible to them.

In a democratic society the status of teachers must be improved, specially those who work in rural areas. Their emoluments and housing needs must be looked after.

The Ramamurthi Report of 1990, again, emphasises democracy as an important objective of education, and has made recommendations very similar to those of the NPE of 1986.

However the policies, structures and administrative measures proposed are somewhat different.

In the area of Early Childhood Care and Education (ECCE) it is recommended that a countrywide network of ECCE be developed. Provision should be made for statutory creches and Day Care Centres in which all labour laws are implemented.

It is recommended that a Central Fund for Child Care services be set up at the natural level.

The Right to Education, according to the Ramamurthi Report should be examined and be included amongst the fundamental rights guaranteed in free India's Constitution. The realisation of this right makes it necessary to take many socio-economic measures.

Navodaya Vidyalyas should be run as residential schools by the states, and the underprivileged children in rural areas should be granted greater access to them.

Movement for Literacy

Democratic ideals have brought about the recognition of the importance of education for the masses. George Washington wrote: "Knowledge is in every country the surest basis of public happiness. In one, in which the measures of government receive their impression so immediately as in ours, from the sense for the community, it is proportionately essential." The chief concern of George Washington lay in educational institutions that would serve as instruments of general enlightenment.

This was the foundation of the movement that led to the establishment of universal education on an ever increasing scale in all civilised countries of the world. The rapid expansion of universal, free and compulsory education has been effectively brought about during the last few decades in the U.S.A., Great Britain, France, Russia, Turkey and Japan, while other countries including our own are trying to follow their example. Not only is education being imparted to children, schools for adults have been opened in large numbers. Evening and night classes for parents are common feature in many progressive countries. The State also makes provision for the education of the physically handicapped, the blind, the defective and backward children, as well as for the specially gifted and talented. Democracy in education thus implies that knowledge and the light of learning must be extended to all types of people. Education is the birth-right of every human being and not the privilege of the few.

Throwing Light on Children

One of the fundamental principles of modern democratic education is that much more attention is paid to the individuality of the child. Opportunities are increasingly provided in order that every child should by able to express his personality and bring it to full development. Mass methods of instruction and organisation in which the interests of the individual child are submerged in the group, are fast disappearing. Teachers have come to recognise the necessity of studying their pupils individually. Knowledge of home conditions, cultural background, psychological traits and temperamental characteristics aid in this task considerably. Intelligence tests are being used to determine the mental ability of each child and to make him work according to his intellectual capacity. Besides, the teacher tries to gain much knowledge about the individual child's health and physical condition through his own observation as well as through the report of the doctor on his medical inspection of every school child.

Aims and Goals

The school is to aid in developing a wide range of wholesome interests in the child by providing for learning through activity, interest and cooperation. The development of interests is not primarily to increase the acquisition of the subject-matter but to enrich the pupil and to improve his conduct. The larger the number of worthy interests that the child has the likelihood is greater that he will be happy, well-balanced and efficient not only as a pupil but also as a citizen.

The development of sound habits of thinking is another aim in democratic education. According to Dewey, "All which the school can or need to do for children, so far as their minds are concerned...is to develop their ability to think." The common belief prevalent in our schools is that before children can progress in thinking, they must learn a large mass of facts through rote memory. They do not realize that projects and problems can provide them quite well with materials for thinking. These enlist the interest of the pupils and in undertaking an activity they face the general problem of carrying it out as well as the several problems incidental to the progress.

In educating for democracy the development of the social outlook is another essential objective. It includes social interests and attitudes, concern for one's fellow beings, sense of obligation to the group, social understanding and the recognition as well as ability to solve social problems. Thus both social spirit and social capability are included in this aim.

Another aim according to democratic principles is that the pupils should acquire mastery over facts and skills that are meaningful as well as individually and socially useful to them. These facts and skills should have a general and a vocational bearing in the higher classes. The progressive educator recognises this objective as being very important and criticises the inefficient way in which it is followed in the traditional classroom.

In other words, the main aim of education in and for democracy should be to develop each pupil into a truly democratic citizen who understands objectively the various social, economic and political problems that arise, who has been trained to think and choose for himself, who is tolerant, who understands his rights as well as duties, possesses courage of conviction, vision of a better world, quality of sensitiveness and who is free from all negative inhibitions—in short, "one who has the creative attitude to life in all its aspects and activities." In India such a pupil will be made to understand the economic, social, political, communal and localitarian factors that have determined the nature of Indian education for years together.

Again, such a pupil will be trained from the beginning to fight such forces as capitalism and the class and caste system in society—the forces which are at once undemocratic and reactionary. What should be the educational needs or objectives of democratic India have been beautifully described by the Secondary Education Commission (1952-53). They say that India has decided to transform herself into a secular democratic republic according to the Constitution. "This means that the educational system should make its contribution to 'the development of habits, attitudes, and qualities of character which will enable its citizens to bear worthily the responsibility of democratic citizenship and to counteract all those fissiparous tendencies which hinder the emergence of a broad, national and secular outlook." Besides, the Commission adds, there is a need for improving productive efficiency, for increasing the national wealth and for reorienting the educational system so as to "stimulate a cultural renaissance and cultural pursuits which are suffering because of poverty." Thus, three aims fit in this democracy: the training of character to fit the student to participate creatively as citizens in the emerging democratic social order; the improvement of their practical and vocational efficiency so that they may play their part in building up the economic prosperity of their country, and the development of the literary, artistic and cultural interests which are necessary for self-expression and for the full development of the human personality, without which a living, national culture cannot come into being.

Prof. K.G. Saiyidain, commenting on the function and aims of education for democracy in "Education, Culture and the Social Order' says that education must be so oriented that it will develop the basic qualities of character which are necessary for the functioning of the democratic life. These basic qualities, are a passion for social justice and a quickening of social conscience, tolerance of intellectual and cultural difference in others, a systematic of the critical intelligence in students, the cultivation development of a love for work and a deep and true love for the country.

Diverse Courses

The curriculum aims at developing in the child attitudes, habits, understanding and ability to enable him to live successfully in a democratic society. We would well recognise first its inclusiveness, for it includes the whole programme of the school, the so called extracurricular activities, the play activities, classroom, procedure and examinations. Thus the curriculum consists of much more than a restricted and prescribed body of organised subject-matter.

The curriculum is also characterised by flexibility. In the progressive schools of America, only the basic or core curriculum consisting of minimum essentials has been prescribed for all pupils; additional subjects are offered only in accordance with the ability, intelligence and the needs of individual pupils.

The social element is also greatly emphasised; the social aim, and social organisation are very noticeable in the curriculum. Besides this, the curriculum lays stress on promoting the growth of the child's intelligence; the business of the teacher is not to present the pupils with readymade ideas, concepts, conclusions and attitudes but to help them to use facts in such a way that they evolve their own ideas and conclusions. A curriculum that most effectively promotes the growth of intelligence is one that involves activity and doing not mere motor activity but meaningful, purposeful behaviour, e.g., solving real problems in arithmetic, telling or writing a story, organising a tea-party or producing a play. These activities mean purposing, planning, thinking and judging.

Concept of Educational Administration

School administration in democracy depends largely on increased opportunity of the teacher and students to share in formulating the policy of the school. Curriculum revision receives particular attention. The guiding principles of curriculum construction are evolved by the teachers and using the principles that they have developed, they actually proceed through their committees to take the leading part in remaking the curriculum. Democracy in administration further means that the teachers are given considerable freedom in classroom procedure. This freedom is noticeably lacking in our Indian schools where inspector and administrators allow very little opportunity to the teacher to plan, to create or to exercise self direction. In a democratic system of education, as Ryburn puts it, both heads of schools and inspectors should give due recognition to any signs of a display of initiative on the part of a teacher.

"The (democratic) administrator will seize on the faintest glimmerings of a disposition to show initiative and will do his best to fan the flicker into a real blaze". The democratic administrator will criticize the work of the teacher but in a constructive and tolerant way. He should lead teachers to evaluate their own work.

"If we wish our administrator workers to be doing their part in preparing for the democratic way of life, we will have to emphasise the necessity of the friendly spirit and the cooperative attitude as the basis." The principal, in democratic administration, thinks of his role as that of one who works within the group rather than of dominating all situations, and, therefore, working on his group. He has to use all talents of the group and has to encourage each member of the group to participate. He succeeds in establishing an attitude of willingness an ability to cooperate. He does not impose a plan upon his group (staff and students). The principal, by imposing a plan on his group, immediately becomes an outsider and is no longer working within the group. Any plan of internal organisation should permit the active participation of everyone, capitalize on all contributions effectively, and allow for continuous improvement in all policies and practices.

The progress made becomes thus, the common achievement of the group. Thus democratic administration seeks to avoid the extreme concentration of power, the unshared responsibility, and the regimentation of authoritarianism on the one hand, and the disorganisation and unrestrained freedom of the laissez-faire concept on the other. There are three practical results which may be expected to follow from a democratic relationship between the administrator and the teacher. First, the teacher can make a distinct and valuable contribution to the policy of the school. All the teachers are in a position to know more about children than the administrator. Secondly, the teacher gains in professional maturity and experience by working with the administrator in purposing and planning. Thus he becomes capable of teaching intelligently instead of plodding blindly. Thirdly, this cooperation between the administration and teachers helps in the development of a democratic spirit between them. Genuine cooperation and diligent application follow from this, raising the moral and enthusiasm of the teachers. The pupils also catch this spirit.

Role of Teacher

In a true democracy the teacher will have status. He is to be the visiting force behind democratic organisation of society. Besides the usual qualifications of a successful teacher, he or she will be well equipped for democratic education. As such he will believe that "environment" is more important than heredity, that every individual is different from every other individual, that everyone is capable of making moral choices, deciding what is true or false, good or bad, beautiful or ugly, that every child has a right to freedom, to think, to choose and to equality of chances. He knows the goal of democratic education—the development of pupils into democratic citizens. He will have "constructive" relations with the community which the school has to serve as a strong supporter of a democratic way of life in cooperation with the parents of his pupils.

Teaching Method

It is democratic administration and supervision which helps to make possible a democratic relation between the teacher and the taught. When democracy permeates the classroom the teacher and pupils-share in planning and purposing. There is a minimum of command and compulsion. Thus, instead of teaching dogmatically and compelling the pupils to imbibe passively the doses of information doled out by him, the pupil is encouraged to take an active part in the learning process. He is given the freedom to ask questions, to reason, to criticise and even to differ in viewpoints with the teacher. The teacher no longer instructs: he guides, directs and encourages the pupil to explore the vast fields of knowledge. We see this spirit in Montessori method where each pupil learns through the aid of the didactic apparatus and only turns to the teacher for aid when in difficulty.

Similarly, complete freedom to choose and purpose is in evidence in the planning and execution of projects, while the assignment system throws the entire responsibility of learning, of discovery and of exploration of avenues of information on the learner himself. Similarly, the heuristic, the laboratory and experimental methods give the pupils an opportunity to experience the thrill of the discovery through self-activity and effort. It is evident that these democratic methods give due recognition to the intelligence of the pupil—the work must be neither too difficult nor unreasonably easy. It must be difficult enough to challenge the child, and to lead him to think but not so difficult as to discourage him. Besides, these democratic methods of caching emphasize the social element in the learning process without undermining the individuality of the child.

New Establishment and Discipline

The modern view of discipline which we derive from Dewey demands the same unity in the educative process and educative materials as is found in real life. The school is a social unit in which social situations are provided to encourage and direct the impulses of the pupils in common purposes through cooperative activities. The school is not merely a place for authoritative instruction but a place for supplying an environment which will give opportunities for character training. Dewey's whole educational theory aims at substituting social for individual control and this is conducive to character training. The teacher's role in this business of social control is not that of a dictator or a policeman; he is a guide who manipulates the environment and makes use of all opportunities to enrich the experiences of the pupils. His main duty is to initiate them into the social processes of life in a democratic world, and they are made to realize their responsibility as members of the school community. For this purpose, various forms and methods of getting pupils to participate in the government and management of the school have been successfully tried during recent years.

The School Council, the Class Committee System, the Parliament, the School City, Homer Lane's Little Commonwealth, the George Junior Republic are all examples illustrating this truth. These institutions of pupils' self-government frame their own laws and decide the forms of punishments for breach of social laws. It has been found that when the child gets a chance in the government of the school, he realizes the need for laws and rules for the successful organisation of the school society. He gladly accepts those rules. "He realizes that he is a member of the school society, the rules he obeys are his own rules and he obeys them willingly." This is self-discipline which is the essence of democracy.

Conclusion : In the end we might restate some of the principles of democratic education.

(1) Democratic education has as its central purpose the welfare of the people.

(2) Democratic education serves each individual with justice, seeking to provide equal educational opportunity for all, regardless of intelligence, religion, social status, condition or vocational plans.

(3) Democratic education respects the basic civil liberties in practice and clarifies their meaning through study.

(4) Democratic education is concerned for the maintenance of those economic, political and social conditions which are necessary for the enjoyment of liberty.

(5) Democratic education guarantees to all the members of its community the right to share in determining the purposes and policies of education.

(6) Democratic education uses democratic methods in the classroom, in administration and in the student activities.

(7) Democratic education demonstrates that far-reaching changes of both policies and procedures can be carried out in orderly and peaceful fashion when the decisions to make the changes have been developed through democratic methods.

(8) Democratic education liberates and uses the intelligence of all.

(9) Democratic education equips citizens with the materials of knowledge needed for democratic efficiency.

(10) Democratic education helps in self-realisation, create respects for humanity, encourages attitudes for friendship and tolerance, makes for occupational efficiency through occupational adjustment and a sense of civic responsibility in every individual who is properly educated.

The Kothari Commission on Education sums up these ideas beautifully:

"We have to cultivate a spirit of large-hearted tolerance, of mutual give and take, of the appreciation of ways in which people differ from one another. This is a very exciting experiment in living that we have launched upon and no education will be worth while if the educated mind is unable to respond to this situation with intelligence and imagination".

Various Norms

Historical Perspective **:** The trials and tribulations of ninety years brought independence to the Indian subcontinent in 1947. It was not an easy task for the people to realize at once that they were indeed citizens of a free country. The formation of the republic of India was a remarkable political achievement and constitutional land mark which other nation marvelled at. However, the people of India were, for a while bewildered and confused by the rapid changes which were taking place in the political and social spheres. Flags, stamps, coins, office letter heads, uniforms and symbols were more easily and rapidly transformed than the conscious recognition and adaptation to change in peoples' hearts and minds. What did independence and citizenship of free India mean to the common man?

For a few years following independence, the effects of the partition of India, the communal riots, the plight of refugees, food and housing problems, rehabilitation, all assumed gigantic proportions; there was a feeling of dissatisfaction at the unsettled conditions that resulted. However, gradually, under the dynamic leadership of Pt. Jawaharlal Nehru and the formulation of the Five Year Plans, gradual prosperity came about and stability was achieved. People became confident that brighter days were ahead for the country. The celebration of each anniversary of Independence Day and Republic Day restored confidence in the minds of people.

Citizenship Concept

According to the modern concept, a citizen is a member of a country or state and enjoys many civil, social and political rights conferred by the state. He is protected by the state, and is provided opportunities for his development.

Rights and Responsibilities of Citizenship : What are the rights and responsibilities of citizenship? The rights and responsibilities of a citizen differ in various countries and states. They also change during different periods in the history of a country. However, there are some rights and responsibilities that are generally common to every country. In a democracy, there are many rights and privileges, which are available to citizen. According to the Constitution of India, every individual citizen has among others, the following rights:

(1) The right to life and liberty.

(2) The right to work and to own property.

(3) The right to education.

(4) The right to vote, to have justice and to petition.

(5) The right to hold public office.

(6) Freedom of thought and speech as well as freedom of the press.

A citizen has also the following responsibilities :

(1) Obedience to the laws of the country.

(2) Loyalty to the country.

(3) Payment of taxes.

(4) Helping in the administration of the country.

Training in Citizenship : Before India gained independence, education for citizenship was unheard of. "Divide and Rule" was the best policy for foreign rulers to observe. In applying for jobs in government service, or in admission to hospitals, schools or colleges, one had to specify in the application forms whether the individual was a "Brahmin or Non-brahmin," "Agriculturist or Non-agriculturist." Even the caste and sub-caste had to be mentioned in many cases. The emphasis on such details, strengthened disparity and consciousness of differences. It in no way encouraged unity or nationalism in people.

The new idea of citizenship, therefore, has taken a long time to be a part of the life and thinking of the people, and has taken still longer to become a part of the school. Most people prefer to think of themselves, their family, group and community in a restricted sense, and hardly in terms of citizens of India, with rights and obligations to the country. The idea of citizenship is too new and too recent to become a conscious part of the lives of people in an effective manner. It is only when a national disaster or emergency occurs, or on independence Day or Republic Day, or when the loss of a loved leader occurs, that people accumulate in large crowds to shout JAI HIND and forget their smaller disparities for a while. But when that moment passes, regionalism and narrow loyalties prevail, language barriers, customs and caste sweep away the enthusiasm for "Bharat Mata."

In short, the idea of citizenship among the people of India is yet not strong enough, and why? Perhaps it is because the feeling of Nationalism is not yet strengthened or developed in us sufficiently.

Training in citizenship, therefore, may well begin with a development and strengthening of nationalism.

Nationalism Reach

Unfortunately, for centuries, the idea of nationhood or nationalism has been obscured by the consciousness and importance attached by people to the states, provinces or regions to which they belonged. It was only after independence that the five hundred or more of princely states merged with India, and the provinces were re-organized. While political boundaries changed, regional, linguistic and provincial loyalties and characteristics of the people did not. Deep-rooted sentiments, traditions and customs cannot be wiped away with political boundaries. In this connection, Pt. Jawaharlal Nehru said:

> "Let us, citizens of the Republic of India, stand up, straight backed and look up at the skies, keeping our feet firmly on the ground, and bring about the synthesis and integration of the Indian people. Political integration has already taken place, but what I am here after is something much deeper than that, an emotional integration of the Indian people so that we may be welded into one strong national unit, maintaining at the same time, all our wonderful diversity." From this speech, delivered a decade after independence, we see that according to Pt. Jawarharlal Nehru, citizenship and nationalism are to be built up though emotional integration.

National Unity

The loyalties of people function at an emotional level in the first instance. Language, customs, region, similarity of dress and food, bind people together and have bound people together for centuries in India. They will continue to do so. It is only a greater sentiment or feeling for unity amidst this diversity which can bring the people of different languages, regions and traditions together. This bringing together and rising above group and regional loyalties with a feeling of unity as a whole—may be called emotional integration. India or Bharat Mata has to be the emotionally integrating factor for the diverse peoples and regions of India. So far, a Malayali may not recognize that he has anything in common with a Punjabi, nor an Assamese have much to say to a Rajasthani, or Gujarati; regionalism, language, disparity and customs stand in the way. How can unity be achieved, except through the emotional integration of these diversities, into a feeling of oneness, as a nation?

Emotional Integration through Education : Dr. K.L. Shrimali, in one of his addresses, emphasised the task of education as a force which can lead to national and emotional integration in India. He said : "If we are convinced that in the present state of our development, we must make a deliberate effort to develop national consciousness among our people, it is a legitimate demand that our educational system should be geared to fulfil this purpose. Educational policies and practices are determined largely by national needs and requirements and our greatest need today is the development of national consciousness among our youth. Schools must become the instruments for the realization of national ideals.

They must give to the youth a feeling of common interest and a sense of belonging to a worthy national community, which had a great past and a present full of hopes and dreams, merging into a glorious future. Education must make the growing youth realize that they are indissolubly bound to the nation and its destiny, its tragedies and joys, its conflicts and settlements they should come to regard it with pride and love—and serve it wholeheartedly."

The Central Government set up an Emotional Integration Committee in 1961, which made a number of suggestions in this regard. In making their suggestions the Committee stated : "We would like to stress the composite structure of Indian culture, and the need to promote unity in diversity by cherishing and respecting equally the various cultural strands which enrich Indian civilization".

Emotional Unity

Aims and Curricula : It was pointed out by Gandhiji in the Wardha Scheme that the educational system failed to stress the culture and aspirations of the people of India. This narrowness of curricula has led to the strengthening of disparity and lack of nationalism. We must introduce to students the concept of India as a whole, composed of a large number and variety of geographical areas, their physical features, occupations, crafts and products. Each region should be studied carefully in detail, and followed by its political and cultural history, its literature, life of the people, arts, crafts, traditions, and language. It is unfortunate that studies in detail of the regions and human geography, cultures and literatures have been neglected for so long. How can there be national unity when there is so much of ignorance about the composite parts of the country?

The pupils' interest in and curiosity about the rich diversity of the country must be aroused through proper study. Often foreign tourists know more about various states and parts of India, than our people themselves. This is often due to lack of curiosity and enthusiasm caused by ignorance. Pictures, slides and films should be used frequently to acquaint students with all human and cultural, historical and geographical aspects of the regions of India.

The study of one or two regional languages, besides the mother tongue and English should be encouraged in the school.

Travel and Tours : A feeling of unity and national consciousness among the young, can also be encouraged through travel, and sight-seeing. Tours of school children at inexpensive rates should be sponsored by the states and local bodies, and pupils should be given the opportunities of visiting states other than their own. Travel and sight-seeing can teach the pupils much more effectively than books, and a feeling for the beauty, variety, and richness of cultures in India can be experienced directly. The emotions of pupils will thus be effected and harnessed in the task of national integration. Much ignorance about distant states and regions will be dispelled. Understanding and appreciation of various regional differences will be inculcated in the young.

Multi-cultural Camps and Student Exchanges : Regional education authorities should promote emotional integration through organizing school camps which will be attended by students of various regions. Cultural exhibits, and performances of various musical and other items can be arranged. These will provide opportunities for student of various states to live together in camps and to cooperate in the performance and execution of many common activities: dances, songs, festivals of the region. Besides this, group of students or individual students may be provided stipends and scholarships for visits to study for a year or so in other states. Exchange of students between one or more states will be valuable experiences for the young.

They will learn to understand and appreciate India much more by this means than by any other. Students who go to another state should live with families in that state. Thus language, culture, traditions and customs will be learnt not only in the school but in the home where a student lives as an exchange student. Such experiments have been tried in International living in many countries including India. Unfortunately this experiment has not been tried within India to promote national and emotional integration among our own students.

Cultural and Co-curricular Activities : While cultural and co-curricular activities occupy an important part of the school curriculum, very little attempt has been made to promote national and emotional integration through these. Instead of emphasising only the particular state's or region's culture, attempts should be made to introduce the culture of other states. Songs, dances, dramas, dresses and cookery from all the states of India should figure on the schools' co-curricular programmes. The parents and community should participate in some of these cultural programmes. This will widen their outlook and teach them many new things about the rest of India.

Secularism, Religious and Moral Education : National and emotional integration has much to do with the development of secularism, religious and moral education. It may appear that secularism, is in direct contradiction to religious education. By religion here, we do not mean dogmatism or superstition. And by secularism we do not mean antireligious feelings. Education in modern, independent India has evolved anew concept of secularism as also of religious education. This concept may well be explained in the words of Dr. Karan Singh.

> "According to this view, the true sanction behind secularism is that all religions are, in fact, so may different approaches towards the same divine reality. As numerous streams flow from many directions to join the same ocean, as many paths ascend from different directions to the same summit, so do the various religions that developed among mankind through the ages, have as their goal the same divine communion. If a divine reality exists,—as I firmly believe it does—it must ultimately be the same for all human beings. Howsoever deep—the differences that divide various religious experiences, these must necessarily be resolved into an integral and transcendent unity."

According to the Sri Prakasha Committee on Religious and Moral Instruction of 1959, there is no real disparity among the different religions. An analysis is made of each religion according to four aspects, according to this Committee: (1) The philosophy of the religion, (2) the personality of the founder, (3) the rituals, and (4) the ethical bias of the religion.

An understanding and appreciation of the lives and philosophical principles set forth by great leaders and founders of religious faiths should be given to pupils, for example, Ramachandra, Krishna, Buddha, Confucious, Zoroaster, Mahavira, Jesus Christ, Mohammad and Guru Nanak. A study of other religious faiths besides their own, will give pupils a broader viewpoint, and develop tolerance, sympathy and understanding. Bigotry and intolerance will disappear among the younger generation if introductory education in the world's religions and their leaders is imparted to them.

It will also be evident from a study of the world's religious faiths that moral and spiritual values are held in common, and that every religion is man's attempt to grasp the ultimate truth and reality.

If national and emotional integration through education is the means of achieving unity and a sense of nationhood among the younger generation in India, and we have discussed some of the ways of achieving it, we come again to the first question, raised in the beginning of this chapter: What else, besides natural and emotional integration, do we need for good citizenship?

Innovative Approaches

Having established the foundations of citizenship among the young through educating for national and emotional integration, what further steps are needed to help in making students good citizens?

Imparting Direct Knowledge and Information : Many people are quite ignorant about the rights and duties of citizens. Pupils can learn about the rights and duties of citizenship in the classroom. In a democracy, the centre, states and local bodies have special duties and responsibilities. The Constitution of India should be studied. Besides, visits to the Central, State, or Municipal Legislative bodies should be arranged for the students. Occasionally, a member of the legislature may be asked to address the students regarding his duties and responsibilities. How and why are laws made? Why do we have to obey laws? What happens when we break the law? Can laws be changed? How, why and by whom? These are questions which should be discussed with the member of parliament or legislator.

Books on citizenship are often dull, but newspaper items and topical articles in magazines, related to the topic of citizenship and similar issues should be read and discussed in the class. Often, only students who study "civics", study citizenship. This is an erroneous attitude, all the students are citizens, and from the primary school onwards, every student should have a knowledge of what the idea of citizenship means.

Encouraging Group and Cooperative Feelings : The individual cannot exist alone in the world. Society requires the development of group feelings and cooperation, for its survival and progress. A good citizen is conscious of the necessity of living and working for the group, while contributing his individual abilities and aptitudes for the good of society and the group. Consciousness of his own rights and those of others must be developed in students along with the duties and obligations attached to them. Discipline, harmony and cooperation are all qualities necessary for good citizenship.

Cooperative group action should follow group feelings in a citizen. Students should be urged and encouraged to explore the community and civic institutions. Observation of how the local government functions, should provide a basis for developing self-government in schools.

Community and civic projects should be undertaken by students, for example, visits to schools for the blind or deaf or handicapped. Visits to schools for the underprivileged, visits to farms, fields and factory areas. Each of these visits should provide opportunities for developing group projects by students, for example, a group of ninth grade students of a school organized a drama project involving children in a slum area.

These children of the slum, after several visits of the students, and much practice, then produced a play, which their parents and other residents of the slum area were amazed to see. On the other hand, a group of seventh class students went on weekly visits to a nearby blind school, where the blind students in return taught them to sing some beautiful songs, the seventh class students in return taught the blind students to speak several sentences in English.

A School Parliament : It is a very useful form of encouraging students to learn the duties and functions of government. Elections are held in the school on the basis of the party system. Members to a legislature are elected. There is a Cabinet of Ministers. Many of school responsibilities—cleanliness, drama, publications, etc., are supervised by a cabinet of ministers elected by students. The meaning of government and citizenship becomes very clear to students by this means.

School-Community Relations : The community and the school should become strongly aware of each other's presence and potentialities, and many school and community activities should reflect this awareness. Young students should realize that this awareness is a part of citizenship; and reflects the democratic nature of society. Involvement of teachers and students in useful community activities is essential. At the same time, all community resources by way of experts and other requisites should be available for the school, whenever, needed.

18

Educational Management

Educational effort in India is organised, administered and supervised by four types of agencies. Their functions and responsibilities, though different and distinct, quite often overlap, for none of them is singly and wholly responsible for policy-making, operation and finance. These four types of agencies are: (1) the Central Government. (2) the State Government, (3) Local Bodies, and (4) Private Enterprise.

Central Authority

Historical Retrospect : During the British regime the alien government was not interested in educating the Indian masses, save some upper classes for the limited purpose of providing junior officials for its own administration and to keep its hold on India. Ripon, in 1883, placed primary education under the local bodies. Educational administration was highly centralised, the provinces were merely carrying out the policies of the Centre. The whole initiative, policy-making, organisation and administration, were dictated by the Centre as it suited their purpose. In 1901 was created the post of Director-General of education, and, in 1910, was established the Department of Education under the charge of a Member of the Viceroy's Executive Council. In the same year, a Secretary was appointed to look after the Department of Education, Health and Lands. In 1921, with the Montford Reforms, education was transferred to the Provinces. With this delegation of authority and responsibility to elected ministers the Centre became totally indifferent to education. The Hartog Committee deplored this apathy as unfortunate. This state of affairs continued till World War II, when the Centre again started taking some interest in education. In 1945, the Department of Education was separated from Health and Lands.

With Independence coming in 1947, full-fledged Ministry of Education and Scientific Research was established. The Centre's interest in education continued to grow. However, we find considerable overlapping in the efforts of the Centre and the States of the Union, specially in the matter of reorganisation of education. The Centre issued directive without sharing responsibility. The Slates looked at this with suspicion.

They wanted to retain the power they had been enjoying for long. The result was that even after the Constitution of India came into force the Centre adopted an isolationist policy and gave no help to the States in the matter of education.

With the launching of the Five-Year-Plans the policy changed. The Centre allotted funds to the States; specially for the expansion and development of universal primary education and social education of the adults. With the control of these grants, the centre started supervising education in the States. The Centre's educational activities expanded and the Central Ministry of Education was reorganised from time to time.

It discharged its responsibilities through the appointment of advisory councils for several purposes and continued to help the States with funds, technical advice, coordination and cooperation. At present, this is done by the Ministry of Education and Social Welfare through its various departments. Of these we are mainly concerned with the Department of Education and Culture.

The activities of the Central Ministry of Education of the Government of India are chiefly directed by the policy flowing from the clauses of the constitution of India.

Policy for Education

The following articles of the Indian Constitution form the bases of the Broad Educational Policy of India.

Art. 28 : (1) No religious instruction shall be provided in any educational institution wholly maintained out of state fund.

(2) Nothing in clause (1) shall apply to an educational institution which is administered by the state but has been established under any endowment or trust which requires that religious instruction shall be imparted in such institution.

(3) No person attending any educational institution recognised by the State or receiving aid out of the state funds shall be required to take part in any religious instruction that may be imparted in such institutions or to attend any religious worship that may be conducted in such institution or in any premises attached thereto unless such persons or, if such person is a minor, his guardian has given his consent thereto.

Art. 29 : (1) Any section of the citizens residing in the territory of India or any part thereof having a distinct language, script or culture of its own shall have the right to conserve the same.

(2) No citizen shall be denied admission into any educational institution maintained by the State or receiving aid out of State funds on grounds only of religion, race, caste, language or any of them.

Art. 30 : (1) All minorities, whether based on religion or language, shall have the right to establish and administer educational institutions of their choice.

(2) The state shall not in granting aid to educational institutions, discriminate against any educational institution on the ground that it is under the management of a minority, whether based on religion or language. Part IV- Directive Principles of State Policy

Art. 41 : The State shall, within the limits of its economic development, make effective provision for securing the right to work, to education and to public assistance in case of unemployment, old age, sickness and disablement.

Art. 45 : The State shall endeavour to provide within a period of ten years from the commencement of this Constitution, for free and compulsory education for all children until they complete the age of fourteen years.

Art. 46 : The State shall promote, with special care: the educational and economic interests of the weaker sections of the people, and in particular of the Scheduled Castes and the Scheduled Tribes, and shall protect them from social injustice and all forms of exploitation.

Entry 63 : The institutions known at the commencement of this Constitution as the Banaras Hindi University, the Aligarh Muslim University and the Delhi University, and any other institution declared by the Parliament by law be institutions of national importance.

Entry 64 : Institutions for scientific or technical education financed by the Government of India wholly or in part and declared by Parliament by law to be institutions of national importance.

Entry 65 : Union agencies and institutions for:

(a) professional, vocational or technical training, including the training of police officers; or

(b) the provision of special studies or research; or

(c) scientific or technical assistance in the investigation or detection of crime.

Entry 66 : Coordination and determination of standards in institutions for higher education or research and scientific and technical institutions.

List II-State List

Entry 11 : Education including universities subject to the provisions of entries 63.64,65 and 66 of List I and entry 25 of List III.

List III-Concurrent List

Entry 25 : Vocational and technical training of labour.

Part XVII-Official Languages

Art. 344 : (1) The President shall, at the expiration of five years from the commencement of this Constitution and thereafter at the expiration of ten years from such commencement, by order, constitute a commission which will consist of a chairman and such other members representing the different languages specified in the eighth Schedule as the President may appoint and the order shall define the procedure to be followed by the commission.

(2) It shall be the duty of the commission to make recommendations to the President as to-

(a) the progressive use of the Hindi language for the official purposes of the Union.

(b) restrictions on the use of English language for all or any of the official purposes of the Union.

(c) the language to be used for all or any of the purposes mentioned in article 348.

(d) the form of numerals to be used for any one or more specified purposes of the Union.

(e) any other matter referred to the commission by the President as regards the official language of the Union and the language for communication between the Union and the State or between one State and another and their use.

(3) In making their recommendations under clause (2) the commission shall have due regard to the industrial, cultural and scientific advancement of India and the just claim and the interest of persons belonging to the Non-Hindi speaking areas in regard to the Public Services.

(4) There shall be constituted a committee consisting of thirty members of whom twenty shall be members of the House of the People (Lok Sabha) and ten shall be members of the council of States (Rajya Sabha) to be elected respectively by the members of the House of the People and the Members of the Council of States in accordance with the system of proportional representation by means of the single transferable vote.

(5) It shall be the duty of the committee to examine the recommendations of the commission constituted under clause (1) and to report to the President their opinion thereon.

(6) Notwithstanding anything in article 343 the President may after consideration of the report referred to in clause (5) issue directions in accordance with the whole or any part of that report.

Art. 345 : Subject to the provisions of articles 346 and 347 the legislature of a state may by law adopt any one or more of the languages in use in the State or Hindi as the languages to be used for all or any of the official purposes of that State.

Provided that, until the legislature of that State otherwise provides by law. English language shall continue to be used for those official purposes within the State for which it was being used immediately before the commencement of this Constitution.

Art. 350 A : It should be the endeavour of every State and of every local authority within the State to provide adequate facilities for instruction in the mother-tongue at the primary stage of education to children belonging to linguistic minority groups; and the President may issue such directions to any State as he considers necessary or proper for securing the provision of such facilities.

Art. 351 : It shall be the duty of the Union to promote the spread of the Hindi language, to develop it so that it may serve as a medium of expression for all the elements of the composite culture of India and to secure its enrichment by assimilating without interfering with its genius, the forms, styles and expression used in Hindustani and other languages of India specified in the eighth Schedule, and by drawing, wherever necessary or desirable for its vocabulary primarily on Sanskrit and secondarily on other languages.

Concurrent List

Art. 346 : The language for the time being authorised for use in the Union for official purposes shall be the official language for communication between one State and another State and between a State and the Union.

Provided that if two or more states agree that the Hindi language should be the official language for communication between such states that language may be used for such communication.

There had been large variations in the curriculum and structure of education, service conditions of teachers, examination systems, staffing patterns and standards of education over the various States of India right from the beginning of the modern system of education originating with the British rule in India. Uniformity in these matters could not be brought about as the education was on the State list and the States were free to make their own rules. It could be brought about only when the Central Government was made empowered to legislate on education. This was possible only when education was placed on either the Union list or on the Concurrent list. Efforts had been made several times, to place education on the Concurrent list, but success was not achieved.

It was only in 1975 that education was voted to be on the Concurrent list. Since then, therefore, the Central Government has been empowered to make legislations, on education also with the provision that if State act comes into conflict with the act passed by the Union Government, the latter act will prevail. This change has been very much welcome by the people of India, particularly the teachers. The present position in this regard after this change stands as follows:

(a) The State Governments even now can make their own legislations on education.

(b) The Central Government is also empowered to get any act about education passed through the Union legislative bodies.

(c) If the State act and the Union Government act happen to be in contradiction, the Union Government act will prevail.

Bringing education on the Union list has been considered a very progressive and useful step in the direction of educational development in India. It may be expected that this will ensure uniformity as well as adequate and desired diversity within the framework of this broad uniformity in the field of Indian Education. It may now be possible for the Central Government to pass a legislation in favour of 10+2+3 system, a uniform structure of education for all states. It may also pass legislations regarding a uniform structure of education for all States. It may also pass legislations regarding a uniform national policy on university admissions, vocationalization of education, teachers service conditions, uniform examinations system, etc. Another great advantage of putting education on concurrent list as put by Shukla (1983) is that this may lead to "Greater responsibility of the Central Government in educational matters. It may even have to find more funds from its own revenue to be spent on education, particularly in respect of those aspects of education which are covered by a Central legislation". He, therefore, considers this change to be in the larger interest of Indian Education.

Centre's Role

It is clear from the above that the Constitution restricts the role of the Central Government to the following activities:

1. The administration of institutions of national importance such as the National Library, the Indian Museums, etc.
2. The financing and supervision of the Central Universities of Banaras, Aligarh, Delhi, Vishva Bharati, JNU, etc.
3. The administration of institutions for scientific and technical education financed by the Government of India.
4. The coordination of facilities and determination of standards in respect of higher education, research, scientific and technical education.
5. Sharing responsibility with the State Governments and private bodies for free, universal and compulsory primary education of all children of the age group 6 to 14 years.
6. Coordination in regard to elementary and secondary education.
7. The administration of award of scholarships and fellowships.
8. Assistance for special provision for the education of the Scheduled Castes and Scheduled Tribes.
9. Cooperation with international organisations like the UNESCO.
10. Financing, directing and controlling of education in the Union Territories.

The role of the Central Government in education is limited to providing leadership, helping the State and Private bodies in expanding and improving education including higher education, maintaining standards of higher education, research, scientific and technical education, administering, expanding and improving education in the Union Territories and preservation of national culture.

The Ministry of Human Resource Development at present looks after about fifty subjects, of which the most important are the following:

(1) School Education, (2) Higher Education, (3) Technical and Professional Education, (4) Social Education, (5) Physical Education, (6) Youth Welfare, (7) Book Promotion, (8) Educational Research, (9) Languages, (10) Cooperation with UNESCO, (11) Scholarships, (12) Exchange Programmes, (13) Cultural Affairs, (14) Archaeology, (15) Museums and Libraries.

The Central Government, discharges its functions and responsibilities through several advisory councils and statutory organisations. Of these the following are the more important:

1. Central Advisory Board of Education (CABE)
2. Central Board of Secondary Education
3. University Grants Commission (UGC)
4. National Council of Educational Research and Training (NCERT)
5. All-India Council for Women's Education
6. National Council for Women's Education
7. Central Schools Organisation
8. Language Centres

Establishment of Administrative Machinery **:** The Central Ministry of Human Resource Development is run by the following administrative machinery as shown in the following table also:

The Minister of Education is a person elected to either House of Parliament. He is chosen by the Prime Minister and appointed by the President. He is responsible to the Parliament and is the executive head of the ministry. He may or may not be of the

Cabinet rank. He is assisted by a Minister of State and two Deputy Ministers. With their help and that of the Education Secretary he frames policies and takes decisions on the advice given by the various advisory councils. He also disburses grants within the framework of the budget.

The Education Secretary is the administrative head of the ministry. He exercises general supervision and control over all the various activities and divisions of the ministry. All the submissions to the Minister have to be routed through him. He is assisted by two joint secretaries, three education advisers and three directors. The work of the various divisions of the ministry' is allocated to these administrative officers. The number varies from time to time.

The Educational Advisers hold charge of distinct divisions of the ministry. They are of the rank of joint secretaries. Besides coordinating the work of their divisions they are associated with the advisory councils, and as their designation implies, their duty is to tender advice on educational matters to the Minister through the Secretary. The advisers are assisted by a number of deputy, assistant and under-secretaries, holding charge of their respective subjects. In this category also fall the Deputy Education Advisers.

The Attached and Subordinate Officers: The HRD Ministry like other ministries, has a number of attached and subordinate offices under its control. Through these offices are conducted the policies, and activities of the ministry. These offices are responsible for implementation of policies and detailed execution of the decisions and programmes of the government.

Criticism :

(1) The Central HRD Ministry has been doing remarkable work. It has widely associated non-official experts and educationists in planning its policies and implementing its programmes. The association of State representatives ensures wide acceptance and cooperation. It makes the fullest use of available expertise and resources. It works in a democratic and constructive way of doing things.

(2) The tendency in the Central Secretariat is, however, developing towards uniformity and rigidity. Quite often,

many good schemes are killed at the altar of bureaucracy and because of paucity of funds.

(3) Some of the advisory councils meet very rarely at long intervals, and work under the influence of officials. They have fallen into the nit of routine.

(4) The policy of matching grants is proving harmful for educational development. Poorer States and institutions, are unable to provide their share and remain backward. Consequently there is an increase in the inequality of educational opportunities.

Suggestions: The desirable improvement in the role of the Central Government in educational matters may be defined thus:

(1) The Education Minister must enjoy a Cabinet rank; this will give prestige and due importance and status to education. The recent reorganization making it a part of the Ministry of Human Resource Development has lowered its prestige and importance.

(2) The Centre should have a continuing and closer concern for education in the States. Reintroduction of the Indian Education Service (I.E.S.) will go a long way to achieve this.

(3) The Centre should provide adequate protection against the possible misuse of the education function. Democratic control should rest with the people and should be further strengthened. Education should not be allowed to propagate the ideology of any political party.

(4) The Centre should equalise educational opportunities all over the States and the whole country, which means giving more funds and encouragement to poorer areas.

(5) The Centre should collect and publish information on conditions and needs of different areas.

(6) The Centre should conduct cooperative research, coordinate and disseminate the findings and adopt means of implementing them.

(7) Some of the advisory bodies need to be raised to the statutory level. They should be made autonomous so that

they become free from bureaucracy and redtapism. They should include the teachers from the field and not only "big" people.

(8) Some more fields of education, such as preschool education and teacher education, etc., should receive closer and more attention from the Centre and in general, it may be said that wherever the States are deficient the Centre must step in.

Bodies of Advisory Nature

The Central Advisory Board of Education (CABE) : The CABE was first established in 1920. Its main function was to tender advice to the provincial governments. It was abolished in 1923 as a measure of economy. Later on, as a result of the recommendation of the Hartog Committee (1928), it was reviewed in 1935, and has been in existence ever since.

The resolution says "The Government of India feels that there was need for review and reform in the system of education, comprehensive examination of educational problems and the central government should play its part in educational reconstruction. The most valuable contribution towards the right development of education in India can come from a clearing house of ideas and information like the CABE.

The Functions of the CABE are:

(1) To advise on any educational question which may be referred to it by the Government of India or by any local government.

(2) To call for information and advice regarding educational development of special interest and value of India; to examine this information and evaluate it with recommendations to the Government of India and the local government.

These functions have been deliberately defined broadly so that the Board remains a live organisation endowed with incentive and growth. It should, however, be noted that the Board's recommendations are only advisory and not binding on the government.

Central Board of Secondary Education : The Central Board of Secondary Education was established to cater to the educational needs of those students who had to move from State to State due to their parent's transfer, etc. It has been making significant contribution towards raising the standard of education, specially secondary education, improvement of curricula, text-books, methods of teaching and evaluation.

In September 1971, it had 781 higher secondary schools, mostly Central Schools affiliated to it. The Board Conducts the All-India Higher Secondary Examination and the Higher Secondary Technical Examination. It also conducts the Matriculation and Higher Secondary (Part I & II) Examinations for schools in Union Territories.

Besides conducting these examinations the other important activities of the Board are examination reform and orientation courses for teachers of affiliated schools. It has introduced physical education as an elective subject for the Higher Secondary Examination and job-oriented courses for its examinations. Work experience has also been introduced in its curriculum.

University Grants Commission (UGC) : As a result of the recommendation of the Sargent Report an advisors' committee was set up in 1945. Its function was to make recommendations for grants to be paid to the various universities. The Ministry of Education forwarded these recommendations to the Finance Ministry, which judged them for itself. Radhakrishnan University Commission (1949) recommended the establishment of a University Grants Commission with its own funds and this was done in 1953. The UGC was established "for the purpose of allocation and disbursement of grants to universities as well as for the purpose of coordination and maintenance of a statutory body by an Act of Parliament passed in 1956 (Act III of 1956).

Composition of the UGC : The UGC consists of nine members appointed by the Government of India. Of these, not more than three are from amongst the vice-chancellors of-universities, two are officers representing the Government of India and the remaining are from reputed educationists and persons of high academic distinctions. The Chairman is a non-official nominated by the Government.

Functions of the UGC : The functions of the UGC may be briefly stated as follows:

(1) Promoting and coordinating university education throughout the country.

(2) Determining and maintaining standards of teaching, examination and research in universities.

(3) Inquiring into the financial needs of the universities (and also colleges), to allocate and disburse grants out of its funds for the maintenance and development of the universities (and colleges) or for any other specific purposes, such as buildings, equipment, libraries, etc.

(4) Recommending to the universities (and colleges) measures for the improvement of standards and advise necessary action in that direction.

(5) Advising the Government of India or State Governments on the allocation of special grants out of their consolidated funds.

(6) Advising on the expansion of existing universities and establishment of new universities in the country.

Criticism : The UGC has been doing great service for the qualitative improvement of higher education. It has been able to introduce the three-year degree course, which is a remarkable achievement. It has helped to bring, about improvement in university curricula, equipment of laboratories and libraries, pay and service conditions of university and college teachers. It has made efforts towards restrictive admission to universities and colleges, medium of instruction, examination reform and introduction of correspondence courses. It has encouraged research in the universities and colleges and by individuals serving and retired teachers.

The present activities of the UGC also include establishment of Centres of Advanced Study, running summer institutes and holding seminars and conferences, teachers' and students' services and welfare, scholarships and fellowships, book production, etc.

Among its recent achievements are raising the salaries of teachers, upgrading their basic qualifications for recruitment and experimentation on internal assessment and awarding grades instead of marks at the final examinations, establishing Academic staff colleges and National Education Testing service.

A very significant step in the direction of upgrading the quality of teacher of higher education has been introduction of the NET examination at the national level.

It is hoped that the Commission would be able to expand and improve its services as more and more funds are placed at its disposal.

National Council of Educational Research and Training (NCERT) : Historical Retrospect: Soon, after the publication of the Report of the Secondary Education Commission (1953), the Government of India paid close attention to the improvement of school education. Education being a State subject, the Centre went about the task in cooperation with the States. The Central Institute of Education had already been established for the training of secondary teachers. From 1954 onwards a number of institutes were started, such as the Central Bureau of Text-Book Research (1954). Institute of Educational and Vocational Guidance (1954). All-India Council for Secondary Education, later converted into the Directorate of Extension Programmes for Secondary Education (1959). National Institute of Basic Education (1955). National Fundamental Education Centre (1956) and the National Institute of Audio-visual Education (1959).

In 1961, all these various institutes were brought together under an autonomous organisation, which enjoyed greater resources of personnel and expertise and larger freedom of operation. This organisation, established in September 1961 was named the National Council of Educational Research and Training (NCERT). The various institutes were put under one banner of the National Institute of Education (N.I.E.). In 1968-69 both the Council and the NIE were reorganised into their present form.

Composition of the NCERT : The council consists of the following members:

(1) President - The Minister of Education and Social Welfare.

(2) Chairman of the University Grants Commission (ex-officio).

(3) Secretary to the Ministry of Human Resource Development (ex-Officio).

(4) Four Vice-Chancellors of Universities, one from each zone, nominated by the Government of India.

(5) One representative of each State Government and Union Territory with a legislature, who shall be the Education Minister (or his representative), and in the case of Delhi, the Chief Executive Councillor (or his representative).

(6) All members of the Executive Committee not included in the above.

(7) Such other persons, not exceeding twelve, as the Government of India may, from time to time, nominate. Not less than four of these shall be school teachers.

There are one whole-time Director and a Joint-Director of the Council who look after the day-to-day administration.

There are two important Committees of the Council, viz., the Executive Committee and the Programme Advisory Committee.

Functions of the Council : The main functions of the NCERT are:

(1) To assist the Ministry of Human Resource Development in the formulation and implementation of its policies and programmes in the field of school education.

(2) To develop necessary research, experiments, pilot projects, advanced training and extension services.

(3) To maintain close liaison between the Central Ministry and the State Education Departments and Universities.

To discharge these functions the NCERT organises and undertakes educational studies, investigations and surveys, conducts pre-service and in-service training of an advanced level, organises extension services for institutions, disseminates improved educational techniques and practices, assists State Education Departments, universities and institutions, publishes books, periodicals and other educational literature and acts as a clearing house for ideas and information on all matters related to school education.

The activities and programmes of the council are carried out by the following Departments and Units of the National Institute of Education (NIE):

1. Department of Educational Psychology and Foundations of Education. (DEPFE)
2. Department of Preschool and Elementary Education
3. Department of Education in Science and Mathematics (DESM)
4. Department of Education in Social Sciences and Humanities (DESSH)
5. Department of Teacher Education and Extension (DTEE)
6. Department of Educational Measurement and Evaluation (DEME)
7. Department of Computer Education and Technology Aids (DECTA)
8. Department of Educational Survey and Data Processing Unit (DESDP)
9. Division of Library Documentation and Information Services (DLD)
10. Publication Division (PD)
11. Department of Educational Research and Policy Perspectives (DERPP)
12. International Relations Division (IRD)
13. Department of Women's Studies (DWS)

Criticism : The NCERT has been doing commendable work in several areas of school education and has been successful in bringing about a lot of improvement. Among its outstanding achievements are in the fields of Science Education Curriculum and Textbooks. Teaching Aids and Examination Reforms. Some of the text-books produced by the Council are really very good, while others have not proved popular in the field. The Council should co-opt more-school teachers on the text-book and curriculum preparation boards to make its output more realistic and fruitful.

The Council is the most important national organisation for educational research and has done considerable and useful work. There is however need for greater stress on the development of basic tools for fundamental and functional research, an area in which India is very deficient. There is also need for coordinating the research being done in the country and to disseminate research findings. The Council has taken an important step in this direction by compiling and publishing the abstracts of degree and doctoral researches. It should also undertake training of advanced research workers.

The Council has launched integrated 4-year courses of teachers' training in its Regional Colleges. Recently a 2-year B.Ed, training programme has also been introduced. It may, however, be recommended that instead of diversification these colleges should concentrate on only a few intensive programmes.

The Council shows promise and much more will be achieved in coming years if it overcomes the limitations of finance and personnel. A possible solution is to associate more and more local persons in its programmes and activities.

Government of State

Historical Retrospect : The State Government stated as units of educational administration with the appointment of Directors of Public Instruction and Inspectors to assist them. They mainly dealt with recognition and inspection of the schools and recommending grant-in-aid. However, the policy continued to be centralised. With Montford reforms education was transferred to the States in 1921. The I.E.S. was abolished. Education was put in charge of elected ministers responsible to the State legislatures.

Role of Government : After Independence the Indian Constitution made the States responsible for education at all stages with certain exceptions, such as the Central Universities at Banaras, Aligarh, Delhi and Shantiniketan. Institutions of scientific and technical education financed by the Central Government, institutions for professional and vocational education, higher institutions for scientific research and technology etc. Thus, education at all stages is a State responsibility, but the Constitution places the responsibility of coordination and maintenance of standards at higher levels on the Centre. Article 45 of the Constitution directs the States "to endeavour to provide, within a period of ten years from the commencement of this Constitution for free and compulsory education for all children until they complete the age of fourteen years."

In recent years there has been a rapidly growing trend of close cooperation between the Centre and the States. The Centre is in a position to give more and more financial help and so it secures their cooperation by appointment of a number of Central Councils and Committees, such as the Central Advisory Board, the All-India Council of Secondary Education (later converted into the Directorate of Extension Programmes for Secondary Education), the National Council of Educational Research and Training. On these bodies there are representatives of the States and the Centre and also some well-known educationists. Cooperation is also secured by exchanging views through seminars and conferences. However, in the present pattern the initiative for education and educational reform and reorganisation lies with the States.

State Administrative Machinery : The machinery for educational administration in the State is composed of the Department of Education headed by a Minister, who is responsible to the legislature and is appointed by the Chief Minister. In some States he is assisted by a State or a Deputy Minister. The Minister exercises his authority through the officers of the Department and other agencies like the universities, statutory boards, etc., and is assisted by the Education Secretary at the secretariat level and the Director of Education, who is the chief executive officer of the department. It may be known as follows:

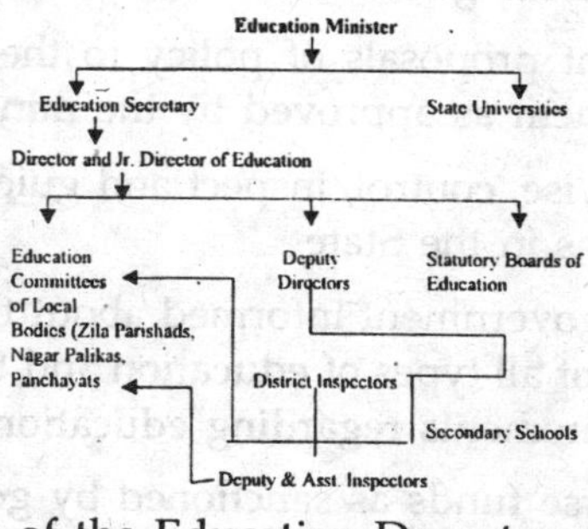

The functions of the Education Department are:

(1) Framing of policies, procedures, rules, regulations and determining standards.

(2) Inspection and evaluation to determine efficiency of operation.

(3) To run schools and colleges established by government and to control private institutions.

(4) To deal with matters regarding curricula and text-books.

(5) To coordinate educational programmes of the Stale in order to promote efficiency.

(6) To provide leadership-for planning and research.

(7) To provide consultative and information services.

The Minister is generally, a non-technical man with almost little experience of either education or administration. He has to lean heavily on the bureaucracy for guidance. He can make or mar the whole education system. "If he is a man of vision, courage and devotion to education, he can provide the leadership for the development of an educational programme in his state which will meet the needs of the individuals and of society..... On the other hand, if he is lacking in vision, courage and administrative ability, the education of the state cannot be progressive."

The Secretary frames policies and passes orders on behalf of the government. He is generally a man from the I.A.S. He acts as a link between the minister and the director. The Director's proposals are critically examined by the staff of the Secretariat before being submitted for the approval of the Minister.

The Directorate of Education is an executive body carrying out the policies of the government. Its main functions are:

(1) To present proposals of policy to the secretary and to execute them as approved by the minister.

(2) To supervise, control, inspect and guide the educational institutions in the State.

(3) To keep government informed about the conditions and progress of all types of education and the people's needs and requirements regarding education.

(4) To disburse funds as sanctioned by government.

(5) To provide expert advice both to the institutions and the secretariat.

The Director of Education is the highest officer of the directorate of education. Recently in some States a director has been appointed from the administrative services, but generally, he is a technical expert and chosen for his long teaching, inspecting and administrative experience in the department. As the highest executive he is responsible for the administration of education in the entire State. Assisted by a number of deputy and assistant directors he performs the following duties:

(1) To supervise the work of the government officials, inspectors, teachers of government institutions and to deal with their leave, transfer and discipline.

(2) To determine and disburse the grants-in-aid to the State Universities, Local Bodies, and the large number of Privately managed institutions.

(3) To supervise, control, inspect and guide the Private Institutions.

(4) To act as Chairman of the State Board of Secondary Education, an examining body, and to administer and exercise emergency powers in this respect. Some Boards of Secondary Education have a whole-time chairman who is not the Director.

(5) To act as a member of the syndicate/executive council of the State Universities.

(6) To frame policies and proposals and submit them to the secretary for the approval of the minister.

(7) To administer education throughout the State.

(8) To organise the training of primary and secondary teachers, where this is not done by the universities.

Inspectors: The function of inspection is carried on by the district inspectors (called District Education Officers in some States). They make a report to the diıector. The headmasters of schools are directly responsible to the inspector for administration and discipline. In government schools he supervises the work of headmasters. In non-government schools administration is carried on by their managing committees and the inspector merely assesses and recommends grants-in-aid. He has nothing to do with university education but in the field of primary education administered by district boards and municipal boards, he provides the inspecting staff, the deputy and sub-deputy inspectors whose work he supervises with leadership and guidance."

Criticism :

(1) The Central financial assistance is leading to the harmful tendency of "regimental uniformity". There is also "an increasing tendency towards centralisation in education in recent years..... the new plans of education in different states are based on the pattern suggested by the Centre." For example, we now have the 10+2 scheme on insistence of the central government.

(2) The minister is committed to the policies of the ailing political party. He is a non-technical man and therefore depends upon the secretariat, which is also manned by non-technical men. There is only a superficial efficiency. With the changes of ministers there is also a change of policy so that continuity is broken. The political ideology of the ruling party dominates educational policy. There is a lack of dispassionate treatment of educational matters on merit.

(3) The secretary is appointed from the administrative service. He lacks conceptual and technical skills, necessary insight, initiative and educational experience. He is with the department of education for a short period and may have to look after other departments of the government in addition to his educational duties. His staff is also non-technical and things are run by trial-and-error efforts.

(4) The Director's assignment of work is much too heavy. Though he is assisted by deputies, he is left with very little time for planning for progress and improvement. He is to work within the steel-frame of the budget. His proposal to the minister are routed through the secretariat, where they are pruned and cut-down beyond recognition. It has been often felt that the Director should have direct access

to the minister. The Sargent Report says. "There can be no possible justification for interposing an officer without an expert knowledge of education between the director of public instruction and the minister of education to whom he should be directly responsible." The Secondary Education Commission too recommended, "where the Director himself is not the secretary of the department he should have the status of a joint secretary and should have direct access to the minister."

(5) Like the Director of education, the inspector has to do much routine work, and even though he is a technical man he has little scope for initiating local plans. Secondary schools are in large number. Administration has to deal with managing committees. The government cannot have effective checks. Very often the plans and policies of the department are opposed by the managing committees. Under such conditions efficiency becomes a casualty.

(6) There is a growing tendency of political interference in educational matters. Local political pressure is rampant. There is also a lot of encroachment on the autonomy of the universities. Being dependent on government grants institutions are hardly free even in academic matters.

(7) More than half a century has elapsed since education was transferred to the States but they have failed to deliver the goods. "The States have also failed to show the educational leadership on which the development of the pupils depends."

Suggestions :

(1) There is need for a consistent educational policy, which is planned after careful thought, vigorously executed and critically evaluated. It should be applied continuously for a considerably long time before being altered.

(2) The policy should be free from the whims of political parties, including the ruling party. In fact, education should be free from governmental and political interference. "Education cannot depend upon the caprice of politicians."

(3) The Department of Education should be strengthened. To be capable of providing the right type of leadership, it should have an efficient and trained staff, adequate in quality and quantity. It should enjoy the confidence of the people and the educators, and freedom from political interference and bureaucracy. As recommended by the Secondary Education Commission the Director of education should have direct access to the minister.

(4) The Director of education and the inspector should be relieved of much of their routine work so that they can devote their attention to the real business of education-purposing, planning, organising, operating and evaluating.

(5) Most attention should be paid to and a large portion of the finances spent on the/improvement of teaching-learning in the schools.

(6) In general, we should agree with Moehlman (1951) that "The education responsibility of the State is to maintain and improve the education function, to remove education inequalities due to economic, social, moral, organisational and educational causes, to provide education leadership to improve the local operation of the education function by providing legal and financial means to assure an adequate education program."

Historical Retrospect: In most countries of the world Local Bodies have been playing a very important role in providing educational facilities, specially in the field of primary education. It has been rightly said that democracy can be exercised best when self-government units are small. This was so in ancient India when every village was a republic. Later on the East India Company did not accept the responsibility of educating Indians. The events of 1857, however, changed the situation. The British planted in India educational practices prevailing in England and adopted the policy of non-intervention in education. Because of the awakening of political consciousness among educated Indians. Ripon was obliged to pass the Local Self-Government Act in 1883 and primary education was entrusted to Local Bodies- municipalities in urban and district boards in rural areas.

Due to the unsatisfactory state of affairs, gradually there

developed a strong reaction against primary education being managed by local bodies. In 1929, the Hartog Committee opposed the practice, and even as late as 1944, the Sargent Report voiced its concern. However, arguments were advanced both in favour and against the practice. The delegation of authority leads to decentralisation and is, therefore, democratic, There is greater sense of participation and responsibility and prevention of wastage of funds.

On the other hand, primary education is an important nation building activity, a source of wiping out mass illiteracy and ignorance, and so it should be handled by a strong governmental machinery. The local bodies have hardly enough resources and competence to bear the burden of universal primary education. Creation of powerful local bodies in the hands of uneducated and ill-equipped members fails to do justice to the important social activity of education.

Under the influence of strong opposition to delegation of powers to local bodies, a rethinking on the problem started and a Committee of the Central Advisory Board of Education recommended withdrawal of powers of inspection from the local bodies. The controversy was, however, set at rest when the Kher Committee of the CABE, in 1952, strongly recommended that "in the interest of mass education and in view of the Constitutional directive on universal, compulsory and free primary education, all types of local bodies should be made to shoulder responsibility for education." Thus, we find that after Independence the role of local bodies in primary education has become more and more active.

Role of the Bodies : The recommendations of the Kher Committee were not universally adopted by all the States. We find that there is no uniform pattern of administration. Even after the reorganisation of the States in 1956, in some parts of the country education is administered by the State Governments while in others responsibility for primary education has been entrusted to Local Bodies. Except Assam and Jammu and Kashmir, however, the major responsibility of primary education rests with the Local Bodies.

In most of the States, municipalities have the legal authority to administer primary education in their areas. In some States (Gujarat and Maharashtra) only the bigger municipalities are authorised to administer primary education and the smaller ones have to contribute their financial share without having any voice in the management. In some States (Uttar Pradesh) municipalities run secondary schools and colleges also.

In rural areas district boards (now called Zila Parishads are made responsible for administering primary education. Some of them run secondary schools also. In some States (Andhra Pradesh and Rajasthan) Panchayat Samities in Block areas and Zila Parishads in non-samiti areas administer primary education.

The educational functions of Local Bodies are:

(1) To organise and administer primary education in their areas.

(2) To implement the Five-year Plans for education.

(3) To provide and maintain accommodation, playgrounds and equipment for their schools.

(4) To enforce compulsory attendance under the prescribed rules and under the special directions of the State Government.

(5) To open new primary schools where needed.

(6) To conduct educational surveys and keep records.

(7) To carry on propaganda for the expansion of primary education.

(8) To recruit and exercise necessary powers over the staff of the schools.

Administrative Machinery : The municipalities and district boards have an Education Committee (or School Board) of elected members. These Committees are responsible for providing and looking after educational facilities in their areas. The budget is decided by the whole municipal or district board, but in a few cases the Education Committees act independently. Some Committees in larger area appoint administrative officers to look after administrative work. In smaller areas administrative work is entrusted to honorary non-officials.

Recruitment of staff is generally done through a selection committee on which the district education officer (inspector) also serves. The State Government is exclusively responsible for training of teachers, prescribing syllabi and preparing text-books and the Local Bodies have to follow them. The State Government gives grants-in-aid to Local Bodies. The district boards receive more generous grants than municipalities.

Inspection of primary schools, is the responsibility of the State and as carried out by the inspecting staff of the State Education Department. Some bigger municipalities (Greater Bombay, Uttar Pradesh, Delhi) appoint their own education officers and inspecting staff. With the introduction of Panchayati Raj and the policy of democratic decentralisation, the Local Bodies have been playing an important part in the maintenance and improvement of primary education. They now have a three-tier system (two-tier in some States) of organisation (1) the village Panchayat at the village level. (2) Panchayat Samities at the Block level, and (3) Zila Parishads at the district level.

Criticism :

(1) The resources of local bodies for financing the programmes of primary education are very inadequate. The pay scales of teachers are poor and they are seldom paid regularly. This very much hampers progress.

(2) The administrative officers and staff are neither well-trained nor competent.

(3) The recruitment, transfer and discipline of teachers are unsatisfactory.

(4) There are pressure groups among the elected members, who, besides being uneducated or ill-educated, misuse the teachers' services for elections and other purposes. Due to this education of the children suffers.

Suggestions :

(1) Democratic decentralisation can be successful only when financial responsibility is centralised, that is, accepted by the State government and the Central government also shares the burden. Pay scales of teachers should be

improved and their service conditions made attractive and satisfying.

(2) For better recruitment of teachers and administrative officers good selection committees of technical persons and experts should be set up and well-defined rules and practices established.

(3) The position of education officers of local bodies must be strengthened and members should be careful to see that discipline among teachers is not weakened.

(4) A uniform administrative pattern should be set up all over the country. Power should be delegated to a powerful local body exclusively set up for education and adequate finances should be placed at its disposal. Building and equipment should be improved. Administration of education should be brought closer to the people and their participation secured.

(5) Improvement of the programmes should include free textbooks, free transportation where necessary, uniforms and mid-day meals. Youth and community recreation centres and rural libraries should be established.

(6) Long-range planning for expansion and improvement of primary education should be undertaken and adhered to. Social education should also be entrusted to local bodies, while guidance, control, finance, and inspection should be the duty of the State.

Agencies of Private Nature

Historical Retrospect: Private, agencies have played a very important role, in education in India. In ancient and medieval times, educational institutions were wholly private. They received land and other grants from the rulers, but were free from their interference. The East India Company being a commercial organisation never accepted educational responsibility. The Christian missionaries, however, worked very diligently to spread educational activities in the country, though with the motive of conversion. Besides them, some British officials and non-officials established educational institutions, perhaps with the idea of encouraging private enterprise among Indians.

A few Indians came forward to establish schools to impart English education. They had to face great odds, which they did with great moral courage. The growth of education continued to remain haphazard till the Wood's Despatch (1854) proposed to give government grants to schools and colleges if they satisfied certain conditions of the government.

The Indian Education Commission of 1882 surveyed the educational activities in the country and recommended that liberal grants should be paid to private agencies which were doing great service to the cause of education. During the period 1882 to 1902, hundreds of Indians created and satisfied public demand for more education and laid the foundation of national life in India. During the early part of twentieth century, education vastly expanded with improvement in both quality and quantity. But later on, during World War II (1939-45) private enterprise had to face great difficulties. The national movement gathered momentum and private enterprise fell from government favour.

After Independence the policy of grants-in-aid became more vigorous. The Government and private agencies have been working together in close cooperation. Private agencies have played a predominant role in all fields of education and at all stages from the primary to the university all over the country and have been specially active in the field of secondary education. There has been a very large expansion both in the number of schools and the students.

Administrative Machinery : Private agencies are registered bodies and have their own elected or otherwise appointed Managing Committees. They are required to fulfil certain minimum requirements for recognition by government to qualify to receive grants: They provide buildings- and equipment from their own resources and employ and control their staff in accordance with prescribed rules.

These private agencies are of several types. Schools and colleges are run by the Christian missionaries, well-established education societies and trusts like the Arya Samaj Ramakrishna Mission, Deccan Education Society, etc. There are smaller registered societies. Then there are the "public" schools providing good education without assistance from the government. Recently there has grown a large number of coaching institutions, which prepare private students to appear at various university and board examinations.

Criticism :

(1) It must be recognised that private enterprise has shown a lot of dynamism and vitality and has proved a valuable asset in the country's educational development. It has played a vital role, specially in rural areas.

(2) The financial condition of a large number of private agencies is not good. Their institutions have poor buildings and the teachers are underpaid.

(3) The majority of private schools lack originality and there is dull uniformity. "They submit to conditions that prevent independence and originality, and their proverbial paucity of funds has always prevented them to risk in such ventures of experimentation as would foster originality."

(4) There have crept many malpractices in some of these private institutions. Some of them charge high fees and capitation charges. There are also instances of irregular and underpayment to teachers with the result that standards are very unsatisfactory.

(5) The unrecognised private coaching institutes are doing great harm to the cause of education. They are generally one man shows with a predominantly profit-motive. Students and teachers alike are exploited to the maximum possible limit.

Suggestions :

(1) The government should come forward to regulate, control and more generously finance private enterprise so that it can make honest effort to share the educational burden of the state.

(2) Private enterprise should be encouraged to develop programmes that would suit the special requirements of their neighbourhood.

(3) It is high time that some measures are adopted to regulate the unrecognised coaching institutes. Their standards must be improved and malpractices curbed. The Delhi

Administration was seriously considering to enact some law in this regard and it would not be too early.

(4) There should be a democratic control of education, which means that it should be administered by a partnership of parents, teachers and private organisations with the sole objective of fulfilling the educational functions and purposes.

In Country's Capital

Historical Retrospect : Originally Delhi was a district of Punjab. In 1912, it was declared a province and in 1952 it became a Part C State with a popular government. On 1st November 1956, It was given the status of a Union Territory. The Municipal Corporation was established on 7th April 1958. It was given the function of running pre-primary and basic education, medical, health, water supply, electricity, etc. Since then three local bodies, the Municipal Corporation, New Delhi, Municipal Committee and Delhi Cantonment Board have been working in Delhi.

The Education Department was established in 1916 under a Superintendent of Education. The post was upgraded and a Director of Education, was appointed in 1949, and he worked as ex-officio secretary of Education to the Union Territory of Delhi. The Director of Education is assisted by a number of Deputy and Assistant Directors and Inspectors of Schools.

Local Bodies: There are three local bodies in Delhi:

The Municipal Corporation has an Education Committee and a whole-time Education Officer. He is assisted by a deputy inspectors of schools also, and a number of assistant education officers. The entire area of Delhi is divided into zones for administrative purposes.

The New Delhi Municipal Committee has also an Education Committee and an Education Officer.

The Delhi Cantonment Board has a very small area. Its schools are administered by the Secretary of the Board.

The Director of Education is associated with all the three above mentioned local bodies.

Primary schools are mainly controlled and run by the corporation.

Private enterprize has been playing a prominent role in Delhi. There are a number of public schools which are recognized but not aided; and a few English Medium Schools prepare students for the Cambridge certificate examination also.

Criticism:

(1) The government is giving considerable grant. Its expenditure is steadily rising. More and more facilities are being provided, yet much remains to be done.

(2) Like all other parts of the country, many schools have no permanent buildings. Some are run in tents and temporary shelters, causing great hardships and frequent breaks during rains and winter. Many of them are poorly equipped. It is strange that private bodies are required to maintain certain minimum standards which the government and corporation do not hesitate to violate. As a consequence standards suffer.

(3) Government domination leads to uniformity and rigidity. There is little experimentations and less research and no application of research findings.

Suggestions:

(1) The improvement of buildings and equipment is an urgent necessity.

(2) There is also much need for improvement of instruction, teaching-learning programmes and techniques, supervision and inspection, experimentation and research.

(3) Teacher education for primary teachers needs a fresh look.

(4) Delhi serves as a model to the whole country. It has, therefore, special responsibility towards setting sound practices. The newly introduced 10+2 scheme requires careful and concerted action. If it is not accompanied by a new outlook and vigorous enthusiasm, it is likely to do more harm than good.

19

Teacher's Responsibility

The institutional framework of the National Adult Educational Programme as visualised by policy makers has already been described. The functions of each administrative unit of the programme are given i.e. at the central level, the National Board of Adult Education, the Central Ministry of Education, The Central Directorate of Adult Education; at the state level the State Board (s) of Adult Education, the State Steering Committees, the State Ministry of Education, the State Directorate of Adult Education; at the District level, the District Adult Education Committee National Service Schemes (NSS), (4) the Nehru Yuvak Kendras and finally (5) through the Integrated Child Development Schemes of the Women and Child Welfare Directorate of the State Governments. A variety of organizations, Governmental, semi-governmental and non-governmental thus, are associated for the first time in the implementation of National Adult Education Programme on a massive scale.

The policy statement on National Adult Education Programme clearly spelt out the arrangements that have to be made to administer the programme. Delineating on the organizational issues, the policy statement says that "from the organisational point of view it is of utmost importance that elaborate preparations are made before launching this massive programme. It is of greatest importance that implementation of adult education programme is decentralized". The policy of associating multiplicity of organization i.e. governmental, semi-governmental and non-governmental raises a number of administrative problems like coordination which is considered as one of the key problems.

Once the goals of the programme have been set, its plans and policies determined, money provided, organization tailored to the need, personnel assigned, directions given, delegations determined and supervision provided for, then the coordination is the means of bringing all those factors together in an interlocking relationship. Coordination has further been viewed as a means by which a blend is secured.

There are a few, generalizations which are usually attributed to the principle of coordination.

1. The more the work of a bureaucracy is sub-divided, the more important it is that the components be assembled in a unified relationship, if the goal of the programme is to be achieved.
2. Coordination relies on the authority that accompanies hierarchy and position, it relies also on individual competence, understanding and voluntary cooperation.
3. The better the goals of the programme are understood and accepted by those who work for it the easier it is to secure voluntary cooperation.
4. Even when conditions evoke voluntary cooperation, coordination is difficult because people in a bureaucracy tend to have a natural desire to be left alone. Consequently, the application of the techniques of coordination is time consuming responsibility of the executive and becomes more so as he (The Executive) rises in the hierarchy.
5. Relatively more time is spent on external coordination than internal coordination.

Administration, therefore, is an attempt to bring diverse units into a working relationship so that, together, they result in achieving the goal. Coordination is viewed as placing the many aspects of an enterprise in proper position relative to each other and to the programme of which they are a part of the policy. In other words, it harmoniously combines 'agents' and 'functions' towards the achievement of a desired goal.

According to professor Mohit Bhattacharya, Coordination assumes importance in organization theory in the context of "intra-organizational interdependencies. Situations of interdependence have to be objectively identified within the organization". Discussing the various aspects of coordination, the author wrote that "coordination is a process of harmonisation of the activities of the different parts of an organization with a view to achieving the goals of an organization".

Keeping in view the above theoretical premise on the principle of coordination an attempt is made in this chapter to study how coordination is secured by the agencies which have run the programme. As the implementation of the programme forms chief concern of the investigator, it is proposed to analyse the problems involved in the following order.

1. The instructors, method of their recruitment, perceptions about the centres, curriculum and learners.
2. The views of the supervisory staff, those of the agencies on the one hand and of the governmental departments on the other about running of the centres (constraints and limitation), instructional material and instructors, mutual perceptions between the two branches of the supervisory cadres to highlight problems of coordination.
3. Structures and functions of the agencies, the opinions of the office bearers and other concerned about the programme and particularly their views on the government's role in organising the programme through the agencies, the problem of coordination in the governmental bodies connected in promoting voluntary agencies in he programme and the agencies themselves, will be highlighted.

Recruitment Method

Instructors or organizers of Animators of an adult education centre is virtually the kingpin in the entire administrative edifice of Adult Education Programme. The policy outline on National Adult Education Programme states that 'the governing consideration in assigning responsibility for instructional arrangements should be (a) the suitability of the persons concerned to organize programmes with a grasp of the conceptual standpoint and with a spirit of commitment'.

Further, the policy planners have identified school teachers, students, village/youth, ex-servicemen and others including retired personnel as the main reservoir from which the instructional cadre can be drawn.

The policy statement as well as the subsequent documents relating to the National Adult Education Programme, however, have not dealt much with the methods or procedures for recruitment to the posts of instructors and thus seems to have left enough autonomy to the agencies in selecting the instructors.

One hardly needs to emphasise the point that the selection procedures adopted by the implementing agencies to recruit instructors would go a long way in ensuring the success of the Adult Education Programme.

In this section, it is proposed to examine the methods of recruitment of instructors adopted by the agencies in the sample. The following table presents the methods followed by different agencies in the recruitment of instructors.

As can be seen from the table, the broad methods of selection of instructor adopted by the agencies in the sample are (1) Interview, (2) Personal contact, (3) Approach by the agency (4) village committees' recommendation.

Method of Selection

Sl. No.	*Agency*	*Inter-view*	*Per-sonal*	*Approach by contact*	*Village Agency*	*Total Comm-ittee recom-mended*
1.	Andhra Mahila Sabha (AMS)	—	8	2	—	10
2.	Bhagavathula Chari-table Trust (BCT)	3	—	—	—	3

Contd...

Sl. No.	*Agency*	*Inter-view*	*Per-sonal*	*Approach by contact*	*Village Agency*	*Total Committee recommended*
3.	Comprehensive Rural Operations Service Society, (CROSS)	—	—	1	2	3
4.	Durga Sangh Seva Samaj (DSS)	3	—	—	—	3
	Total	6	8	3	2	19 (100.00)

The method of selection of instructors through interview was followed by only two agencies in the sample. Each of these agencies has given wide publicity to the programme and this has attracted quite a few applicants for the posts of instructors. While the Bhagavathula Charitable Trust (BCT) did not specify preference in selection to the instructors posts, the Durga Sangh Seva Samaj (DSS) specified that it would give preference to the teachers, retired or in service. About 50 applications are said to have been received for 30 posts of instructors in the case of Bhagavathula Charitable Trust. The selection committee of this agency consisted of the project officer, Director of Adult Education, Andhra University (Vishakhapatnam) and its own officials in charge of horticulture besides block level official incharge of agriculture and education. All the three instructors in the sample reported that they were interviewed on such wide ranging issues like problem of illiteracy, economic development, poverty etc.

The Durga Sangh Seva Samaj also received around 50 applications for the post of instructors out of which 30 were selected. As has already been mentioned, the agency gave preference to teachers, retired as well as those in service. The selection committee constituted by this agency included the Project Officer, the supervisor, block level official incharge of education. The candidates were examined on general topics.

Coming to other agencies, the Andhra Mahila Sabha did not seem to have followed formal methods of selection. A majority of the instructors in the sample (8 out of 10) reported that they were appointed by 'personal contact.' The supervisors visited the villages and ascertained the willingness of people, who in their view, would satisfy the requirements to work as instructors. However, in two centres, where the supervisor found it difficult to appoint instructors the project officer and the supervisor together approached a few candidates and after getting their willingness appointed them as instructors.

As far as CROSS is concerned, a different method of selection is adopted. This agency has established 'Village Sanghams' (associations) in a good number of villages in Bhongir Samiti which is its main area of operation. These 'Sanghams' were informed by the agency about National Adult Education Programme and were asked to suggest the names of those interested for the post of instructors for undertaking teaching in the adult education centres. The candidates whose names were suggested by the Sanghams were selected by the agency and were appointed for two centres as instructors. In the case of the third centre in the sample, as the village Sangham could not arrive at a consensus about any candidate, the agency picked up a candidate who incidentally was also acceptable to the Sangham.

Thus, the methods of selection adopted by all agencies in the sample differed though not drastically. By and large, they have been guided by the exigencies of the situation. No doubt the investigator come across instances of nepotism and also role of subjective factors in the selection especially in the Sirsilla area where Andhra Mahila Sabha implemented the programme. As far as other agencies are concerned, the method of selection adopted by the Bhagavathula Charitable Trust has proved to be more rational compared to Durga Sangh Seva Samaj and Andhra Mahila Sabha. In the anxiety to entrust the job of teaching in the Adult Education Centre only to persons belonging to teaching profession the Durga Sangh Seva Samaj seems to have ignored other factors like age, interest, motivation, ability to teach and the capacity for running the Adult Education Centre.

In the case of the Andhra Mahila Sabha also the investigator noticed such instances like selecting the instructors without taking into consideration their interest in the job. With this, we shall now turn to the socio-economic background of instructors.

Varied Social Factors

In this section, an attempt would be made to know the general background of the instructors. The standard variables that are usually employed to determine the socio-economic status like Age, Caste, Sex, Occupation, Education, Income are taken into consideration besides the teaching experience.

It is evident from the table that half of the male instructors in the sample fall in the age group of 15-25 years. Further, about five male and three female instructors are aged between 26-36. The sample also consists of two instructors (12.50 per cent) who are above 48 years. It may be recalled that the Durga Sangh Seva Samaj has given preference to teachers in appointments to instructor posts. There were two retired teachers who are above 65 years.

The Drawbacks

Among nineteen instructors in the sample, 16 are male instructors and three (15.78 per cent) are female instructors. Regarding caste background, about 5 male instructors (31.25 per cent) and 1 female instructor (33.33 per cent) belong to scheduled caste, about 31.25 male instructors hail from backward classes. The representation of forward castes among instructors is about 37.50 per cent male and 66.27 per cent female.

Thus, scheduled castes and backward castes constitute about 62.50 per cent among male instructors and 33.33 per cent among female instructors which is in conformity with the policy objectives. The female instructors are lesser in number in whole sample. With great difficulty, the investigator could contact three instructors. The Government while admitting the agencies for grants stipulated that about fifty per cent of centres should be earmarked for women. None of the agencies in the sample could satisfy this requirement because of non-availability of women instructors and also learners.

An analysis of the occupational background of the instructors is considered necessary in order to understand which occupational group is showing interest towards the adult education programme. The policy makers, as has already been pointed out, identified school teachers, students, village youth and serviceman and retired personnel as the instructional cadre.

Of all the categories, educated unemployed constitute more than half of the instructors in the sample (56.25 per cent). About three instructors (18.75 per cent) of the sample belong to the small farmer category. There are three in-service teachers in the sample. Of them, one is male instructor and two others are female instructors. Retired male teacher constitute about 12.50 per cent. It will be interesting to not that there is one agricultural labour who has been given opportunity to teach the adults by one of the agencies.

Thus, an analysis of the occupational background reveals that majority of the instructors in the sample are educated unemployed followed by small farmers and retired teachers.

Fiscal Facet

The data on income of the instructors is gathered in order to ascertain which strata of income group is showing interest towards the programme.

As can be gleaned from the table, an overwhelming majority of instructors in the sample fall in the income range of Rs. 101-500 per month. While out of 16 male instructors 14 (87.50 per cent) earned between Rs. 101-500, all the female instructors belong to this range. Only two instructors have comfortable economic position as they belong to a higher category of income (501-1000). Thus, the income level suggests that a majority of the instructors hail from very poor economic background.

Educational Status

A study of the educational background of the instructors reveal that they possess sufficient educational background to teach in Adult Education Centres. The following table gives the agencywise details of the educational qualifications of 19 respondents in the sample.

Educational Status of Instructors

Sl. No.	*Agency*	*Qualifications*							
		S.S.C.		*Inter*		*College*		*Total*	
		Male	*Female*	*Male*	*Female*	*Male*	*Female*	*Male*	*Female*
1.	A.M.S.	2	3	4	1	—	—	6	4
2.	B.C.T.	2	—	1	—	—	—	3	—
3.	CROSS	2	—	1	—	—	—	3	—
4.	D.S.S.	3	—	—	—	—	—	3	—

A majority of the instructors (63.15 per cent) in the sample possess secondary qualifications i.e. either tenth class or matriculation. The remaining instructors have done up to intermediate. Thus, the sample consists of fairly educated instructors which is considered as a good catchment area for implementation of Adult Education Programmes.

Earlier Successes

It is widely believed that it is relatively easy to shape a person with some experience and with some amount of educational background for adult education work rather than a notice. With this in view, the interview schedule canvassed to the instructors carries a few questions relating to the previous experience in teaching.

The instructors were asked to state the reasons for accepting the appointment as instructor. Eight out of ten instructors appointed by Andhra Mahila Sabha stated that they took up the job to supplement their income. Two instructors have cited that they were very much interested in teaching adults. The instructors appointed by B C T stated that they took up the job because it afforded some financial assistance, but also because it gave them an opportunity to take part in the developmental activities of B C T. They felt that besides providing some financial relief, the agency also gave them a chance to participate in its activities. It may be recalled here that the B C T has been a well-reputed organizations and a majority of the people in Yellamanchili area knew various activities of the agency. Similarly, all the three instructors in the Bhongir area which is the main operational area of CROSS stated that they were interested in taking any activity sponsored by the agency. Incidentally, this organization places high premium on education of masses as a liberator from exploitation. The researcher noticed commendable identity of the instructors in the sample with the main objectives of the agency. Coming to the instructors of Durga Sangh Seva Samaj which has implemented the programme in Gannavaram block, out of three instructors in the sample two stated that they took up the job only to supplement their income. The other respondent cited his keen interest in the programme.

Thus, nearly half of the respondents stated their interest in the programme the remaining half cited economic and other reasons.

Concept of Teacher Training

Training occupies an important place in the adult education programme as the National Adult Education Programme is stated as qualitatively and quantitatively superior to earlier Adult Education Programmes. The training of instructors is considered critical for the success of the programme as he/she is the key level or frontline worker. Further, the policy makers of the programme viewed training programme as an exercise in self knowledge or value clarification to the trainees.

Besides, it has been observed in one of the documents released by the Directorate of Adult Education that the training programme "is fundamentally a process of . . . education and has to reflect the main characteristics of the methodology that the functionaries would have to follow while working with the learning groups at the block level".

All the instructors reported that they had undergone training after induction, although differences as to the length or duration and training among the agencies is noticed. While the B C T arranged a training programme for 27 days, the Andhra Mahila Sabha, the Comprehensive Rural Operations Service Society, and the Durga Sangh Seva Samaj arranged training programmes for 15, 14, 15 days respectively. All the agencies in the sample trained their instructional cadre in two phases. The venue for the training programme is their head quarters in case of two organizations.

The B C T at Yellamanchili and the CROSS at Bhongir while Mahila Sabha and Durga Sangh Seva Samaj conducted training programmes closer to their areas of operation.

The content of the training programme for instructors did not vary much from among the sample agencies. All the agencies in the sample arranged lectures by experts from outside. However, B C T and CROSS have taken special care to make the training programmes 'discussion oriented' rather than lecture-oriented. The participants were encouraged to simulate the situations usually faced by illiterate adults in rural areas. The project officer and others clarified doubts raised by the instructors." The instructors in these two agencies (BCT & CROSS) seem to have been extremely satisfied that is the case with other instructors of other agencies in the sample. The respondents in the sample were asked by the investigator to comment on the utility of the training programmes. About 9 out of 10 instructors in the centres run by Andhra Mahila Sabha and Durga Sangh Seva Samaj rated their programme as 'not adequate' while all the instructors of BCT and CROSS rated them as 'extremely useful'.

While the instructors of centres under A.M.S. and D.S.S. rated their training as 'inadequate' others confined its utility. Training as a critical input to achieve the policy objective appears to have been very well articulated by the organizers of the programme in BCT and CROSS.

The Difference

In order to gauge the difference between NAEP and the earlier programmes to educate illiterate adults, the investigator asked a few questions about the objectives of NAEP. All the instructors of Andhra Mahila Sabha in the sample stated that literacy is the main objective. Only four out of ten could tell the other component the functional education and much less could tell (only two) the third component of the programme i.e., the awareness. In contrast, the instructors under B.C.T., CROSS, and D.S.S. listed out all the components of the programme. One major difference between the earlier programmes to educate illiterates and NAEP is that while the earlier one's focussed mainly on literacy (or 3 R's) the NAEP widened it and included functionality and social awareness also besides literacy. Absence of appreciation of the other two points out to the inadequate training programmes of some agencies.

The Importance

Regarding weightage to each of the three components stated above, 7 out of 10 instructors under Andhra Mahila Sabha told that more weightage was given to literacy component and three reported that along with literacy, functional education also was given coverage Only a couple of instructors at least felt the need to give equal weightage to all the components of the programme.

Coming to B.C.T. although preference seems to have been given to literacy, the other two components are not totally neglected. Since B.C.T. has been engaged in some productive programmes, which are found to be useful to the people in general in that area, it has succeeded to certain extent to motivate learners to attend Adult Education Centres.

The agency has announced through its instructors that preference in admission to carpentry training centres run by it would be given to those who continuously attend Adult Education Centres for ten months. Moreover, the Project Officer, Supervisors and others have taken interest in arranging lectures pertaining to social awareness. The learners were also taught some rudimentary techniques in carpentry, pottery and other such trades.

As far as CROSS is concerned, we notice relatively more emphasis on literacy and next to literacy, the awareness component seems to have been given preference. The instructors reported difficulties in implementing functional education component mainly owing to lack of study material as well as infrastructure.

The instruction by Durga Sangh Seva Samaj also gave importance to literacy component as attested by instructors. Two out of three instructors brought to the notice of the investigator the limitations in the implementation of functional education and social awareness components. Only one instructor stated that in his instruction all the three components were covered with only marginal success.

Thus, the perceptions of the respondents on the objectives of NAEP are not very satisfactory. By and large, the agencies have given preference to literacy component alone. Further, excepting B.C.T. and CROSS other agencies did not seem to have accorded priority to other components of the programme. This points to the inadequacies in publicity to the NAEP in general and non-appreciation of the value of functional education and social awareness to the cause of adult education. If policy components are not fully comprehended, there may arise a problem when they are being implemented.

Knowing about the Students

A majority of the instructors (14 out of 19) adopted the method of identification of learners enrolled in adult education centres through personal contact. Some instructors reported that they orally enquired about the age, caste, interest and former educational background of adult illiterates in their villages. All the instructors belonging to B.C.T. were asked to conduct a survey of the entire village. CROSS, however, entrusted the task of selecting learners to its village sanghams with the help of instructors. All the ten instructors in the sample belonging to Andhra Mahila Sabha (AMS) relied on the personal identification method. In the case of the Gannavaram block where the Durga Sangh Seva Samaj (DSS) conducted the programme, two instructors told the researcher that they 'knew' all the adults who were illiterates and felt no necessity for a survey. However, one instructor in the sample told that he selected learners after enquiring about their background.

It appears that the 'survey' for identification of learners in AMS, DSS is not foolproof and reflects the agencies' casual way of treating the most important aspect of the programme.

Here, it must be pointed out that apart from their regular tasks of giving instruction in the curriculum, the agencies included some supplementary device; aimed at motivating the learners to go through and benefit from the programme. In this, the instructors are again to play a vital role. It is about this supplementary tasks towards motivation that we now deal with.

There are broadly two methods adopted by the agencies: (1) personal contact between learners and the instructors, (2) arranging frequent contacts between the officials of the agency and the learners. The instructors of AMS and DSS as has already been stated relied heavily on personal contacts in which the instructor was told continuously to highlight the benefits of adult education. Eight out of nineteen instructors reported using various methods like persuasion to attract and retain learners, while six instructors of the BCT and CROSS highlighted the role of their respective agencies in the development of the locality, and the people that is by projecting their agencies role as 'change agents'. By this method, they succeeded, to some extent, in controlling the dropout problem. This has been corroborated by learners also. Some of the instructors under BCT, CROSS reported that those who attended adult education centres for 10 months will be offered loans and various other inputs. Instructors of other agencies in the sample have not shown keen interest in motivating the learners except by occasional lectures. Thus, we notice prevalence and different methods of motivating.

The investigator sought suggestions for motivating learners. An interesting aspect to be noted here is that the instructors belonging to BCT and CROSS recommended for a preferential treatment to the learners in the distribution of loans and other benefits which these organisations arrange for, besides equalizing the 10 month course with 5th class in the formal system so as to enable the learners to get into such jobs like watchman, gateman etc. The instructors of other agencies suggested economic incentives to the learners. These suggestions reveal that there is not one single method of motivating adults either to attend or to continue in the programme. The trend confirms the popular view that incentives of some kind motivate villagers to take interest in any developmental programme.

Concept of Teaching Aids

The views of the instructional cadre on the material used are elicited with a view to improving them. All the instructors in the same reported the receipt of teaching material. However, they differed on the relevance of study/teaching material. A large number of instructors of the centres under Andhra Manila Sabha reported that the material supplied to them deals mainly with aspects relating to agriculture. The same appears to be the case with the teaching/learning material supplied by CROSS, which has incidentally prescribed the material produced by AMS. The BCT prescribed and supplied books prepared exclusively for N A E P by Adult Education Department of the Andhra University. Although the instructors were not unhappy about the contents, out of three responding to the queries, two complained about the small size of the print of the material.

On examination of the material supplied to the learners by the Andhra Mahila Sabha, it was found that the books were prepared keeping in view a specific project i.e. Farmers Functional Literacy (FFL). Needless to say that the objective of FFL Programme and N A E P are different. Some of the instructors as well as supervisors who earlier worked in F F L programme corroborated this fact. When the investigator enquired about the material, the authorities concerned had not given a convincing answer. This would prove how organizations tend to perceive the policy objectives. Though one may argue that the material is not totally irrelevant, one gets an impression that the attitude of AMS is one of easy taking of the new policy to educate illiterate adults.

The Programme

One of the ideas of policy planners of NAEP is to make the programme as broad based as possible thereby putting an end to the tendency of treating adult education as the concern of education departments alone. The investigator attempted to ascertain the cooperation received from other departments especially the local leaders and other developmental functionaries of the government. Though the instructors reported good cooperation from their superiors within the organization, almost all were sore about the indifferent attitude of the government officials toward the programme (16 out of 19). A good majority of instructors rated as poor the cooperation given by local leaders (14 out of 19). They felt that their supervisors helped them in many ways in organizing and location of centres, in enlisting the support of local political functionaries as well as in keeping up the morale of the instructors.

A few instructors (5/19) also reported the authoritarian attitude of the supervisors as well as project officers. It is interesting to note here that the instructors who were selected on the recommendations of their local leaders, received some support in running adult education centres." Some instructors faced a tough problem in locating an adult centre owing to the stiff opposition of local leaders. A few instructors narrated how the elite disliked the very idea of educating adults. Some brushed aside the idea of adult education, while others warned the consequences of imparting education to the illiterates in their areas.

Their main fear as reported by the instructors was, that, if the masses are educated, it will not be possible for the vested interests to deal with them in the way they do when they are illiterates, uneducated and ignorant. That is why, according to some instructors the local leaders opposed establishment of centres in their villages. When the instructor refused to listen, he was harassed in many ways asking him to pay back all his dues, transferring him to a remote place, suggesting that the loan amount be paid from adult education funds, or from learners. Further, the learners were advised not to attend and when they flouted the writ they were asked to immediately repay their loans. In such hostile environment, the instructor, howsoever effective he is, fails to find a solution and prefers to close down the centre for sometime. Some learners held him responsible for bringing in a new set of problems for their already problem-ridden life.

Such situation further demoralised the instructor. As for the cooperation of government officials, as stated earlier only three out of the nineteen respondents stated that the officials were extending the necessary cooperation. However, there are some saving features. For example, in the centres visited by the governmental functionaries, the instructors reported good reception to the lectures by them. Thus, a majority of instructors feel that more cooperation is needed from local leaders and government officials in running adult education centres effectively.

Consequent Problems

All the instructors are expected to approach their supervisor first and then the project officer in case they experience any difficulty in running adult education centres. This supports the view that, even in non-governmental agencies, the practice of respecting hierarchical norms and bureaucratisation is present.

The type of problems which occasioned the instructors seeking the guidance of their immediate supervisors related to matters like fall in the attendance of the learners and how to retrieve the situation. Non-cooperation of village elite/leaders in running adult education centres and also deliberate attempts to close down the centres in some instances, delays, and difficulties in the receipt of learning material and in matters relating to the availability of other material facilities like lighting and problems with the behaviour of learners in the class rooms instances of learners coming under the influence of drink and teasing of women participants in coeducation classes did arise occasionally.

The response of the supervisors on the whole is reported to be encouraging. In many cases complaints about material necessities were personally solved by the supervisors themselves intervening either with the government officials or with the local elite. This was particularly visible in the case of supervisor, belonging to BCT and CROSS. The role of supervisors belonging to Durga Sangh Seva Samaj and AMS seems less encouraging. Where the village elite/leaders attempted to close down the centres, the supervisors and project officers visited them and attempted to persuade them. In some places it worked and in some others it led to further trouble.

Thus, coordination between the instructor and his immediate supervisors appears satisfactory. Further, there is evidence that good rapport existed between the instructors and the supervisors in general. It is more or less a uniform opinion of the instructors in the sample that supervisors were sincere in exhorting the instructors to operate the programme in the proper spirit by constant reminding of the ideals of the programme. A general spirit of confidence was thus instilled in the instructor thanks to the positive interaction between the instructors and supervisors.

On the issue of the desirability of transfer of instructors from one centre to another for every three months nearly half of the respondents (8/19) did not agree with this, only one fourth

(5/19) favoured it, others remained non-committal. One respondent, however, pointed out the practical difficulties of 'in service' teachers who cannot move around. The practice however, has been that the instructors were allotted to particular centres and no transfers were made. While the opinion of the instructors on transfers was largely negative, some instructors, however, agreed to the suggestion of the researcher that a periodical change of instructors would be better as it would expose them to different types of people. There is, thus, a clear difference in the views of the instructors on this issue.

The learners too were divided on this issue. Whatever be the merits of `transfer', it would appear that, given the fact that some instructors are only part-time with a separate full-time job, transfers would prove to be extremely inconvenient to them. Apart from this practical difficulty, as the recommendation is that instructors should be drawn from the locality and community in which the centre is located, policy-wise too transfers are perhaps undesirable.

The Remarks : An overwhelming majority of the instructors (18/19) felt that at least 50 per cent of the learners acquired the skills of reading and writing and some amount of knowledge in arithmetic. An interagency comparison reveal that the instructors of BCT and CROSS are quite positive about the impact of literacy component on the learners. The instructors of DSS and AMS, however, felt that only 40-45 per cent of the learners enrolled in their respective adult education centres could improve their reading, writing and numerical abilities.

Almost all learners (17/19) pointed out the difficulties involved in imparting skills in functional education and in raising the awareness. The main reasons for their failure is lack of infrastructural facilities and proper learning materials. Some instructors regretted that instruction was confined to face-to-face teaching. Except black board no other teaching aid is made available. Perhaps audio-visual aids like radio, tape recorder, VCR and TV would go a long way in sustaining the interest of the learners. Thus the instructors were modest about their claims as far as achievement in the three components of the programme are concerned.

Views on job satisfaction as expressed by instructors show wide variance. A good majority of the respondents (12/19) reported that they were satisfied with their jobs. The remaining (5/19) were totally dissatisfied with their jobs for a host of reasons which include meagre remuneration, heavy work, apathy and politics played by the local leaders 18 and indifference of the government officials and authoritarian attitude of the supervisors and project officers. Two respondents have refused to react on this question.

The Guidelines : The suggestions given by the instructors touch several aspects of the programme administration. An overwhelming majority (87.8 per cent) wanted increase in the honorarium. Most of them said that an honorarium of Rs. 50/- per month was very meagre (it was enhanced to Rs. 100/- recently) and the requirements of the job demand lot of their attention and time. About 48.9 per cent suggested that unless some economic incentives were offered to the learners, it would be difficult to sustain the interest of an illiterate adult. A good percentage of instructors (46.9) also suggested the need for more diversified teaching and learning materials. Some suggested association of village level politicians with all aspects of programme management. The other suggestions include strong linkages with other development programmes (22.88), proper lighting facilities (52.33), increasing the involvement of government functionaries (70.3) and cooperation of village elite (57.33). Suggestions like less paper work, conducting regular tests, motivating the learners who show encouraging improvement by offering economic incentives are grouped under "other" suggestions which constitute about 43.81 per cent.

The instructors' reactions in the sample on various aspects of the programme thus suggest that there are clear gaps in the training programme, conducted by some agencies. However, it should be remembered that they were not totally disoriented towards the programme. It was given to understand that lectures as part of the training programme arranged by Andhra Mahila Sabha and Durga Sangh Seva Samaj are mostly stereotyped. And this had produced a negative effect on the trainees. As has aptly been commented by one of the trainees, "It appears silly if a resource person tells me how to look after my agricultural farm or how and when the paddy should be cut as a good number in the group hail from agricultural background". The agencies which organized training programmes have not even used audio-visual aids to sustain the interest of instructors. A couple of instructors were frustrated at the general attitude of the village elites. They felt that good programmes like adult education fail because of polluted political atmosphere. Thus, the training programmes appear to be not strong enough especially with regard to a couple of agencies in the sample. The Durga Sangh Seva Samaj in particular does not seem to be knowing that the NAEP is not a literacy programme alone but also contains two other components, functionality and awareness. The agency does not also seem to be aware of the fact that mere literacy drives will not succeed.

Coming specifically to the problem of coordination, we notice that purely in terms of the instructors on the one hand and the supervisors on the other, there has been adequate coordination. But coordination does not merely pertain to rapport and personal relationships. A greater effort on the part of the agencies to equip the centres would not only improve the programme but will contribute to increased morale in the instructors. In other words, a more intensive and constant interaction between the agency and the centre would generate a correspondingly greater degree of involvement as far as the instructors and other cadres are concerned.

Diverse View

In the organizational framework of NAEP, the tasks of supervisors would be concerned with making instructors effective in the field. The supervisors are expected to guide and support the work of a cluster of about 30 adult education centres as visualized in the administrative structure of a project. The main functions of the supervisor as conceived by the policy makers of NAEP include (1) to enlist community cooperation and support, (2) to help in the survey of the area and assess the learners' needs, (3) to help in the training programmes of instructors, (4) to help prepare flexible and need based curricula and materials, (5) to plan and organize the programme, (6) to keep open the channels of communication, (7) to evaluate and guide the work of the centres and (8) to take steps to give wide publicity to the programme.

The supervisors are expected to perform the above functions with the support and cooperation of project officer, development departments of the government, the instructors, resource persons from among the local people and above all with the help of the community.

In this section, an attempt is made first to analyse the socioeconomic status of the supervisors, their perception about the objectives of NAEP, their selection, recruitment and training methods of supervision, comments on resource material, steps initiated to secure coordination internally as well as externally, mechanisms to monitor the programme, job satisfaction and finally their impressions and suggestions.

Social and Economical Facets

Thus, such standard variables like age, caste, and sex, education, economic, occupational status of the four supervisors in the sample will be briefly analysed in order to determine their socio-economic profile.

Age: Of the four supervisors two belong to the age group of 25-34 years and the other two fall between 35-44 age group. The supervisory staff' of all the agencies therefore satisfied the requirement prescribed by the policy planners that the supervisors should at least be of 21 years.

Sex and Caste: All the supervisors in the sample are male. Among them three are from forward castes and one belongs to backward caste.

Educational status: All the supervisors are fairly educated. Three out of 4 are graduates while the fourth one has studied up to twelfth class (or plus two equivalent). The supervisory cadre of the sample possess more than prescribed qualifications for the post which is in consonance with the policy objectives of AEP.

Occupation: Occupation wise, two supervisors are teachers and one a homeopathic doctor and the other an employee of the agency. Among the two teachers one is working as a full time employee of the agency on deputation from Zilla Parishad School. The other one is just attending to work on part-time basis.

Income: All the supervisors belong to middle income group.

Previous experience: On the experience in adult education work, two out of four have previous experience in adult education and the other two are new to the job.

Thus, the socio-economic background of the supervisors reveals that all of them are in the prescribed age group, and a majority are graduates. All of them belong to middle income group.

The Objectives

All the supervisors are aware of the three main objectives i.e. literacy, functional education and social awareness. However, they are divided in their opinion about the weightage to be given to each of the three components. The supervisor belonging to B C T drew the attention of the investigator to the impracticability of implementing functionality component as it involves large scale preparation. The supervisor of CROSS on the other hand is of the opinion that awareness is more important than functionality. Coming to the D S S though the supervisor is aware of the three components, he appears to be more interested in imparting three R's rather than the other two components. The case with the A M S is altogether different. The supervisor of this agency said that for imparting any thing, literacy is most important. In his opinion the material supplied by his agency to the learners is out of tune with the objectives of N A E P and hence questions on weightage does not arise at all.

Selection Process

The criteria for selection and recruitment of supervisors as conceived by policy planners of the N A E P is as follows:

(1) As far as possible, the supervisors should be drawn from among the ranks of experienced and successful adult education teachers, extension workers, N S V S, N S S and Community Social Service Volunteers, social workers and also those who may have academic qualification in adult education.

(2) They should be familiar with the local language, and as far as possible be residents of the project or a similar area. They must be willing to live in the cluster area to which they are eventually allotted.

We also find reference to modern methods of recruitment in various policy documents. One of such method is to ask the interested candidates for the post of supervisors to submit in advance a full and honest account of their understanding of the N A E P, the tasks of the supervisor within this and the assessment of their suitability for the post.

Coming to the response from the supervisors about their selection, one supervisor (belonging to B C T) replied that he was just asked to look after the programme through an official memorandum. Further he said, he happens to be one of the coordinators of the agency put in charge of rural leadership programmes. The agency might have thought that he can look after the adult education programme as well. As has already been pointed out in the last section of the first chapter on profiles of the agencies, the Bhagavathula Charitable Trust is engaged in implementing a variety of programmes/projects in Yellamanchili block. That way this agency is placed in a better position vis-a-vis others in the sample. As part of the developmental programmes the agency sponsored and ran a few non-formal adult education centres too. The supervisor of N A E P of this agency looked after those centres and the same person was made Project Officer-cum-Supervisor of the N A E P of this agency. Hence, no formal method of selection of supervisor was felt necessary by the agency.

The Durga Sangh Seva Samaj too did not follow any formal methods in the selection of supervisors. In fact the Honorary Project Officer in charge of the A E P appointed his own son as the supervisor. It is also noteworthy that the project officer himself is none other than Director of the agency. This instance brings to light the special problems or considerations that arise when a voluntary social service agency undertakes the adult education work as one of the items of its activities. In some cases, the head of the agency can himself become the head of the adult education programme. This has the advantage of solving the problems of coordination as the head of the agency himself is incharge of the

A E P. On the other hand, this may mean that the programme may not receive the requisite attention given the project officer's busy engagements with other activities.

The supervisor of N A E P for this agency is full time teacher in a school in Vijayawada which is about 20 KMs from the area of operation. In spite of his best efforts, he could not strike a balance between his official responsibilities as a teacher in a school, and as supervisor of an adult education project. Some adult education centres are located as far away as 35 to 40 KMs. Distance naturally deterred the supervisor from undertaking frequent visits to adult education centres which are so necessary for ensuring their effective functioning. The Project Officer is quite an aged man and visits by him are totally ruled out. With the result, there is noticeable laxity in supervision. These things point out how voluntary agencies exhibit tendencies which may have negative effect on the objectives of a qualitative programme like adult education. It is not to say, that the agencies suffer from such an inadequacy.

The Comprehensive Rural Operations Service Society appointed the coordinator of its adult education programmes as the supervisor. The agency did not follow formal methods for selection of its supervisor taking into consideration the experience of the candidate.

With regard to Andhra Mahila Sabha, it has advertised the posts of supervisors and selected three candidates out of fifteen applied. The selection committee consisted of the Chairman and Secretary of the Literacy House (which looks after education programmes as the name itself indicates) and the Project Officer. However, it was given to understand that no expert in adult education seems to have been associated with the selection committee.

Thus, the method of selection of supervisors through advertisement was followed by only one agency. The other agencies in the sample selected and appointed the supervisors without official formalities. The reason could be that these agencies had more confidence in the personnel readily available in their organisations.

The training programmes to supervisors are intended to increase the understanding about the N A E P and the needs of the community and learners, impart the ability to prepare material work out, methods of organizing adult education centres, evolve techniques for gaining community support, increase their ability for planning the follow up programmes, develop skills arranging training programme for Instructors and finally enhance competence on various ways of achieving the coordination with other developmental programmes/departments. Besides these, the policy makers of N A E P recommended provision for practical experience in order to acquire skills necessary to perform their functions with confidence.

The organisers of the training programmes for supervisors are expected to arrange:

(1) Visits to villages for getting an acquaintance with the needs of learners and learning environment;

(2) Development of suitable programmes based on the field data collected through surveys;

(3) Preparation of need-based curriculum or adaptations of existing, available curriculum;

(4) Evaluation of the available teaching/learning material;

(5) Acquaintance with the procedures of monitoring (monthly, quarterly and annual reports);

(6) Preparation and use of simple visual aids.

The above are some of the functions that are supposed to be experimented by the supervisors in the course of the training programme.

The Central Directorate of Adult Education suggested that there be a two or three phased training programme, for supervisors starting with a three day initial orientation programme followed by two week pre-service training and further followed by a "process of recurrent training sessions through monthly meetings, refresher courses and correspondences".

Thus, training for the supervisors was visualised as a process of continuous learning.

Now, coming to the training part of the supervisors in the sample, it was found that all the supervisors did undergo training at the Sri Venkateshwara University, Tirupati. The State Directorate of Adult Education, Government of Andhra Pradesh sponsored the training programme. The State Resources Centre, Tirupati conducted the programme. The duration of the programme is spread over a period of 10 days. The supervisors of B.C.T. and D.S.S. attend the training a few weeks before the inauguration of the adult education programme in their area. The supervisors of CROSS and AMS, however, could attend the programme after the starting of the adult-centres in their areas.

All the supervisors opined that the training programme attended by them was mainly lecture oriented. They were not given an opportunity by the organisers of the training programme to narrate individually or collectively to share their experiences for the benefit of the fellow supervisors in adult education work. In fact, a supervisor called the whole training a 'farce'. Coming to the utility of the lectures delivered in the training course, out of four supervisors, three felt that these were 'idealistic', miles away from realities in rural areas. Two supervisors felt that they did not understand some lectures owing to language problems. The regional language being Telugu, it is no wonder that the supervisors experienced some difficulty in following lectures in English. The investigator was further told that the supervisors in the training programmes were not encouraged to participate, be it in the form of discussions or other simulation exercises.

The whole programme was a one-sided affair. A supervisor summed up the programme saying that the organisers of the training programme should first attend programme on how to organise training programmes to the key level functionaries of the N.A.E.P. Questioning the methods of training, yet another supervisor felt that the grasp of the organisers of training programme about rural areas in general and about the psychology of rural people in particular is so poor that he felt like withdrawing himself from the training programme half way through.

Regarding the material that they are supposed to receive, all the four supervisors said that they did not receive any. When a supervisor asked the organisers about the material, it seems he was told that he would get them by post. He waited for three months and got reconciled to the indifference of the organisers. On the utility of the lectures, two supervisors said that whatever little they could understand sounded 'upstartish', to them. A particular mention need to be made about "how to organise training programmes to the instructors". Two lectures, it seems, were given on the above theme. The supervisors were told that they should involve other developmental functionaries in the programme. A respondent in the sample remarked that the indifference of the developmental functionaries was experienced by the organisers of the training programme as out of five lectures arranged to such developmental personnel only two turned up. And, their performance was also poor. Thus, the supervisor told the investigator that "it is very easy to preach than to practice". Enquired about the field visits they were supposed to undertake during the training programme, all the supervisors in the sample said that they were not taken any where.

The above instances show the gap between the directives of the policy planner and the implementors. What is the main reason for the discontentment of the supervisors about their training ? The trainees say that it was because of the halfhearted efforts of the organisers. It surprised the investigator as to how the personnel of S R C could be so indifferent even to the medium of lectures. The fact that a good number reported their difficulties in following the lectures in English on the first day of the training programme itself and the consequent failure of the organisers to remedy the situation, clearly exhibit the formalistic/ritualistic response of the organisers of training programmes. Further, the failure to encourage participation in debates and discussions reveals the unchanged nature of the organisers towards training programmes. As aptly summed up by a participant, "the commitment of N A E P which they often exhorted us to cultivate, appears to be lacking in them".

Different Approaches

The effective supervisory methods seen to have been by almost all respondents in the sample. These include (a) regular visits (scheduled and surprise) to the A E C under their control; (b) checking the attendance, (c) guiding the instructors on methods of teaching, (d) getting the feedback on regularity of instructor;

(e) method of teaching and (f) enquiring about the difficulties faced by learners.

Interagency comparison, however, proved that the two supervisors of B C T and CROSS are far more effective vis-a-vis their counterparts in Durga Sangh Seva Samaj and Andhra Mahila Sabha. In terms of number of visits to A E Cs the investigator noticed that the supervisors of the B C T and CROSS checked more number of centres in a day than the other two supervisors in the sample, which is of course made possible mainly due to the fact that the supervisors of BCT and CROSS are provided with vehicles. Because of this, on an average they could visit six centres per day. The supervisors of A M S and D S S could visit only one or two centres per day as they have to commute the long distances by other modes of transport. That is why, instructors of the B C T and CROSS reported a more number of surprise inspections by their supervisors. In case of instructors of A M S and D S S, this was not the case and they could not take up as many 'surprise' visits as was the case with the supervisors of B C T and CROSS. Moreover, as the two agencies (BCT & CROSS) are involved in a number of economic programmes and a readily available infrastructure running Adult Education programme posed no fresh infrastructural and other problem. Each agency as a matter of fact has got two to three motor vehicles besides jeeps etc. That is why, they could be able to maintain an effective supervision. So it must be understood that factors like conveyance also play an important role in ensuring effective supervision.

Guest Teachers

We have mentioned earlier how the policy planners visualised A E P as the concern of the departments and should not be viewed as the job of educationists alone. Involvement of others like the Block Development Officer (BDO), managers of banks, project officials and small farmers development agency and other officials incharge of agriculture, animal husbandry etc., is regarded as crucial for the success. The supervisors were asked about the role of other developmental functionaries. A number of reasons were cited by the supervisors for their inadequate role. The first is the indifference. Only one supervisor belonging to B C T could succeed to some extent, in persuading the officials in the block to visit some of the centres. But it was mainly because of the image of the agency in that part of the state. Right since its inception, it made sincere serious efforts to associate the block level officials in almost all its activities. The rapport it has established over a period of time was utilised by the supervisor at least to some extent which resulted in getting some cooperation from them.

But coming to the other two agencies, Durga Sanga Seva 'Samaj and Andhra Mahila Sabha, they do not have strong roots in the areas where they have implemented the programme. And naturally they had to encounter difficulty right from starting the project. These two agencies could not involve the block level functionaries in the programme to the extent they desired partly owing to 'unacquaintance' with the area and also partly due to indifference of the local level village elite. Further the investigator came to know that the agencies did not seek cooperation from either local leaders or officials.

With regard to CROSS, it could not involve block level developmental functionaries for a very significant reason. The very fact that CROSS's long standing work in the area seemed to have led to strained relations between block level officials and CROSS. This is because CROSS in pursuing the other aspects of its activities and as a matter of fact had on many occasions crossed swords with the block administration. For example, on issues like fertilizer distribution CROSS did not fight shy of taking up matters with the block officials wherever malpractices in distribution of fertilizers were identified. In any case, the block officials got the impression that there were instances of CROSS instigating some rural sections to vocally complain against block officials. This is an interesting instance of close contacts between a voluntary agency and a rural government resulting in estrangement rather than cooperation. To an extent, this should be assumed as a given factor. In such circumstances, problems of coordination in the implementation of a policy like Adult Education, arising out of the lack of rapport between the agency and the government becomes inevitable. The agency organized several processions against rise in prices of essential commodities, for establishment of fair price shops in villages, for distribution of fertilisers with subsidy to the needy etc. It brought to the notice of higher officials in the district about the rampant corruption at village and mandal levels and demanded stern action against corrupt administrators. Thus, CROSS has established itself as an agency of masses and earned the name of crusader for justice to the unorganised rural people. The activities of the agency to an extent antagonized the local bureaucracy. The landlords joined with police and taluq officials made several efforts to close down the agency by using all sorts of pressures and attacks but they could not succeed. This only shows how dedicated voluntary agencies are harassed with a view to continuing the status quo.

Thus, the methods of supervision adopted by the supervisors in the sample seem to be satisfactory. The checking of attendance registers and paying surprise visits did to an extent keep the instructors on alert. However, coming to the checking of the drop out rate is concerned, where the instructors failed, the supervisor also did not succeed much. Except the supervisors of the BCT and CROSS who tried and succeeded to some extent in helping the learners in their problems like securing a loan, settling disputes between two castes etc., the other supervisors in the sample could not do anything as they neither have access to other institutions which could do something to the learners nor could act in cooperation with officials concerned at the block/taluq level in finding a solution to some of the problems faced by the learners.

On the whole, one comes to the conclusion that the supervisory methods are satisfactory but there is a limit to what they can do as the problems of increasing the effectiveness of supervisors would depend on various other factors which are mostly beyond the control of the supervisor.

Material for Learning

All the supervisors reported that they distributed teaching/ learning material for instruction to the instructors. Regarding the source of the material, the Andhra Mahila Sabha produced and supplied to the learner the material prepared by it. The Department of Adult Education, Andhra University prepared primers for learners in the centres run by it under N A E P University Adult Education Programme. The same material was ordered and used for its learners in Centres under the Bhagavathula Charitable Trust. The Comprehensive Rural Operations Service Society supplied to its learners the material prepared by Andhra Mahila Sabha. The Durga Sangh Seva Samaj acquired the material prepared by a private publisher. An attempt is also made to elicit the views of the supervisory personnel on utility and the relevance of the material in general. Of the four supervisors in sample, two supervisors felt that the material supplied is not totally irrelevant and felt that much needed to be done to revise or refashion the material in the light of the feedback from the learners. The other two supervisors opined that the material supplied meets the occasion.

All the supervisors reported the receipt of the material in adequate number. However, as has already been observed, the A M S in this respect is in a better position compared to others in the sample. The material which was prepared by it for another programme (Farmers Functional Literacy Programme) was reprinted at its own press in Hyderabad and it did not face any problem in its supply. It distributed a set consisting of six books to each learner. But the B C T and D S S distributed one book to each of the learners and CROSS distributed two books. The supervisors were by and large satisfied with the distribution part.

Concept of Cooperative Method

As has already been discussed, the success of programmes like N A E P depends to a large extent on how best the coordination is achieved or secured. The investigator examined the operation of the principle of coordination in the implementation of N A E P through voluntary agencies in the sample.

In this section, an examination of the mechanism created by each agency for achieving coordination is attempted. Broadly, there appears to be two bodies for securing coordination. One at the agency level for the purpose of the study called 'project level committee' and the other at the village level or adult education centre level, called 'village level committee'. It must be remembered that not all agencies have a two-tier co-oridinating bodies. Again, these bodies are referred to with different names.

Of the two bodies intended to secure coordination, discussion is more on project level committee, as the village level committees of almost all the agencies in the sample remained dysfunctional.

The discussion that follows begins with the structure and functions of the Project Level Committees (P L C's). It must be mentioned that the functions of the P L Cs are not precisely and exhaustively given in any documents relating to any of the agencies. It is possible to identify them both from what is contained in some other documents and from an informal study of their functioning.

The main functions of the P L C's include (i) to secure coordination between adult education programme and other programmes by the other development agencies; (ii) to ensure coordination between adult education programmes and other formal systems of education; (iii) to create necessary administrative infrastructure and supervision; (iv) to arrange lectures by resource persons and identifying the persons belonging to the developmental departments of the government for the same; (v) to make arrangements for the supply of reading material to the learners; (vi) to fix criteria for selection of supervisors, instructors and arranging for their training; (vii) to lay broad guidelines for managing day-to-day administration; (viii) to continuously monitor the progress by adhering to the proforma; and (ix) to take steps to associate local elite in the programme.

The membership of the P L Cs varied from one agency to the other. The Chairman of this body in BCT and CROSS was the Secretary and the head of the agency respectively. The Chairmanship of the P L C of D S S was kept vacant. The Project Officer is made as the Convener of the body. However, the A M S nominated the President of the Panchayat Samiti of the Sirsilla Block as the Chairman of its P L C. Regarding membership, the B C T had involved the supervisor and one third of its total number of instructors.

For every three months, the representation of instructors changed and almost all instructors took part in the deliberations of the body at one time or the other. Local leaders and learners are also associated sometimes with the P L C meetings.

The Project Level Committee of the CROSS comprised the Chairman, Supervisor and three instructors besides other functionaries. It is given to understand that the learners are also invited sometimes to the meetings. But the criteria of learners/ instructors representation is not clear. As pointed out earlier, the

Andhra Mahila Sabha made the President of the Sirsilla Panchayat Samiti as the Chairman of the Project Level Committee. The Project Officer, Supervisor, some officials of block level administration are the members. The P L C of the Durga Sangh Seva Samaj consists of Convener, Supervisor and two women members and the Extension Officer incharge of Education of Panchayat Samiti.

There is, thus, a variation in the composition of the P L Cs constituted by the agencies in the sample. As for the Project Level Committee (PLC) meetings, again going by agencywise, the PLC of BCT met at the beginning of every month.

A cursory glance at the agenda of the monthly meetings of various agencies in the sample revealed that a number of problems were brought to the notice of the P L C for a decision. These include (a) dropout problem; (b) non-cooperation of village elite; (c) non receipt of grant from the Government; (d) trooping of children into adult education centres; (e) absence of instructors without intimation; (f) clash in timings of adult education centres and other developmental programmes of the agency; (g) criteria for consideration of applicants who also happen to be learners for loans; (h) non functioning of village level committees; (i) indifference or non-cooperation of the developmental functionaries to visit adult education centres for giving lectures etc.; (j) arrangements for inspections by the officials of the adult education directorate and other district officials; (k) arranging lectures by the functionaries incharge of agriculture, animal husbandry etc., within the agency, and other problems.

The usual procedure for conducting the meetings of PLC is first to listen to the instructor followed by the supervisor on various aspects of the programme management. On several occasions, there was a difference of opinion and in such a situation the Chairman tried for a consensus. The methods of finding solution to the problem are through discussion, dialogue with the concerned and between the concerned.

As the Chairman of a P L C rightly summed up the "committee looked at each problem with an intention to solve it." Very often, the patience of the Chairman was put to test. Placed as he was in a difficult situation, conducting meetings with a widely stratified members is "a tight rope to walk on." On the whole, the P L C served the purpose for which it was created. An agency involved in diversified activities naturally confronts special problems of coordination which for that very reason may find solution easily. The organizers of the programme were once faced with the problem of finances. The second installment of the grant for running the programme was not released.

The P L C of that agency took a decision to divert the funds from other sources. The agency could have closed down all centres after five months and could have shifted the blame on the government, but the organisers observed that it would have dampened the enthusiasm of learners. Moreover, it was feared that the other educational programmes of the agency may not succeed and secondly winding up a programme for lack of funds would impair the image of the agency. Thus, it can be seen that the P L C of one agency i.e., B C T was favourably situated to arrange coordination amongst its different activities. The village level committees of this agency however have not functioned to the extent the organisers desired.

Coming to CROSS as already stated, the P L C was not as broad in its composition as was the case with B C T. Problems similar to B C T were faced by this agency also, except in one area. The local leaders have not cooperated much with the agency, The wide network of village sanghams are a constant source of tension between the agency and local level bureaucracy on the one hand and between the local leaders and the agency on the other. This agency too, sponsored several economic programmes like B C T. At the end of every month, the meetings of the P L C were held and problems of adult education centres were brought to the notice of the Chairman through the supervisor.

Solutions were worked out to overcome problems and efforts were made to avoid clash with the adult education centres activities and other activities of the agency. Criteria for the processing of applications for loans to banks was framed and guidelines were formulated. Project Level Committee (P L C) prepared a list of resource persons for lectures in adult education centres. Methods of motivating and attracting illiterate adults were discussed and measures were suggested to the instructors to sustain the interest of learners. The members of the P L C visited some centres and recorded their satisfaction on the progress. Thus, the mechanism for achieving internal coordination is sound and produced the desired effect. But as far as external coordination is concerned, the agency found it difficult to secure.

The environment around the agency is hostile. Local elite to a large extent suspect the agency. According to reliable source, the block level bureaucracy envies the agency for its initiative, boldness and result orientation. It was given to understand that some vested interests wrote letters to the Government urging it to stop the grants to CROSS for its antigovernment activities. Pressures were brought on police to wind up even the agency. CROSS has some sort of a village level coordinating committees also and these are called village level -sanghams. As regards the operation of P L C of A M S in Sirsilla, as pointed out elsewhere it was headed by a local leader as Chairman. It may be recalled that the Andhra Mahila Sabha is not new to organizing literacy programmes. The investigator hoped that with its vast experience, this agency would run the programme more easily and effectively. However, this very agency started facing problems right from the beginning. The PLC has not laid down a proper criteria for location of adult education centres keeping in view the local conditions. With the result, some centres had been shifted, closed down and reopened. The policy guidelines on location of centres seemed to have been ignored.

The problems that arose in the implementation of the programme were not attended to. The PLC itself rarely met and naturally several problems of coordination emerged which called for higher policy direction. The Project officer tried several times to make the PLC to meet regularly. When it met, the Chairman was always in a hurry to leave. Hence, no proper discussion used to take place. The whole management of running 100 adult education centre fell on the Project Officer who, though had sufficient experience, was relatively young in age. In the absence of regular mechanism for coordinating the work, the programme could not be implemented effectively. The developmental functionaries have not shown any interest in the programme in spite of the fact that the President of Panchayat Samiti was associated with the programme. According to the Project Officer, the Chairman is so indifferent that on one occasion he suggested to the project officer to take his signature on all papers/cheques once in four months so that the work did not suffer. Thus, the PLC of the A M S largely remained on paper. As regards village level committees, A M S did not seem to have taken any initiative to organise them.

In the case of Durga Sangh Seva Samaj too, the investigator noticed the ineffectiveness of the PLC. The convener of the committee is also the director of the agency. When enquired about the PLC, he observed that the matters relating to the PLC are confidential and will not be revealed. The investigator through other sources was informed that the PLC met only once at the beginning of the programme. The non-functioning of the PLC has adversely affected the functioning of the programme. The major casualty of non-functioning of PLC was internal as well as external coordination.

Issues like the criteria for recruitment to the instructor's post, whether it is desirable to recruit the retired teachers, the quality of the teaching material, location of centres, lighting facilities, the problems involved in opening adequate number of women centres, the problems with regard to arranging lectures by resource persons etc., should have come up before the PLC as in the case of other agencies. In the absence of this vital coordinating body, the organizers were forced to look for ad-hoc measures to cope with exigencies which led to lot of dissatisfaction among learners as well as the instructional cadre. Thus, the agency failed to take the advantage of an important body like the PLC.

Concept of Interrelationship

As regards coordination with other developmental departments of the Government, the supervisors cited several reasons. Giving benefit of doubt to the governmental servants, the supervisor of BCT and CROSS opined that the governmental functionaries did not have much time and the orders of the district collectors/director of adult education programme are not binding on them. The overburdened developmental bureaucracy hardly have any time to participate in adult education programme enthusiastically.

The supervisors of DSS and AMS stated that the block level functionaries wanted them to arrange conveyance to visit centres which they just could not do. The supervisor of AMS said that though his agency owned three imported two wheelers (gifted by Canadians) not even one was sent to the field in spite of several requests. When this question was put to the officials of the agency, they said that "the vehicles get spoiled if driven on dirty village roads" which left investigator to wonder as to the very purpose of keeping idle the vehicles at headquarters when the work is actually being executed in the field. The supervisor of the DSS said his agency did not have a vehicle.

The BCT, however, used its vehicles for bringing resource persons like block level officials. This enabled the officials to participate to some extent in the programme by giving occasional lectures and by answering several questions raised by learners. Presence of officials enthused learners to such an extent that they were feared to answer tough questions like the reasons for the administrative delay in processing their applications for loans etc. This trend in fact had produced a negative effect also on the involvement of officials as they felt that these centres had become a 'nuisance' to them and they stopped visiting on various excuses. This, however, does not mean that all officials felt shy to face learners.

With regard to coordination with other agencies implementing NAEP, none of the project officers in charge of adult education centres directly under the government cared to visit centres under the voluntary agencies. Adult education programmes sponsored by the Government of Andhra Pradesh are going on in places close by to those operated by agencies. When the investigator enquired about it, the Project Officers of the Government replied that to visit all the 300 adult education centres directly under their jurisdiction is proving to be an uphill task and, therefore, the question of visiting centres under 'others' according to them was unimaginable.

The same trend is noticed more or less in case of all the agencies like Universities & Colleges, NSS, ICDS Schemes etc. The involvement of developmental functionaries as envisaged in policy statement (and in other documents subsequently released by the Government of India) too had not materialised to the extent desired.

The reasons for their partial involvement were already discussed. With this, let us move on to the systems of monitoring and evaluation.

Concept of Supervision and Measurement

One of the main functions of the supervisors is to ensure that they follow the reporting systems i.e. monthly and quarterly reports. All supervisors reported compliance with the instructions in this regard and all instructors sent the reports in time. It appeared that the formats for reporting too were lengthy. On this the supervisors felt that it should be smaller in size. Two out of four supervisors admitted that the instructors' reports did not exactly reflect the facts relating to daily attendance, dropouts etc. The position with regard to other two supervisors is interesting. They told the instructors that if they reported correct situation they would be rewarded and they would be punished for wrong figures. This seems to have led, at least to some extent, to correct reporting.

All the supervisors have stated that they are satisfied with their jobs. The supervisors of BCT and CROSS said that a little more cooperation from the government would have made them much more satisfied.

The supervisor of AMS felt that the officials of his agency should pay more interest towards programme by visiting some adult education centres. On the whole, all the supervisors observed that they derived a lot of satisfaction from their jobs.

General Concept

All the supervisors opined that the success of the programme in terms of targets was commendable as they said that they could make at least 50-60 per cent of the enrolled literate. Most of them, however, are sceptical about success of other two components. Further, the supervisors of BCT felt that there were several limitations to put into operation functional and awareness components. To some extent, he viewed that the functional education component was attempted by admitting some learners in carpentry training centres but only after they completed ten month course. On awareness component, he said it would take some more time.

All the supervisors have unanimously endorsed the view that the NAEP would succeed if more voluntary agencies are associated. They further felt that the progress though not a spectacular success, it definitely resulted in creation of a favourable environment as anticipated by policy makers.

The supervisor of BCT suggested that the present policy of extending education 'free of cost' to adult illiterates calls for a thorough review. The value of education according to the respondents will be realised only when the learner pays from his pocket. The government may supply all resource material like books etc., but the honorarium must at least be met by the adults out of contributions or else it is difficult to check the casual attitude of the illiterates.

Furthermore, the supervisor suggested that government must take into confidence the voluntary agencies which were given permission to implement adult education programme. It should create 'demand' for education by equalizing the qualification acquired by adult illiterate to seventh or fifth class.

The supervisors from other agencies in the sample suggested effective involvement of developmental functionaries of government. This gained currency owing to reports that teaching by an instructor continuously may lead to monotony and the lectures by "others" might arouse interest. The other suggestions include change in pattern as well as emphasis on training, modification in resource material, relaxation of procedures for obtaining grants and other financial assistance for carrying follow-up or post-literacy programmes, delegation of powers from the PLC to the supervisors to selrct the instructor, supply of audio-visual equipment free of cost by the Taluq Public Relations Officer etc., provision for vehicles for effective supervision.

An analysis of the role and functioning of the supervisors reveals that they have a fairly good grasp and understanding of the NAEP all of them belong to the prescribed age group and the investigators noticed certain amount of commitment. Their dissatisfaction with the training programme has to be taken note of as it greatly helps them in appreciating their role as key level functionaries and directly contributes to increasing their effectiveness.

Sincere attempts by all the supervisors of all the agencies seemed to have been made to involve the developmental personnel at the block level but success in this regard varied. While the supervisor of the BCT, because of his good rapport with block level personnel, could involve at least some of them, the supervisor of DSS and AMS could not do much to involve them as the officials of their agencies themselves were not seemed to be aware of the benefits accruing from that. The limitations cited by the supervisors in imparting functional education and increasing awareness must be examined more deeply.

Interagency cooperation may yield better results in this regard. With regard to monitoring and, evaluation, the view of the supervisors that the instructor is overburdened with paper work merits serious consideration. The study also revealed as to how effective supervision depends on provision of conveyance facilities. Average number of visits by the supervisors belonging to two agencies in the sample to centres under their control are much higher than the case with other two. The fact that one agency got the vehicles and is not thinking of giving them to supervisors further reveals the agencies' belief in effective supervision. No doubt, there may be more number of supervisors than vehicles. But the solution does not lie in keeping the vehicles idle. Moreover, it appears that it is not a difficult problem to tackle.

As regards coordination, the project level committees attached to each agency need to be activated. Instead of meeting only once in 5 months as was the case with a couple of agencies in the sample, it should meet once in a month. Regular meetings of PLC's facilitate quick decision making pertaining to the project. The methods adopted by BCT for securing coordination appear to be more effective and hence deserve to be emulated by others in this regard.

After the discussion on the role, functions, problems of the instructors and supervisors of the adult education centres, we now turn to matters relating to the target group i.e., learners, dropouts and potential learners. In fact, any meaningful, measurement of the impact of policy can be evaluated only with the responses gathered from the 'target' group.

20

Modernisation Process

Modernisation of the society is one of the aims of education in a democracy like India. It is one of the national objectives. The concept of modernisation is to be understood.

The Concept

1. Modernisation is not westernisation. People consider that thing modern which is western. This shows that we have not understood westernisation even properly. Westernisation is generally understood in bad sense. This is not to be so. Western people love certain values and die for them. Just imagine the character of British race: Who can match them in their sterling qualities? Patriots to the core and hard working people. This is a thing to be cherished and not loose sex morals.
2. Modernisation is not out and out industrialisation. Industrialisation is one component of modernisation. We have not to become robots. We may use science and technology.
3. Modernisation is not just superficial acquisition of certain values or isolated traits and elementary characteristics of more advanced societies. We have to be very judicious

in integrating those values, mere ways of life in our society. It has wide implications if we go ahead blindly.

4. Modernisation does not mean a refusal to recognise the importance of or to inculcate necessary moral and spiritual values and self-discipline. Modernisation is to derive its strength from spirit.

5. Modernisation does not mean outlandish dress and bookish behaviour.

What then is modernisation? Various models have been put forward in the books on Society, Sociology of Education. Diverse models are there. In all countries of the world, it need not take a uniform and unburial course. The West European and North American model is one. USSR is another, Japan is the third. We can know about these models by knowing the alternatives of modernisation or qualities or characteristics of a modern society.

Guidelines of Kothari Commission : The features of modernisation or modern society according to Kothari Commission, are as under.

Science-based Technology : Modern society adopts science based technology. It is this which has helped such societies to increase their production so spectacularly.

Explosion of Knowledge : In a modern society, the stock of knowledge is far greater and the pace of its growth is infinitely quicker. One of the main tasks of education in a modern society is to keep pace with this advance in knowledge. The knowledge stands discovered.

Rapid Social Change : Another feature of modern society is the quick, almost breath-taking rate at which social change takes place. In a traditional society, change is so slow that the conservation of educational system does little harm. In a modern society, on the other hand, change is so rapid that the school must be always alert if it is to keep abreast of significant changes.

Need for Rapid Advance : Two things are to be understood here: (a) Firstly, once a society launches itself upon a programme of modernisation, there is no turning back, no halfway house where we can arrest the process. In the initial stages such a change must disturb the traditional equilibrium. The attempt to create a new social order is bound to create unexpected economic, cultural and political problems and if you falter, new situation may turn out to be the worse than the old one. (b) Secondly, the only solution to transitional problems is to search on. Move rapidly forward to create a new situation.

Economy of Plenty : Modernisation aims at creating an economy of plenty which will differ to every individual a larger way of life and a wider variety of choices.

Modernisation and Educational Reconstruction : The progress of modernisation will, therefore, be directly related to the place of educational advance and the one sure way to modernise quickly is to spread education, to produce educated and skilled citizens and train an adequate and competent intelligentsia. It we want our society to be modern-the Kothari Commission says-spread education-spread secondary and higher education-let 10% people as at present 2% pass higher education classes. There must also be changes in the skills and fields of specialisation to be cultivated. We have got to be technical. Some major universities in the country which attain standards comparable to the best in the world will have to be established. This is one of the basic reforms needed in our systems of higher education.

In short modernisation is to be understood as:

1. Modernisation is a type of social change. It is change for the better, for the positive.
2. Modernisation is characteristic of the present.
3. Modernisation does not mean rejection of all that is old or traditional. It means improving upon the old. Accepting what is good in the old.
4. Modernisation is an attitude of mind. It is between two ears. It has nothing to do with your dress or style of walking.
5. Modernisation is eternal process leading to modernity.
6. Modernisation does not mean leaving our own culture. The best example of modern society in Asia is that of Japan. They are modern yet very much Japanese.

Model of Shipman : M.D. Shipman in his book "Education and Modernisation" published by Faber and Faber. London lists the following as the attributes of modernisation.

Change in Society : Change is must in modern society. Here it means changes in religious, political and economic life of the society. A static society is a dead society. Once a minority bent on change achieves political power, the path to modernisation is open. Rising productivity and rising living standards influences the attitudes to change.

Mobilisation : Mobilisation is a continuing process. After the initial transformation of traditional society, there is continuing change, accelerating under technology and its use. It involves surrender of old loyalties, relationships and life styles and the learning of old ways. Mobility (movement) is symptomatic of industrial societies. Movement from village to town, between towns, between communities and social classes, from old to new occupations, across national boundaries and away from parental and ancestral homes has become common communication and its means-rail, bus, shift work assembly lives have brought in rapid mobility.

Modern Society is a World of Organisations : In politics, religion, occupation, economy, social welfare and ensure organisations have come up in large numbers to solve the problems of urban and industrial living. The family in traditional society could satisfy most human needs. It does retain its basic position or core position in socialisation of the young but it is supported by an assay of organisations ranging from family planning clinics to old peoples homes. At every stage-from wedding to the death there are welfare, educational and financial supports. And an organisation further has its specialists branches. Specialists serve in these organisations.

Modernisation is Specialisation : It is an industrial society and industrial society cannot exist without specialists. It is true that the values become uncoordinated in such a specialists role but that is the price which we pay. It is specialisation all the way. It does lead in disorganisation of personality and personal stress but one has to cope with it and integrate oneself.

Modernisation Town life : It brings modern social order which has its own features such as:

(a) Living in town requires a different discipline from that appropriate in villages. Urban life is symbolised by the clock. Meal times and tea breaks are fixed. There is precision in urban life. There is discipline in urban life and it is to be learnt.

(b) Town life is frequently impersonal. People feel isolated. Neighbour's know little of each other, personal warmth is missing.

(c) In town, town life causes initial disruption and persistent friction in cultural heterogeneity. The village is socially one but the town is divided into different parts, each with a predominance of different religions, classes, languages and customs. Groups come. Groups are assimilated. Groups come again. Clashes occur. High density is there.

(d) In town people are socially mobile. Social mobility increases as the range of occupations increases. Once these are open to competition, kin of the same generation can occupy different positions. This social mobility also means learning of new life styles.

Modernisation is tension, struggle to achieve more with proper sense of differentiation. We are not to forget this differentiation—choice, choosing.

Modernisation involves better social control. Social control should be from within.

Model of modernisation listed in Papers on Sociology of Education in India-Edited by M.G. Gore & I.P. Desai.

The model is listed in terms of Attributes.

These could be called the psychological Attributed indices of modernisation

(i) Empathy

(ii) Mobility

(iii) High participation

(iv) Interest articulation
(v) Interest aggregation
(vi) Industrialised political competition
(vii) Achievement orientation
(viii) Rational ends and means calculation
(ix) New attitudes towards wealth, work, savings and risk taking
(x) Faith in desirability and possibility of change
(xi) Social, economic and political discipline
(xii) Capacity to put off immediate and short run satisfaction for higher satisfactions in the longer run.

Vital Points

Empathy : Empathy means participation in the feelings of other people. We should have the liberty to think in terms of "I feel". It opens up one's mind and equips him for rational, situational and structural choices.

Mobility-explained-mobile Personality : A personality that moves.

High Participation Means Conscious Participation as Social Strain : One person who is modern must have healthy adjustment to his rights and duties.

Rational Thinking and Actions : It means making of rational choices in reference to ends and means. This attitude has to be there. The point is that we tell others to think rationally but we ourselves do not behave like that. We teach lessons to people but we do not follow those ourselves.

New Attitudes towards Wealth, Work, Adventure : This means that work, wealth, rest, adventure, sayings and enterprise have to be viewed in new prospective. No work is small. It is how you do it. Still we have some types of work and glorify others. The right attitude of modern man should be that we should not shirk any work.

The case and for seventh attribute achievement orientation

has been presumably convincingly argued by McHeland. Concerned with "inner concerns" that motivate and sustain economic growth, he demonstrates how a achievement the need for achievement plays a crucial role in this process. People in a achievement category learn faster and work harder motivated not by rewards but by a covert feeling of personal accomplishment.

The rest of the attributes last five in number in the list concern attitudes values and motivations. They have been articulated in different contexts and terms in the growing literature on the social and cultural implication of modernisation. Several interacting transformations are thus called for personality must open up, values and motivations must change and institutional arrangements must be revolved.

Indian context is unique. We have pockets of modernisation against a vast hinterland of tradition. Development is not keeping pace. Slogans will not do. We have shape and reshape our priorities. Education has a role to play. S. Verma in his article "Modernisation and Teachers" as it appears in sociology, of the teaching profession in India published by NCERT says:

Modernisation, it must now be pointed out, is a multidimensional phenomenon; as a process, it is made up of many subprocesses. These subprocesses are economic, political, social and cultural. Each of these dimensions/processes has its own indices of modernisation. We shall examine these indices:

Economic Dimension : Process of modernisation has the following attributes:

1. Industrialisation, implying machine production under factory system and increasing automation.
2. Urbanisation and urbanism-city dwelling.
3. Money and market economy, implying production including agricultural production, for exchange and not for direct consumption.
4. Mass production.
5. Specialisation which implies increased division of labour and vice-versa.
6. Occupational mobility.

Political/Administrative Indices

1. Nation State of Secular Disposition.
2. Enlargement of state functions so that they include not merely maintenance of law and order and external security but also cover education, health, employment, housing etc.
3. Democratic set up.
4. Equality of opportunity implying absence of discrimination on the basis of sex, age, caste, colour etc.
5. Bureaucracy.
6. Equality before law which is impersonal and predictable.

Social

1. An open system of stratification, which considers social mobility desirable and makes it possible-mass society.
2. Achieved status.
3. Contractual social relations (in marriage and employment, for example).
4. Nuclear and functionally specialised family having equalitarian patterns of relationships.
5. Emphasis on personal freedom in matters of sex, marriage, religion, occupation etc.
6. Levelling, which Kierkegaard defines as the process of creating equalities and similarities in the midst of inequalities.

Cultural and Psychological

1. Multiplicity of Alternatives.
2. Emphasis on change as a value; innovative mentality and secular outlook.
3. Rational and scientific approach to life and its problems (not accepting things blindly).
4. Cosmopolitan outlook.

5. Rise of material aspirations which leads to "Consumption Orientation."
6. Mass culture.
7. Pragmatic Orientation which implies the ascent of Vita activa (action) over vita contemplation (pure thought)

Conclusion : The ultimate goal of modernisation as agreed upon by social scientists is a general transformation of the conditions of life and the ways of personal and social life for the better. It is a 'total' transformation of a traditional or pre-modern society into the types of technology that characterise the relatively advanced, economically prosperous and politically stable nations. Modernisation may start in a variety of ways or in various aspects of social structure, and may operate in several of them simultaneously.

Objective based Modernisation

Education thus should be such which brings in modernisation in today's India. We should come out of the hold of conservative values, out of the hold of religion and religious dogmas out of taboos and rituals. We should learn to think rationally. We should believe in change. A feeling of empathy is to be inculcated. It is an age of specialisation. Education should play a role. How?

Change Child Rearing Practices : We begin at home. The parents have to be educated about various child rearing practices. So that modernisation begins right at home. And when he comes to the school, he should be a mini, modern citizen. Repression in homes must go. Puritanical upbringing has to go. The relations between parents and children will have to be more on mutual respect, regard and enjoyment. He is to be educated about sex. Parenthood, childhood and school days have now to be enjoyed. Light-headed and curious children will make right modern citizens.

Open Schools : Family has ceased to be a unit of work, worship personal welfare and education. The role has shifted to school. Modernisation can be achieved through schools. Let there be a network of schools with well-qualified staff. Let people come and mix. Right type of socialisation will also take place. People will go enlightened. Universal schooling should be there.

Specialise Education at Higher Level : Things should not end with schooling. Let there be opportunities for specialisation. Specialisation is an essential attribute of modernisation. Skill teaches pride to youth. They are respected also. Highly professional people in all branches have to be produced.

Organise Education Properly : Let not an organisation organise education to suit its interests e.g. church, army to quote only two. Things should be properly organised. Legal and administrative duties should be clearly demarcated. Rule and regulations should be put in writing. Better organisation-better output. There are wars or infights to control various educational institutions. This spoils atmosphere. You can come across two managing committees for one school or college. This shows that organisation is not proper. Students suffer and modernisation also suffers.

Education should ensure that crucial parts of a culture are thoroughly learned. It forms human personalities. Curriculum has to be reframed.

In education for modernisation-talent has to be recognised. Look for the creative, gifted children. Train them. New loyalties have to be built. Ambitions have to be matched. Do it.

Education is not to be used for indoctrination.

Education is not to over a modernise the society. Even on modern society has its own checks and balances. It has its inhibitions. It has its form of social control. This is a warning which has got to be heeded.

Further, the school not only occupies a central place in the maintenance of social order in modern societies, it also typifies the way organisations work as agents of social control. We live in a mass society. Mass society lives on school and on mass education. As such education has all role to play in modernisation. Bureaucracy is not going to modernise society, only Education will do.

Role of the Teacher/Intellectuals in Bringing Modernisation : Let us define intellectuals. These are persons, scientists, philosophers, artists, thinkers, analysts, theorists, journalists, whose role is to interpret the world to their society, fashion its world view and make it aware of possibilities and alternatives. In doing so they make ideologies.

Now what can such a person do?

Again to quote S.C. Verma, the intellectual/teacher must:

Break Resistance : Break the psychological and emotional resistance or barriers to change. This can be done by exposing the uselessness and outdatedness of traditional ways and scheme of things and by stressing the inevitability of change in human affairs.

Inculcate Modern Outlook : Inculcate a modern outlook in people. This will require the intellectuals to impart information and education in modernism.

Face Problems : Face practical problems of modernisation and development. This implies that the intellectuals must bridge the gap between theory and practice, associate themselves with policy making, and impart training and education in developmental skills and techniques. Examine Models of Development and their costs and implications.

Awaken Mass: Awaken and arouse masses. This can be done by making the masses aware of their potentialities and/or the possibility and desirability of rationally and consciously directed change.

Make an Objective Evaluation of Socio-cultural Changes : It takes place under the impact of developmental plans and modernisation. For this, the teachers, the intellectuals, must have a scientific temper and a rational approach to personal and social life and its problems.

Bibliography

Awasthy, G.C. : *Broadcasting in India*, Allied Publishers Private Ltd., Bombay, 1965

Bantock, G.H. : *Education in an Industrial Society*, Faber & Faber, London, 1963.

Bloom, B.S. : *Human Characteristics and School Learning*, Harper, New York, 1976.

Brown, J.W. Lewis, R.B. & Hercleread. A.V. : *Instruction: Materials and Methods*, Mc Graw Hill Book Co., New York, 1964.

Brubacher, John S. : *Modern Philosophies of Education*, Tata McGraw Hill Publishing Company, New Delhi, 1978.

Chatterjee, R.K. : *Mass Communication*, National Book Trust, India, New Delhi.

Chaube, S.P. : *Philosophical and Sociological Foundations of Education*, Ravi Mudranalya, Agra, 1981.

Cook, L.A. & Cook, E.F. : *A Sociological Approach to Education*, McGraw Hill Book Co., New York, 1950.

Cream, David : *Explaining Teaching Machines and Programmes*, Featon, San Fracisco, 1961.

Curtis, S.J. : *An Introduction to the Philosophy of Education*, McMillan, New York, 1958.

Dale, Edgare : *Audio Visual Method in Teaching*, Dryden Rinehart and Winston, New York. 1969.

Dewey, John : *Democracy and Education*, The McMillan Co., New York, 1961.

———— : *Philosophy of Education*, Little Field-Adams & Co., New Jercy, 1961.

Eby, Frederick : *The Development of Modern Education*, Prentice-Hall of India (P) Ltd., New Delhi, 1964.

Eshwar Bhai Patel : *Report of the Education Review Committee*, 1979.

Haban, Charles, F. : *Movies that Teach*, New York, Dryden Press, 1945.

Hancock, Alan : *Planning for Educational Mass-Media*, Longmans London, 1977.

Kaul, B.N. : *Studies in Distance Education*, Association of Indian Universities, IGNOU, New Delhi, 1988.

Kilpatrick, William Heard : *Philosophy of Education*, McMillan Co., New York, 1961.

Kinder, James. S. : *Audio-Visual Materials and Techniques*, American Book Company, New York, 1959.

Kothari, O.S. : *Report of the Indian Education Commission*, New Delhi, 1966.

Kulkarni, S.S. : *Teaching Learning Process: A Systems Analysis*, UNESCO Regional Office for Education in Asia, Bangkok, 1975.

Lowman, J. : *Mastering Techniques of Teaching*, Prentice Hall India, New Delhi, 1987.

Mac Iver, R.M. & Page, C.M. : *Society*, Macmillan, London, 1950.

Matheson, Alastair : *The Communication Materials and Methods*. Mc. Graw Hill Book Company, New Delhi, 1964.

Mc. Whinnie, Donald : *The Art of Radio*, Faber & Faber, London, 1961.

Menon, Narayan : *The Communication Revolution*, National Book Trust, India, New Delhi, 1976.

Mohanty, J. : *Current Trends in Higher Education*, Deep & Deep Publications, New Delhi.

———— : *Educational Guidance, Measurement & Statistics*, Takshashila, 1996.

———— : *Educational Technology*, Deep & Deep Publications, New Delhi, 1991.

————: *Studies in Distance Education*, Deep & Deep Publications, New Delhi.

———— : *Studies in Educational Broadcasting*, Deep & Deep Publications, New Delhi.

Munn, Norman L. : *The Fundamentals of Human Adjustment*, Houghter Miffin Co., Boston, 1965.

Ottaway A.K.C. : *Education and Society*, Routldge and Kegan Paul, London, 1962.

Rao, V.K.R.V. : *Education and Human Resource Development*, Asia Publishing House, Bombay, 1966.

Raymont T. : *The Principles of Education*, Orient Longman, Calcutta, 1957.

Rewntreu, Desk : *Educational Technology in Curriculum Development*, Harper and Row Publishers, London.

Ross, James S. : *Ground work of Educational Theory*, George S. Harrap Co., Ltd., London, 1954.

Rusk, Robert R. : *Philosophical Bases of Education*, University of London, London, 1956.

Sampath, K. : *Introduction to Educational Technology*, Sterling, New Delhi, 1981.

Schramm, Wilbur : *Programmes Instruction: Today and Tomorrow*, The Funds of Advancement of Education, Newyork, 1962.

Sharma, G.D. & Ahmed, S.R. : *Methodologies of Teaching in Colleges*, UNESCO UGC & NIEPA, New Delhi.

Vedanayagam, G. : *Teaching Technology for College Teachers*, Sterling Publishers, New Delhi, 1989.

Report

Report of the Education Commission (1964-66): Education and National Development, Delhi: Government of India Press, 1966.

Report of the Committee on Emotional Integration. Ministry of Education, Govt. of India, 1962.

Report of the Secondary Education Commission (1953), Ministry of Education, Govt. of India, 1958.

Report of the University Education Commission (1948- 49), Delhi: The Manager of Publications 1950.

N.C.E.R.T.: Teacher Education, New Delhi.

Index

❑❑❑